A GENERATION OF SCHOOLING

HARRY JUDGE

A Generation of Schooling

ENGLISH SECONDARY SCHOOLS
SINCE 1944

Oxford   New York

OXFORD UNIVERSITY PRESS

1984

372.942
J 92

Oxford University Press, Walton Street, Oxford OX2 6DP

London New York Toronto
Delhi Bombay Calcutta Madras Karachi
Kuala Lumpur Singapore Hong Kong Tokyo
Nairobi Dar es Salaam Cape Town
Melbourne Auckland

and associated companies in
Beirut Berlin Ibadan Mexico City Nicosia

Oxford is a trade mark of Oxford University Press

First published 1984 as an Oxford University Press paperback
and simultaneously in a hardback edition

British Library Cataloguing in Publication Data
Judge, Harry
A generation of schooling.—(Oxford paperbacks)
1. Educational sociology—England
2. Education, Secondary—England— History—20th century
I. Title
373.42 LC191.8.G7
ISBN 0–19–219175–6
ISBN 0–19–289180–4 Pbk

Library of Congress Cataloging in Publication Data
Judge, Harry George.
A generation of schooling.
Bibliography: p.
Includes index.
1. Education, Secondary—England—History—20th century I. Title
LA634.J82 1984 372.942 84–7939
ISBN 0–19–219175–6
ISBN 0–19–289180–4 (pbk.)

Typeset by Oxford Verbatim Limited
Printed in Great Britain

CONTENTS

*I am grateful to Stuart Maclure
for reading an earlier version of the text,
and rescuing me from several errors,
to Valerie Clark for making
legible the illegible, and to
many friends for their
conversations*

CHAPTER 1

Origins

My secondary education began in Cardiff in September 1939, a few days after listening to Neville Chamberlain's broadcast. England was now at war with Hitler's Germany, and would be so for the next six years. Three days after my sixteenth birthday, in August 1944, Butler's Education Act received the royal assent. The face of secondary education had been permanently changed.

On the Sunday after the beginning of the War, with his son wearing the embarrassingly new cap and blazer that were then the proud symbols of recruitment to the grammar-school élite, my father drove my grandmother back to her home village of Kidlington in Oxfordshire. The journey in a Morris Ten-Four around the Bristol Channel, with no Severn Bridge and no motor-way, was never rapid. Nor was there usually any reason why it needed to be. On this particular occasion it was doubled in time by the long army convoys crawling up the hills out of Lydney and Chepstow as the machine for war was ponderously assembled.

Kidlington was the village in which my father had been born in November 1886. His sisters had curtsied to the vicar; his brothers had gone to war in 1914, and one of them had died at Vimy Ridge; his father had been a farm bailiff and died in 1911 after being bitten by a horse (misnamed Lucky). My father, the one scholar in a large family, had caught the eye of the village schoolmaster and been coached by oil-lamp in the evening for an examination offering access to that rare privilege for the children of the poor, a secondary-school education.

For the villagers of Kidlington in the 1890s that privilege was not only rare, it was also a startling novelty. The better-off farmers could send their sons as fee-payers to endowed grammar schools (in Thame or in Oxford itself); the gentry could take advantage of the railways and dispatch their sons to boarding-schools further afield. But for the vast majority, in the towns but especially in the countryside, no such opportunities existed. But in 1888, two years after my father was born, the newly constituted county councils were created and Oxfordshire was systematically governed for the first time. Within ten years those youthful county councils had been empowered by Parliament to levy a rate in order to provide scholarships for pupils in elementary school to attend secondary schools. A door had been prised open.

On 5 February 1900 Mr Thomas Box, then headmaster of Kidlington School, made this entry in his log-book:

Severe weather and a poor school. George Arthur Judge a VI Standard boy in this school has gained an Oxford County Council Junior Scholarship of £30 per annum for four years tenable at Thame Grammar School. The Governors of that institution have, owing to the favourable report of Rev. A. E. Shaw, the Headmaster, awarded him a further exhibition of 25 shillings per annum for books.

In 1902, when my father was at Thame, only 9 per cent of his contemporaries were receiving full-time education of any kind. He, busy with Euclid and Latin, did not notice the passage through Parliament of Balfour's Education Act of 1902—which had a profound effect on the shape of secondary education throughout Britain, and therefore in Oxfordshire. But he did notice the growing financial difficulty of his parents—unlike his son in 1939, he was required to be furnished with a top hat for use on Sundays. His career at Thame had been full of promise, attested by the Oxford University Local Examinations certificate framed on the walls of the terraced house in Cardiff in which I grew up. In later and easier days he would certainly have studied mathematics at university, but instead left school when he was seventeen. He had passed the examination to join the clerical staff of the Great Western Railway. Social historians would note that between 1889 and 1911 the number of clerks employed in Britain increased by 37.5 per cent.

That is why, a few years later, he settled in Cardiff and married into the Welsh. But every year, and often more than once, he made the pilgrimage to Kidlington in Oxfordshire and on one of those visits (I cannot have been more than eight years old) took me to Thame and showed me his name on the board as head boy. On another occasion, walking across the water-meadows away from Kidlington church towards Hampton Poyle, he told me how (during one of the school holidays) he had read Thomas Hardy's *Jude the Obscure* and, at the end of the day, had climbed a haystack. In the distance, five miles to the south, a glow in the sky represented Oxford.

But it was to be Cardiff and not Oxford, railways and not mathematics. In Cardiff I went to the local elementary school and in 1939, in the competitive scholarship examination, won a special place at Cardiff High School. Much had changed since 1900 in the world of secondary education.

The most obvious, but not the most superficial, of those changes related to the multiplication of opportunities for access to second-ary education. In 1902 the county councils were given responsi-bility for the planning and provision of secondary education. They could already, of course, provide scholarships and other forms of support, but they had hitherto enjoyed neither the right nor the duty to provide secondary schools of their own.

It was not, save by a few visionaries, supposed that these secondary schools should be provided for everybody, nor that they should be free. Entry should be selective and competitive and the curriculum of the secondary school followed closely those successfully established lines of the traditional Public and endowed grammar schools. A secondary school would, however, not be eligible for grant support unless (after 1907) at least 25 per cent of its places were free and available in open competition. Although these rules were constantly adjusted under pressure, it was not until 1932 (when I was four years old) that the principle of free places in selective secondary academic schools—grammar schools, for short—was directly challenged. Free places were to be replaced by special places: still open to competition, but with the added requirement that parents should nevertheless pay an approved fee, to be adjusted according to the means of the family. That was the kind of 'special place' I secured at Cardiff High School, and my parents paid ten guineas per annum. Guineas always sounded more genteel than pounds.

These restrictive measures, sponsored by Ramsay MacDonald, which are never to be forgotten or forgiven by the Labour party, were defended as the inevitable product of the continuing economic crises of the 1930s. Underlying them, of course, were attitudes and principles still visible and audible half a century later. Not only should parents pay when and what they could, and so inhibit the assumption of paternal responsibility by the State. It was also important to restrict access to secondary education.

Stanley Baldwin had argued in 1923 that it was not 'wise, as some suggest, to give everybody a secondary education. It is no good forcing every kind of ability into one form of education if the result is going to lower the standard which it is in the interests of the country to maintain.' The measure of 1932, which marked profoundly the discussions leading up to the Act of 1944, was bitterly resisted (especially in Wales) and led the President of the Board of Education to argue in the Commons that secondary education should be reserved for 'selected children, the gifted and the intellectual' from whom 'we expect leaders of industry and commerce in the coming generation'. Seven years later, I was presumably one of those.

I was also part of a problem (although it was no problem then) of falling rolls. In 1928, 620,627 live births were recorded, compared with 950,782 in 1920. Such a dramatic decline made possible an improvement in the opportunity index, the measure of the percentage of all eleven-year-old children going on to secondary education. In 1920, it had been 9.5 per cent. By 1938, my last complete year in a city elementary school, it was 14.34 per cent for England and Wales, but 25.89 per cent in Wales alone. (Wales, in this respect like Scotland, has always taken education more seriously than England. Moreover, the Welsh Intermediate Education Act of 1889 gave authorities a flying start in establishing publicly provided secondary schools.) By 1938 98,280 eleven-year-olds in England and Wales could be admitted to secondary schools. Nearly half of them had 'special' places, and in many schools (like Cardiff High School) there were only special places.

In others, however, fee-payers (who may or may not have been among 'the gifted and the intellectual') existed alongside those who had won places in the eleven-plus competition. It followed that some schools were more competitive and selective academically than others: those which had no fee-payers (in the pre-1932 sense) were startlingly similar in character and purpose to the type of post-war grammar school of which, very much later, I became a head.

I went, therefore, to one of the country's 1,398 secondary schools in September 1939. In the deceptive lull of the Phoney War, Cardiff High School was very much as Goronwy Rees remembered it:

The High School at Cardiff, at the time when I attended it, between 1923 and 1928, was indeed an excellent one . . . In the classics, in mathematics, in history and in English we were taught by men of quite exceptional ability and qualifications: my history master later held a university chair and became a Welsh historian of the greatest distinction . . .

Most of all they were marvellously responsive to any sign of talent or ability and were wonderfully generous in the pains they took to foster it . . .

I do not know what kind of verdict would be passed on the school if it were judged by modern educational standards. I imagine it might be said that it was too insistent on formal academic instruction, that it took things like examinations very seriously and prided itself on its academic record; yet in fact the education it gave was surprisingly wide and varied . . . Even to-day I am still surprised that our history master should have thought it worth while to include in his course a class in Plato's *Republic* . . . or that our English master should take me to his home to show me his excellent library and especially his fine editions of Blake and Donne.

If that is how Cardiff High School was when Goronwy Rees knew it in the year of my birth, then it was not very different eleven years later. W. Dyfed Parry dignified the teaching of English, Walter Jones enlivened history (which should be, but is not always, the brightest of subjects), S. S. Michaels brought to the classics a massive learning and a sharp yet generous wit. The headmaster, Cliff Diamond, universally known as 'The Boss', was youthful, with a background of Cambridge and Public Schools. He always wore a gown, he beat boys whenever he thought it necessary, he did not need to assert that his was the best school in Wales, if not Britain. Everybody knew it. Rugby was played vigorously, music flourished, the school plays were of high quality.

I recall those things because of their typicality: this is what the English and Welsh grammar schools were like, and (more surprisingly) were still like when I began to teach in them ten years after the 1944 Act. They represented what T. S. Eliot was to call 'the happy combination of privilege and opportunity', and it is hardly surprising if many older people now look back on them with gratitude (which is justified) and a regretful nostalgia (which, I shall argue, is not). Like my contemporaries I first attended an elementary school, about which I remember only three things. An attempt was made to teach me Welsh, mostly by the reading aloud of stories from *The Mabinogion*—in English. I suspect this, like compulsory religious education, gave me a lifelong scepticism about obligatory elements in any curriculum. Second, I remember the *frisson* when my Welsh (and therefore maternal) grandfather extracted me from a class in order to take me home early for tea. He, a bearded evangelical with a taste for rhetoric, was an Attendance Officer—or 'whipper-in'. He was therefore paid to oblige others to do something which my Oxfordshire grandfather, living in Hornton north of Banbury, had no opportunity of doing. He had no choice but to work on the land, and to live the life described by Flora Thompson in *Lark Rise to Candleford*. But third, and most powerfully, I remember working for 'the scholarship exam', direct predecessor of the eleven-plus. We worked in a special class and at a cracking pace—with a man called Harris, who had none of the contemporary difficulties about aims and objectives. Everything seemed to depend, although I don't suppose it did, upon activities called mental arithmetic and spelling.

It was important to pass the examination—and not only that, but to be near the top of the list in order to be assured of getting through the door of the right secondary school. Boys who did not, remained in the elementary-school system (in, as will appear, most cases) to linger on like dispossessed giants until the system and my grandfather let go of them at the age of fourteen. Indeed, on 1 September 1939 (by the Act passed in 1936) the school-leaving age would have been raised to fifteen—without much preparation, it seems. But at 4.45 a.m. on that Sunday morning German tanks crossed the Polish border.

That event (apart from the lines of groaning trucks on the hills of Chepstow and Lydney) made surprisingly little difference to the 100,000 of us who began their secondary education, in England and Wales, in that month. Masters must have disappeared to the War, sixth-formers had their carefully laid plans disrupted over-night, and yet . . . For as long as Chamberlain was there with his umbrella and the Phoney War lasted the surprisingly robust life of schools continued.

Dunkirk in the early summer of 1940 meant the arrival of an exhausted Belgian soldier, who was a teacher and helped me with my French. He was called, inappropriately, Victor. The hot summer of 1940 I spent in Kidlington, listening during those suspended August days to the radio bulletins on the Battle of Britain.

The raids on the British cities were another matter. I cycled to school one morning through streets littered with glass, and past a little Nonconformist chapel, in which everything had been destroyed except the far wall with its multi-coloured and scrolled message 'God is Love'. I stood one night outside the air-raid shelter which we shared with neighbours, looking towards a great glow in the sky. Bristol was burning, and these were not the lights of Oxford with a message of unattainable ambition. Cardiff High School lost most of its windows, but Latin grammar went on. Another secondary school was destroyed, and the buildings were shared—one school in the morning, another in the afternoon.

There is nothing heroic, but something reassuring, in the per-petuation of routine. The grammar-school pulse kept beating, pumping up (a selection of) 'the gifted and the intellectual' into the universities and desirable occupations. I was placed in an express stream, specialized in arts subjects, after four years took nine subjects in the School Certificate, and then specialized still further to take English, history, and French for two years in the sixth form. It would be a long time before all of this changed very much—and certainly it had not by the time of the Crowther

Report in 1959 (see Chapter 8). In some senses, indeed, the great
Act of 1944 did not fundamentally modify some of the basic
assumptions about the nature of a 'good' secondary education.

I took my School Certificate, immediate ancestor of the
O levels, in the summer of 1943—one of the papers being interrupted by an air raid, with interesting problems for invigilators
and examiners. For our part, we all sat in a cellar and talked about
other things (I think). Early in 1944 the Russians advanced into
Poland, opening another chapter in the history of that tortured
country. On 6 June, in a year when I had no public examinations
and (like so many others) was busily occupied ruining floral
wallpaper by sticking pin-flags into maps of Europe, the Allied
forces landed in France. On 1 August, Warsaw rose in rebellion
against the Germans, hoping for an early relief by the Russians—
who had their own plans. Two days later the Education Act of
1944 received the royal assent. In May, the McNair Committee
had reported on the future of teacher training; late in July the
Fleming Report suggested some of the ways in which the Public
Schools might be integrated into the national educational system.
These three themes—the legislative and organizational structure
of education (and especially secondary schooling), the 'problem'
of the Public Schools and the underlying dilemmas of comprehensive education, the nature and purpose of teacher training—are
central to the narrative of this book.

Why in 1944, when there was so much else to think about and
to do, did those three key documents appear? (I need hardly add
that, at the time, I noticed none of them.)

Attempts to reform the education service in the 1930s had been
frustrated by financial stringencies (of the kind, for example, that
led to the substitution of special for free places in secondary
schools), by the conservative indifference towards education that
marked the National Governments of the decade, and, perhaps
most decisively, by the persistence of religious difficulties. These,
although complex in their manifestations, are relatively simple to
explain. The village school attended by my father was a Church
school: it had been founded and was originally funded by the
National Society for Promoting the Education of the Poor in the

Principles of the Established Church (was there ever a more eloquent title?). Since the 1830s, these schools, and other denominational schools, had received government grants. In 1870 school-boards were established with the right to levy rates to support secular elementary schools, where the provision for denominational schools was inadequate. In 1902, when my father was at Thame, Balfour's Education Act transferred these board schools to the county councils (with some exceptions) and to the county boroughs.

Balfour's Act moreover transferred to those same county councils the duty to provide rate support for the denominational schools, which nevertheless kept a considerable degree of autonomy and their particular religious character. The cry 'Rome on the Rates' contributed to the defeat of the Conservatives in 1906—which Churchill for one never forgot.

Any attempt, in the period between the two World Wars, to raise the school-leaving age or to provide secondary education on a more generous scale was for these reasons bound to encounter sustained political opposition. More secondary education must mean more provision by the Churches as well as by the State. If the Churches were given further subsidies, their political critics would protest. If they were not, then the voluntary bodies would be unable to match State provision and must therefore oppose any substantial alteration to the status quo.

The unlocking of this particular problem owed much to the skill of R. A. Butler and William Temple, the Archbishop of Canterbury. But it is doubtful whether they would have had any opportunity even to attempt that massive task if the years of the War had not profoundly changed public attitudes, and even softened the mind if not the heart of that great enemy of education and old boy of Harrow, Winston Churchill.

Historians lack the skills, or the evidence cannot exist, to settle in any precise way the question of *why* and *how* conditions of war seem propitious for social reform. Yet the evidence of such changes in the period 1914–18 are clear enough and have been well documented. They issued in, among many other reforms, the Education Act of 1918, introduced by Lloyd George's Minister of

Education, H. A. L. Fisher (who was knocked down and killed in the black-out in April 1940). The tasks of reconstruction were perceived as equally urgent in the period 1939–45, even if the rhetoric of building a land fit for heroes could not be plausibly employed for a second time. Labour members of Churchill's coalition would be particularly, but not exclusively, concerned to redress some of the injustices of the Dark Ages and to earn a reputation as determined and competent reformers.

The clearest evidence of such a change is proclaimed, of course, in the general election of 1945. Behind that lie the less easily quantifiable facts of the effects of war service in mingling classes and breaking attitudes, the powerful if vague sense that sacrifice and austerity required a matching improvement in the quality of life in a free society, and the experience of life under siege as contributing to a stronger sense of community and fraternity. It is surprising that the Government should have failed to understand the public enthusiasm for the Beveridge Report, when it was published in December 1942. Even a schoolboy, preoccupied with his own small affairs conducted against a background of global danger, registered the importance and appeal of a plan which would offer security and dignity 'from the cradle to the grave'. As for the future of schools themselves, one effect of a report requiring a massive expenditure of public funds was to turn political attention (by those to the right of centre) away from threatening plans for universal social security towards the milder, and less expensive, alternative of educational reform. The Act of 1944 remains the one substantial legislative achievement of the wartime coalition.

The conduct of the War required fiscal policies sufficiently egalitarian to appease the conscience of even the most austere socialist. Food rationing generally, and especially the 'Points' system operated as a supplementary—and unambiguously 'egalitarian'—currency. The notion that money alone could or should buy things—like privilege, or secondary-school places (whether at Public School or not), or priority of treatment—was correspondingly diluted. T. O. Lloyd points to the queue as a symbol of wartime Britain 'and its implicit values—fair shares, peaceful and patient waiting and no advantage for the rich—were part of what the country was fighting for'. It could certainly be argued that those values and attitudes—fairness, change without violence, deference for order—marked the discussions both preceding and following the 1944 Act. The girls no longer curtsied to the vicar in an Oxfordshire village, but the grammar school powerfully survived as the symbol of 'the happy combination of privilege and opportunity'. Other voices could be heard, of course, but they were attended to only later—when I had returned to Oxfordshire as a headmaster.

National service, imposed sacrifice and sharing, Points and queues, idealism in the face of a pernicious enemy, the dynamics of coalition—all contributed to the sense that, in education as elsewhere, something could and must be done. So did the evacuation of schoolchildren. In September 1939, 764,900 schoolchildren were evacuated from vulnerable into safe areas. Immediate bombing attacks were expected, and when these did not take place the evacuees began to trickle back. Numbers were down to 420,000 by January 1940 and, although there were fluctuations as bombing began in earnest, by the end of 1942 only 220,000 remained. But a great impact had been made. Parents and families in the reception areas were shocked by what they saw and heard, incredulous that they could until then have been ignorant of the deprivation within a society which they thought they knew well enough.

I had an uncle who, like my father, had become a railway official and lived a quiet and decent middle-class life. Among the three-quarters of a million evacuees was one, whom I remember only as Ron, and who was drafted to my uncle's home. He lacked many of the plainer necessities of life, and of ambition he was totally innocent. I remember my uncle pointing towards plain and simple opportunities—through education—of attaining a (slightly) better life. He, while happy to be of some use, was not content that inequality on this scale should persist—inequality of opportunity, of course, for as a station-master he was a hierarchical man.

Ron and his peers were not the only ones to be obliged to move by the War. Most of the senior officials of the Board of Education were evacuated to a Bournemouth hotel, leaving as their man in London, R. S. Wood. He had, from the beginning, no doubts of the direction in which it would be necessary and right to move: the War, he argued, 'is moving us more and more in the direction of Labour's ideas and ideals'. Central to those ideals had been—at least since 1922 when Tawney published his *Secondary Education for All*—the extension of secondary schooling (although, less precisely, not all of it of the grammar-school variety) to the whole of the population. Embedded in that plain proposition were problems of administrative structure, with anomalies surviving from the Acts of 1902 and 1918, and of religion. The latter proved crucial in the wartime debates, with the Churches unwilling to see their influence diminished but unable to finance its support, and their critics unwilling to direct public money to denominational ends. R. S. Wood and his colleagues saw a further advantage in a firm initiative by the Board: they looked wistfully back to the days of central power as exercised by Morant in the shadow of the 1902 Act, and believed that the Local Education Authorities created by that Act had become too powerful. The spirit of mobilization as well as of equality (or, at least, fraternity) was in the air.

R. S. Wood himself, occupying a central position in more senses than one, wished to see a transfer of all pupils at the age of eleven to a common secondary school, followed by transfer for a selected minority at the age of thirteen to either a grammar or a technical school. At one extreme, within the committee of officials charged with reshaping the national educational system, was the isolated Cleary who saw the common school at the age of eleven gradually extending itself across the whole of the secondary age range. Standing in determined opposition to him was G. G. Williams who, anticipating many of the protests of the 1960s (and later), objected that 'the parity of esteem is purchased at the expense of the grammar school'. He was entirely comfortable with the predictable opinion of the Senior Chief Inspector of Schools who confessed that 'I am not much moved by what appears to sacrifice the interests of the few in favour of the many when one result is certain to be that the quality of the person required to fill posts of great importance and of a highly specialized nature is likely to be degraded.' The Permanent Secretary himself, Maurice Holmes, came down closer to Williams than to R. S. Wood (and nowhere near Cleary) by ruling that there should be selection and transfer for all at the age of eleven, to schools of various types, with a review at the age of thirteen of all pupils who might have been initially misplaced. So the matter was settled on the sea front at Bournemouth.

Most of the work was completed by February 1941, and the *Green Book* was prepared in June as a basis of discussion. Butler became President of the Board of Education in July and saw the purpose of a discussion on the Book as being 'to sound for shoals, as it were'. He soon discovered where they were, lifting the curious secrecy in which the Book (to the annoyance of the *Times Educational Supplement*) had been shrouded in the hope of achieving a 'reform representing the whole English character'.

R. A. Butler was no warm friend of Churchill, the Prime Minister, whose politics on India he had stoutly opposed in the 1930s. Churchill was contemptuous of Butler for occupying so marginal a Cabinet post—'wiping the children's noses and smacking their bottoms during war-time'—and exhorted him to steer well clear of the Public School question and, even more, of the religious settlement. The Chancellor of the Exchequer was a little more friendly since he 'would rather give money for Education than throw it down the sink with Sir William Beveridge'. Especially if it was much less money, too. The Chief Whip was prepared, when it became necessary, to make parliamentary time available on the delightful ground that 'We have got to occupy the parliamentary members somehow during the war.' It was as well that Ernest Bevin was a strong ally, and that the President could rely upon his (Labour) Parliamentary Secretary, Chuter Ede. The Conservative party was not yet the party of Edward Boyle—nor was it long to remain so.

At the centre of the web of religious issues lay the problem of the 'single-school district'. If, as was proposed, denominational schools should have a choice of status—effectively inside or outside the *fully* provided and supported system—what should happen in those districts where the *only* school was a Church school? Should parents and children there have no choice whatever? The so-called *White Memorandum* (March 1942) proposed that in such districts the Churches (in practice, the Church of England) must give up their schools. The scale of the problem was imposing. In 1939, of 20,906 schools 10,553 were 'non-provided', that is under some form of Church or voluntary control and yet receiving considerable sums of public money. 12 per cent of these schools were Roman Catholic, and presented a further range of problems. There were 4,000 single-school areas.

A fiery dispute here might consume energy and inhibit the reform to which Butler was so committed—strengthened by his walks in the woods with Winant, the US Ambassador, and convinced (alone, he says) that Churchill would be succeeded by the socialists and that educational reform should be completed now. He persuaded senior ministers that only the unusual conditions of a wartime coalition could permit the religious question to be solved. Churchill was increasingly restive—'it was a case of Rome on the rates and Rome on the taxes'—and, what was more, he was in favour of fee-paying by parents.

The Conservatives were critical of the appointment of William Temple as Archbishop of Canterbury in April 1942. Temple had opposed Baldwin's Act in 1936—on the grounds that it permitted exemptions to the raising of the school-leaving age, planned for 1939—and had been deeply influenced by his undergraduate friends, Tawney and Beveridge. His commitment to the reform of secondary education was unrelenting; his position as Archbishop placed him at the heart of the religious problem; his alliance with Butler—for whom he was 'all bulge and brain'—eventually tamed the opposition of the Churches.

But not without difficulty and not until Butler had assembled a complicated financial package which included generous loans to enable the voluntary bodies to build or convert schools for secondary purposes. (Whereas 62 per cent of council elementary schools had been reorganized into a junior/senior pattern, only 16 per cent of the voluntary provision had been so reshaped). The Roman Catholics were particularly vulnerable, yet impossible to dislodge or ignore, and when Cardinal Hinsley wrote a letter to *The Times* in November 1942, Churchill cut it out, pasted it to a piece of cardboard and sent it to Butler with the cheerful note: 'There you are, fixed, old cock.'

But Butler had already made up his mind. 'Basing myself on long experience of Churchill over the India Bill, I decided to disregard what he said and go straight ahead.' In July 1943 he publicly accepted the commitment to legislate by publishing the White Paper, *Educational Reconstruction*. Ten days later the so-called Norwood Report was published (for which see Chapters 2 and 7). The prophet Tawney, now writing for the *Manchester Guardian* and still committed to an extension of grammar-school opportunities could, on the twenty-first anniversary of *Secondary Education for All*, write: 'Now, at last, the reign of organised torpor masquerading as statesmanship shows signs of ending.' . The Bill was published in December 1943, and its slow progress through Parliament alarmed Chuter Ede. The end of the War was at last in sight, and with it breaking of the electoral truce. Anything might happen if the Bill was lost. Religious grumbles continued, but the Government's only serious defeat was over equal pay for women teachers. The defeat was reversed on a motion of confidence; and the Bill became an Act on 3 August 1944.

What, in its final form, did it prescribe? The ambitions of the civil servants were realized. The President became the Minister of Education with the duty to secure the effective execution by local authorities, under his control and direction, of the national policy for providing a varied and comprehensive educational service in every area. 169 authorities (147 boroughs and 22 urban district councils) having responsibility within counties for elementary education were abolished, leaving 63 county councils and 83 county boroughs with a unified responsibility for all the stages of education within their boundaries. Without that elimination of the anomaly created in 1902 the necessary reconstruction could not have been accomplished.

The principle of 'dual control' (by the public authority and by a voluntary body) was extended for the first time to secondary schools. The non-provided schools, unless they were absorbed totally into the public system, had a choice of status. Some became voluntary aided, preserving a considerable measure of autonomy, receiving full support for all their annual running costs and a generous subsidy (at first 50 per cent, but in later decades rising to 80 per cent) towards the capital costs of building. Many became voluntary controlled, with more carefully circumscribed independence and total support from public funds.

The category of 'elementary' was abolished, and all schools should be separately organized as successively primary and secondary. Each authority should within a year produce a development plan showing how these changes would be achieved—some laggards took until 1951. All fees were abolished—they had gone from elementary schools in 1918, at the end of the First World War, and now parents in Cardiff would not have to pay ten guineas per annum for access to Blake and Donne. More important, fee-paying parents in other areas (and in schools like Thame) would no longer be able to buy a grammar-school place for children who had not 'passed the scholarship'. The 'Points' system had indeed triumphed, only it was IQ points that could now be accumulated.

The school-leaving age—without the exceptions opposed in 1936 by the Local Education Authorities, the National Union of Teachers, Harold Macmillan, Walter Citrine of the TUC, and (of course) William Temple—was to be raised to fifteen on 1 April 1947, and to sixteen as soon as it became practicable (which, in the event, was not until I had completed my teaching career in secondary schools). 300,000 school places had been destroyed during the War, and 350,000 additional ones would now be needed.

Nor was the Act the only important educational publication of the year. The McNair Report on teacher training (see Chapter 9) appeared in May, but both it and the Act were apparently overshadowed in public interest by the Fleming Report on that subject of endless fascination to the English, the Public Schools. Their place did not, however, become central to disputes about the essential nature of secondary education until the secondary schools themselves established under the Act were subjected to dramatic change (see Chapter 6).

Later in the month of August 1944, Paris was liberated. I caught the sense of victory in seeing the film of *Henry V*—just as I had supposed that all schools were like that of *Goodbye Mr Chips*, which I was taken to see in 1939. William Temple, to whom the Act owed so much, died on 24 October 1944. In 1945 I worked hard at my Higher School Certificate subjects of English, French, and history—the Tudors and Stuarts, of course—and tried to decide whether I should have preferred to be Thomas Wolsey or Thomas More. I celebrated VE Day with my friends on 8 May, and VJ Day in September. Every street in Cardiff had a party, and no traffic moved. My father said, for the second time in his life, that it could not all happen again.

Between the two days of carnival, on 26 July 1945, the results of the general election—delayed by the counting of servicemen's votes—were announced. It was a landslide: 393 seats for Labour, 213 Conservative, 12 Liberals, and 22 others. It would be a Labour government that would put into effect the Act of 1944, and much else besides. Was the first and outgoing Minister of Education tempted to return to Churchill's piece of cardboard—'There *you* are, fixed, old cock'?

CHAPTER 2

Peace

From 1945 until 1951 the Labour party was in power in Britain. It carried through, under Clement Attlee as Prime Minister, a wide range of reforms and established a framework of government and welfare which survived unchallenged until the 1980s. Even its controversial plans for the nationalization of major industries came to be accepted as part of a world built upon consensus. The leaders of the party, although idealists and orators flourished among them, were perceived as sober statesmen dedicated to parliamentary procedures and seasoned by their years of experience within the wartime coalition. Most of them would be unlikely to sponsor a wholesale reconstruction of the educational system and were content to work strenuously within the generous limits of the new Act of 1944. In any case, there was more than enough to do in repairing the faults of the existing system and correcting the injustices which they and their predecessors had been denouncing since the 1920s.

Moreover, the reforms had to be achieved with resources severely diminished by the efforts of war and with the pound at an uncomfortably high rate against the dollar ($4.03 until the devaluation of September 1949). The Bank of England was nationalized, as were the coal-mines (unhappily for public relations, in the cripplingly cold winter of 1946–7), the railways, electricity, gas, and—with much more contention—steel. In 1946 general effect was given to the recommendations of the Beveridge Report, Aneurin Bevan tamed the recalcitrant self-interest of the doctors, and the main outlines of the Welfare State were definitively drawn.

Bread rationing continued until July 1948, and clothes rationing until 1949 (when the University of Keele was founded and Orwell's *1984* published). These were at-home years of high purpose, tough conditions, and not very much humour—marked by the austere image of Stafford Cripps, of whom Churchill observed 'There but for the Grace of God, goes God.' Ellen Wilkinson, for two tragically short years until her death in the frozen February of 1947, sat in the place which Butler had created at the Ministry of Education. 'Red Ellen' had long been in the public eye—notably as the figure at the head of the Jarrow March in 1936 bearing down upon London to protest against the enormity of unemployment. A grammar-school pupil going on to Manchester University through the sacrifices of an elder brother, she fought the cause of Labour through the trade-union movement and into the House of Commons. She supported her ungenerous lover Herbert Morrison against the rival claims of Attlee, and spent the war as a junior minister. By 1945 she was already ill and exhausted. By 1947, when she was succeeded by George Tomlinson, the mould of secondary education had been set.

The Left in British politics had never had, nor needed to have, any single clear view about the structure of secondary education: the imperative was to provide it for all, and to provide it free. That had been the central claim of Tawney's *Secondary Education for All*, made in 1922 and constantly reaffirmed since. The Hadow Report of 1926, and its successor the Spens Report of 1938, had envisaged that not all children would want or could profit from the kind of schooling which was available in Cardiff in the 1930s or in Thame in the 1890s, and that different kinds of pupils deserved not only various curricula but also distinctive types of school. When the White Paper on Educational Reconstruction was published in 1943 it contained references to three possible 'types' of secondary schools—grammar, technical, and modern.

The Norwood Report which was published ten days later, and (somewhat improperly) enjoyed the status of an official document, elaborated a justification of this manner of classification in terms of distinct styles of mind and temperament. Sir Cyril Norwood was the head of an Oxford college who had been the head of a Public School and written about leadership.

Groups like the National Association of Labour Teachers had, even before the War, urged the importance of the common or unified secondary school. But the Labour party was emotionally more committed to the plain principle that the workers should have access to the good things which in the past could be bought for money—health, security, places in grammar schools. The more radical critics within the party did nevertheless ensure that the reference to three types of school did not appear in the 1944 Act (or, indeed, the 1943 Bill). Butler, as Minister in Churchill's caretaker government, authorized the publication of 'The Nation's Schools', and Ellen Wilkinson followed this later in the same year with *The Organisation of Secondary Education*. Grammar-school places should be provided for not more than 25 or 30 per cent of the age group: the new orthodoxy was canonized. She brushed aside criticism at the Party Conference of 1946 by asserting of the different types of school:

If the teachers get the same pay, if the holidays are the same and if, as far as possible, the buildings are as good in each case, then you get in practice the parity for which the teachers are quite rightly asking.

Holidays had symbolic importance: then, as now, the more prestigious an educational establishment then the shorter its terms. Criticism was effectively silenced for the rest of the Government's life, but a buried ambivalence persisted in Labour attitudes.

Things may have been different under another Minister, or under the same one in happier and healthier days, but it seems doubtful. The post-war years were marked by a dislike, even a hatred and fear, of novelty—as was amply demonstrated in the reception of the Picasso–Matisse exhibition in 1945. Novelties such as comprehensive schools for all would certainly have been distrusted by the civil servants who had drafted the Green Book. They were now joined by John Maud as Permanent Secretary, who soon found that his Minister—not particularly well informed on educational matters, although still capable of righteous passion in the face of wrong—was content to learn rather than to lead. There was plenty to keep them busy. Bombing during the war, the inadequacy of school provision as it had existed in 1939, evacuation and the neglect of repairs, intense pressure upon the resources and materials available—all these combined to face Red Ellen and her Permanent Secretary with a formidable task. The school-leaving age was raised, and the birth-rate remained high throughout the period 1944 to 1949. Small wonder that there was little time or taste for theorizing about ideal forms of secondary education.

A great deal of deep and genuine idealism nevertheless dignified the effort to provide quickly an adequate and free form of secondary education, as an alternative to the existing and enlarged grammar-school provision. These were the golden years of the secondary modern school—a school which was to be free, so it was thought, from the cramping effects of competitive examination. Valiant attempts were made to develop a humane and worthwhile schooling for the majority who were not selected into grammar schools by the sophisticated operation of an eleven-plus examination.

The danger, of course, was that the new schools would be little more than half-hearted extensions of the former senior elementary schools—by 1938, 63.3 per cent of pupils beyond the age of eleven were in separate senior elementary schools and all that was at first formally required was that such schools should change their labels. A few shillings sufficed to repaint the notice-boards. To give body to the reforms new building was needed on a massive scale. Priority was given over grammar-school building. Yet even by 1961, when there were 3,872 secondary modern schools, there were still 1,026 unreorganized schools—schools, that is, which (although not secondary schools) included many pupils of secondary-school age. The Burnham Committee, which had since the First World War been responsible for determining the salaries of teachers, now produced a unified scheme, making no formal distinction between the remuneration of teachers in primary, secondary modern, or grammar schools. Serious attempts were made to level up the resources for secondary modern schools, in order to make them comparable with grammar schools, and so achieve that parity to which Ellen Wilkinson was openly committed. In the county of Kent, for example, in 1938 the expenditure per pupil in central schools (in effect, senior elementary schools attempting to provide a serious alternative to the grammar schools) was only one-half of that for each grammar-school pupil. By 1948, in the same county, the proportion for secondary moderns had risen to three-quarters.

Nevertheless, the gap remained wide. It was calculated that 170 per cent more on books and other educational materials was spent on grammar than on secondary-modern pupils. Even when the reorganization of schools was complete the 29 per cent of pupils who were in grammar schools absorbed 49 per cent of the costs for all secondary pupils. Staffing ratios were generally better in grammar schools than elsewhere, and even the Burnham system favoured (as it was meant to do) schools with a larger proportion of older pupils, especially if they were in those sixth forms which continued to stand at the peak of a meritocratic secondary system. Twenty years later, when the divided system was beginning to crumble under public and political pressure, 73.9 per cent of grammar-school teachers were graduates, and therefore receiving extra pay and were (although by no means in every sense) better qualified. The corresponding figure for modern schools was 15.7 per cent.

Such harsh realities made the dream of parity, and still more of equality, seem remote, and allowed later critics to denounce it as a sham. Inevitably, the great majority of pupils left at the age of fifteen and without any formal qualifications. The very nature of such schools placed a ceiling upon ambition and aspiration. Small wonder, then, that A. J. P. Taylor's advice was to 'run away to sea rather than go to a secondary modern'. That advice was given in 1957, and captured a reality described more soberly six years later by William Taylor: 'The ideals of the period [after 1945] involved not only a concept of the Modern school, but also a concept of society, in which the strains and stresses of occupational and social competition would be considerably reduced, and motives higher than those of profit and personal gain would direct human endeavour.' Butler was, perhaps, not saying anything so very different when he observed that 'equal educational opportunity is not identical educational opportunity'.

But what kind of an opportunity, then, should the secondary modern school offer? First, it was assumed, the opportunity of a transfer for the more able to grammar school at the age of thirteen (or, very much later in the story, at the age of sixteen). But that, of course, is an answer which bites its own tail—the 'opportunity' in the secondary modern school is the chance to get out of it into something better, namely a grammar school. *The New Secondary Education*, the pamphlet approved by Ellen Wilkinson and issued in 1947, observed somewhat unhelpfully: 'The Modern School will be given parity of conditions with other types of secondary school; parity of esteem it must earn by its own efforts.' The first promise was, of course, never fulfilled. What was done to achieve this elusive parity of esteem which was required if the new schools were to be acceptable to parents and pupils?

It was always easier to say what such a school should not be, rather than what it should be. *The Nation's Schools*, Butler's official pamphlet of 1945, gestured vaguely towards freedom and liveliness, but not much else: 'Free from the pressure of any external examination these schools can work out the best and liveliest forms of secondary education suited to their pupils.' A headmistress in 1946 said that same thing at greater length, but in doing so collapsed into meaninglessness:

In my opinion, such a school should not be an imitation of the old Secondary School [that is, of the grammar school] . . . Exterior examinations have no place in the modern school . . . Highly intelligent and academically minded children should not be in this school . . . The modern school must, to my mind, stand or fall by what it does for the worst-equipped children. Our aim must be to turn out a fully developed person to the limits of his or her personality. We are not concerned to turn out good workmen or even good citizens, but a complete individual. Education should make Mary Smith more Mary Smith.

But how? Brave attempts were made to give some of the schools a particular flavour by linking them to particular emphases, or even particular careers. Could area schemes be developed on this kind of a basis? Might farm schools have a part to play? Could schools be built around the project method, in which the tyranny of traditional subjects was loosened? But it was not long before the harsh facts of economic and social life exerted their pressure. Central government and received opinion were powerless against that pressure, which expressed itself most clearly in the urge to enter secondary-modern pupils for public examinations. The introduction, in 1951, of the General Certificate of Education made it easier to enrol secondary-modern pupils for such examinations, since at ordinary level (O level) the more able among them could now take one subject or a few subjects, without having to take a whole group of subjects at the same time.

Her Majesty's Inspectors frowned upon this distortion of the purposes of the new school, but proved powerless and in 1955 a Government Circular gave modified approval to the introduction of examination courses in the schools. In 1953 there had been 4,068 subject entries from secondary modern schools; by 1966 there were 22,000, the floodgates were open, and alternative public examinations were being developed nationally.

At the same time, the schools developed a whole series of vocational courses. The secondary technical schools anticipated in 1944 had not been created in significant numbers, and the modern schools were required to fill the gap. These schools therefore, and inevitably, developed within themselves quite different curricular packages—some of a grammar-school type, some of a technical or vocational variety, some designed to fill in time in the least troublesome way for growing adolescents. The ideal of the secondary modern school was disintegrating, and the lack of a clear mission contributed to a steadily growing disenchantment with some of the consequences of the 1944 Act. It was, doubtless, agreeable for Mary Smith to become more Mary Smith, but that process did not enable her to find a job or make a living.

Government, in carrying through into the late 1940s the orthodoxies of the 1920s, had trapped itself into what was to prove an untenable position. The years 1945–51 were not a period for new ideas, but for remedial action. Nor were new ideas produced by the Labour government for the general elections of 1950 and 1951. After all, the leading ministers had been continuously in office for the past ten years, and had achieved many of their declared objectives. Their parliamentary majority was reduced to a handful in February 1950 and eliminated in October 1951. The underlying shift in public opinion should not be exaggerated. As a result of the well-publicized vagaries of the British electoral system the Conservatives did indeed have more seats than Labour (321 to 295) although Labour had more votes in the country as a whole (13.9 million to 13.7 million). The Labour share of the popular vote had fallen from 50.4 per cent in 1945 to 49.2 per cent, but the party had lost nearly 100 seats. The Conservatives were to rule for thirteen years, with Churchill as Prime Minister for the first three and a half. Churchill made Butler his Chancellor of the Exchequer, and Florence Horsburgh became Minister of Education.

She was still in that office when, in January 1954, I became a secondary-school teacher. The world of secondary schools was one from which I had been absent for eight years and it had in the mean time greatly expanded, so that the new secondary modern schools now occupied most—although not necessarily the most strategically important—territory. When Clement Attlee became Prime Minister in 1945 I had just completed my Higher School Certificate in the traditional three subjects, with a year to spare before being called up for National Service. It had always, I think, been assumed that I might try to get to Oxford, and history (by an equally mysterious process) became the subject of my choice. It was quite unclear where the money would come from, but the first necessity was to secure a place and preferably an award. Oxford admissions were even more complicated then than now, and the preferred route was by taking scholarship examinations after completing Higher School Certificate. It was possible to make two, or even three, attempts in any one year—in December, January, and March. The colleges, then as now, were arranged in groups for these purposes.

Autumn 1945 in Cardiff High School was a season of intensive preparation for a small group of us who were to make that attempt. We worked very hard, and most of us that season appeared in Oxford at least twice. We travelled, of course, by train and behind a steam-engine, and ate very sticky cakes in a café in the High Street. Most of my friends stayed in colleges, but I stayed with an aunt in Victoria Road and was very much warmer in consequence. Several three-hour papers were answered in large, cold halls smelling of kippers: the open fires were large, decorative and ineffective. All I can now remember of questions and answers is writing a three-hour essay on 'Security', and I cannot think that it was very good. In December I was interviewed on a dark evening at Trinity by a group of Fellows, one of whom wore enormous boots and all of them seemed amused by my belief that there were no good books on eighteenth-century English history. They offered me, in due course, a commonership—that is a place. That was something to cheer Christmas 1945, but not quite enough and in the new year I was back again, once more taking the No. 2 bus from Summertown to Carfax.

This time Brasenose College was to decipher my handwriting, and I was interviewed by the Principal and Fellows in the Tower Bursary. A dozen of them sat there and terrified me, although several were later to become my friends. They raised the offer to a college exhibition, and much of my future—more than I could have guessed—was then determined. Back in Cardiff, my name went up on the Honours Board and my father, in the last year before his retirement, quietly enjoyed the thought that I was to spend at least part of my life in the county in which his father had been born. For the first half of 1946 I remained at school, where the privileged handful of us who had won our places at Oxford and Cambridge did no work, read widely, cycled to the seaside. I wrote to my tutor at Brasenose asking for advice on what to read, and he suggested some 'shorter essays' such as Gibbon's *Decline and Fall of the Roman Empire* (in six volumes). There was not much time for that after the summer of 1946, for in September I travelled north along the Welsh borders to join the RAF.

During my two years of national service I became first a radar mechanic and then an Education Sergeant, leaving in 1948 to start reading History at Brasenose. There I remained for five years, going on to Theology after History. Oxford, after the War and after national service and in spite of the minor irritations of having to carry into Hall private rations of butter and sugar, was a place of freedom. It was a curious mixture of determined work, for many undergraduates had lost five years or more, and of equally certain enjoyment, for the lost years had to be made up in

other ways too. I was lucky in my tutors and my college, and like
so many young men before and since fell in love with the place.

> Know ye her secret none can utter,
> Hers of the Book the Triple Crown?
> Still from the tower the pigeons flutter,
> Still by the gateway flits the gown.

And on Sunday afternoon I often went to Kidlington , to eat large
teas and remember another world.

They were, of course, not comfortable years for the world. In
June 1948, just before I bought a gown, the Berlin Airlift began
and continued until the autumn of 1949. Visions of the future
were often black and in 1949 Orwell published *1984*. In 1951
Burgess and Maclean fled to Moscow; Aneurin Bevan and Harold
Wilson resigned from the Labour government in protest at the
imposition of charges within the National Health Service, which
they saw as an attack on the principles of the Welfare State. Many
of us read C. P. Snow's *The Masters* and snatched an intriguing
glimpse of what the old universities were really like. The Festival
of Britain sought to persuade us of the imminence of a better and
less contorted world. In February 1952 King George VI died, and
an Old Testament lecture I was attending stopped in the middle.
In Oxford the new Queen was proclaimed with due ceremony,
several times. The last London tram ran, and *The Mousetrap*
began its record-breaking run in London theatres. Stalin died in
1953, and Hillary climbed Everest 'because it was there'. Intending
to be a priest of the Church of England, I lost my faith, slowly but
painfully, and at the end of the summer left Oxford and the house
in Norham Gardens in which I had been living for two years and
in which, by a curious turn of fortune, my office now is. My
puzzled parents welcomed me home and, after a reassuring three
months tearing up confidential papers for the Civil Service, I
joined the staff of Emanuel School, London, in January 1954. It
was, predictably, a grammar school but of course by then part of a
system in the capital in which secondary modern schools (with
some novel comprehensives) predominated. Yet, like so many
others brought up through an older tradition, I was only indirectly

aware of their nature, or even of their existence. Emanuel and the London school scene of which it was part illustrate well the unsteady evolution of the system through and beyond the 1944 Act.

The remote origins of Emanuel School lay in the sixteenth century and a small charitable foundation for the elderly and the young. Emanuel Hospital, as it was called for two and a half centuries, lived quietly in Westminster into the nineteenth century and until a more elaborate scheme was developed by the Endowed Schools Commission. In 1882 a larger and at that time healthier site was purchased on Wandsworth Common, and the new school opened with 271 boys—most of them boarders, but 80 day-boys. Very few stayed beyond the age of fifteen. After the Education Act of 1902 the London County Council made available each year a number of scholarships for brighter boys from its own elementary schools, but the school (like Lord Williams's School at Thame) remained formally independent. Scholarship boys replaced the boarders and the school became steadily more successful as a grammar school of the Public School type. Traditions were culti-vated and invented. The headmaster from 1927 to 1953 (from the year before I was born to the year before I joined the staff) was C. G. M. Broom: a scholar of Brasenose and, like all his prede-cessors, a classic in the old manner. During his headmastership eighty-five open scholarships to Oxford and Cambridge were won by boys at the school: the spirit of the place in the 1930s, however different the forms of independence, was very close to that of Cardiff High School at the same time. In 1932 Broom was elected to the Headmasters' Conference and the school therefore became officially a Public School—albeit in a somewhat special sense. In 1938 the ordinary fees were twenty-one guineas a year, and for those who paid fees this made Emanuel rather more expensive than the general run of London County Council secondary schools. There were 550 boys in the school, of whom 40 per cent had free places.

During the War the whole school was evacuated to the green safety of Hampshire, and celebrated its return to London and normality with a commemoration service in Westminster Abbey and a luncheon at the Dorchester Hotel. R. A. Butler, as President of the Board of Education, was the principal guest. The Act which he had just steered through Parliament faced Emanuel with difficult choices: should it remain fully independent and operate outside the State system, or should it be incorporated within the local provision of schooling and become a voluntary-aided school? The response of the London County Council to the 1944 Act had been to propose 'a system of comprehensive high schools'. The London County Council, for long a stronghold of the Labour party, was one of the relatively few authorities to press firmly in this direction in the immediate post-war years. Its plans were, however, for long inhibited by the existence of fifty-five voluntary-aided grammar schools, of which Emanuel now prudently decided to become one. Fees were abolished for all pupils, entry to the school was by the competitive eleven-plus examination. In London as a whole the grammar schools (twenty-one of which were directly maintained by the London County Council) were for many years to admit 17–20 per cent of each age group, and the movement towards comprehensive schools was painfully slow.

Meanwhile, Emanuel School and the other grammar schools continued to dominate the peaks of the academic market. Most of them, protected by their voluntary-aided status, resisted for twenty years and more all attempts to change their fiercely academic character or to entangle them in vague schemes of amalgamation or co-operation with secondary modern schools. The new head-master of Emanuel in 1954 had himself taught at Harrow, where the strains of 'Forty Years On' stirred his memory and his loyalties, and was an old boy of Emanuel: nothing would be deliberately done to loosen the ties with the past. Moreover, the liberals on the staff were sensibly content that the reforms of 1944 had eliminated all fee-paying from the school, and that they could deliver a first-rate academic education to the brighter boys of Battersea. It was, in these years, a good place in which to work. I had the good fortune to work with a brilliant head of department, and paid £10 for a 1927 Austin 7 in which I drove uncertainly every day from Wimbledon.

After five terms I moved into Surrey to become head of the

history department in Wallington County Grammar School for Boys and to work away for five years at doing what grammar schools were most proud of: helping boys to win awards at Oxford or Cambridge, urging ever-growing numbers of them successfully through public examinations, encouraging that sense of discipline and order which characterized the traditional Public and grammar school, wearing a gown, sustaining the prefect system. These tasks ruled my life at Emanuel and Wallington, from 1954 to 1959. My faith in grammar schools remained robustly intact.

In October 1954 David Eccles succeeded Florence Horsburgh as Minister of Education. In November Churchill paid his annual visit to his old school at Harrow, where the boys sang for him a special verse:

> Sixty years on—though in time growing older,
> Younger at heart you return to the Hill:
> You who in days of defeat ever bolder,
> Led us to Victory, serve Britain still.
> Still there are bases to guard or beleaguer,
> Still must the battle for Freedom be won:
> Long may you fight, Sir, who fearless and eager
> Look back to-day more than sixty years on.

The bases were, in the event, guarded by Eden, who succeeded Churchill as Prime Minister in April 1955. A mood of relaxed and optimistic nostalgia was abroad, and gentler songs were sung by those who flocked to see *Salad Days*:

So, if I start looking behind me, and begin retracing my track,
I'll remind you to remind me we said we wouldn't look back.
And if you should happen to find me, with an outlook dreary and black,
I'll remind you to remind me we said we wouldn't look back.

In 1956 Nasser nationalized the Suez Canal. The House of Commons debated the crisis on 2 August, and on the same day I was married to Mary Patrick in Southport, formally recording my profession as 'Schoolmaster (Grammar)'. These distinctions were still, it seems, important to the Registrar General. In the autumn, the Hungarian crisis broke and British and French troops landed in Egypt. They were obliged to withdraw from one of the last (but not quite the last) imperial adventures, and Eden resigned. Harold Macmillan became Prime Minister, with Butler as Home Secretary. Lord Hailsham was appointed Minister of Education. Edward Boyle, who had resigned from the previous Government over its management of the Suez crisis, became his Parliamentary Secretary. John Osborne's *Look Back in Anger* set a new style for the London theatre, and introduced a new harshness into the contemporary idiom: 'There aren't any good, brave causes left.' Boyle, of course, did not agree.

Galbraith's *The Affluent Society* was published in 1958, shortly after Macmillan had reminded his fellow countrymen that they had 'never had it so good'. 1958 and 1959 were boom years, and my pupils got into Oxford and Cambridge. Wallington flourished under a headmaster who had been there before the War, who grew roses under the class-room windows, and trees around the playing-field. One Friday afternoon, I looked steadily at one of those great green trees for ten minutes, and knew then I would not want to teach in grammar schools for ever.

Thame, Cardiff, Emanuel, and Wallington all flourished within the grammar-school tradition and 1959 is a good moment—before the critical voices drown the subtleties of that tradition—to try to define it, to place it in its historical and social context, and to prepare the scene for the massive reorganization of secondary schooling which marked the 1960s. The English grammar school— like the Public School (of which more will be written in Chapter 6) and unlike the secondary modern or the comprehensive school— was the product of adaptation rather than invention. Much about its character after 1944 is explained by its previous history. In its origins, it was indistinguishable from the institutions which became the independent Public Schools. Its name referred to its function in teaching the elements, or grammar, of learning and the typical medieval or Elizabethan grammar school was often the fruit of private beneficence or testamentary endowment. The will of Laurence Sheriffe, for example, who died in 1567, allowed for the support of 'a free grammar school chiefly for the children of Rugby and Brownsover'. The three hundred or so grammar schools which existed in the late Middle Ages were mostly local and small. Eton and Winchester, foundations designed to be of national significance and high quality and therefore directly linked with sister foundations at Cambridge and Oxford, were the exceptions. Harrow was the first of the 'local' grammar schools to approach these great national schools in reputation.

Thomas Arnold, although the significance and peculiarity of his personal achievement at Rugby may have been exaggerated, typified the attempt to meet the demands of a rising middle class by moving the local grammar schools into the national, or 'Public', category. The Clarendon Commission (1861–4) examined the larger Public Schools. The Taunton Commission (1864–8) was critical of the impoverished inefficiency of Thame and led to the reform of Emanuel. But the distinction between Public and grammar remained unclear, although the lines were sharpened by the creation in 1869 of the Headmasters' Conference and the consequent definition of an inner circle of boys' Public Schools, properly so called.

Public Schools and grammar schools provided, or sought to provide, the same curriculum: it was traditional, and innovations (like science, modern languages, or geography) were stoutly resisted over many years. An association with middle-class aspirations and a dedication to classics and mathematics were the mark of such schools. It was the kind of secondary schooling that the Local Education Authorities wanted for their new secondary schools created or adopted after the Act of 1902, and by 1944 the image of the grammar school as the path to success was finally embedded in popular imagination, and in the practical politics of the Labour party.

By 1939, nearly 80 per cent of pupils going on to secondary schools came from public elementary schools and the balance from private schools of various kinds. Of that total 46.2 per cent were paying full fees, 45.0 per cent no fees, and 8.8 per cent part fees. From one fairly typical grammar school, studied by Colin Lacey, the fee-payers had almost disappeared as early as 1925. That school, like many of its contemporaries, was essentially a 'professionalizing' school preparing its better students for the more dignified occupations, rather than for higher education (a development that was not to be fully realized until after 1945 and the expansion of the universities). The award of the first State scholarship, providing access to a university, was celebrated with a day's holiday for the whole school in the 1930s.

Fees were abolished in 1944 in secondary schools within the national system, but (even then) not in the direct-grant schools. Many of these schools—Bristol and Manchester Grammar Schools, for example—epitomized the virtues of the grammar schools, were not formally controlled or financed by LEAs, yet were often an important part of local provision and had fee-payers in them. Their anomalous position illustrates the danger of reading back (even into the 1950s, let alone the 1930s) the more precisely defined contemporary categories, and eventually exposed them to abolition. They were left on an indefensible island where the main streams of the Public School—independent and fee-paying—and the grammar school—maintained and free—diverged.

Nobody had, it appears, intended to create a category of direct-grant school: they owed their origin to an attempt to secure administrative and financial tidiness. Before 1902, no general grants were paid, either by central or by local government, to support secondary grammar schools. After 1902 such grants could be paid to schools which were formally independent (i.e. not 'county' schools) either by the Local Education Authority, or by central government, or by both. Many schools preferred at that time to have two paymasters rather than one, but in 1926 they were obliged to choose: those which thereafter received grants from the Board of Education in London, and not through the Local Education Authority, were reasonably enough known as direct-grant schools. Most of them did not differ greatly from most other grammar schools, which also (of course) enrolled fee-payers. The arrangements needed to be further refined after 1944, and the number of direct-grant schools fell from 232 in 1943 to 164 in 1952. By 1968, that total was 178.

Regulations required the direct-grant schools to set aside, without fees, 25 per cent of their places for pupils who had completed two years in an elementary school. The Local Education Authority had the right to take up another 25 per cent of the places (the so-called 'reserved' places). If the governors of the school agreed, yet more places (the 'residuary' places) could be brought into the same category. For the remainder, the governors could admit whom they chose and charge fees on an approved scale. They received a capitation fee for every pupil—in whatever category—in the school. Even fee-paying pupils could, if parental circumstances entitled them, receive full or partial remission of fees at the public expense. Friends of these schools rejoiced in this subtle mixture of independence, fee-paying, support for deserving pupils with poor parents, academic excellence, and adequate support from the tax-payer. Their critics (but not yet) disliked them as examples of heavily subsidized privilege.

Eighty-one of the schools were for boys, ninety-five for girls, and two were mixed. They varied in size from 200 to 1,400 pupils. Two-thirds of the schools had no boarders, and most were situated in the towns—especially in the North of England, where many were Roman Catholic and so represented a useful variant of the religious settlement which Butler incorporated in the 1944 Act. Although they contained only 30 per cent of the whole secondary-school population, they marshalled 10 per cent of all sixth formers —pupils, that is, voluntarily staying on to the age of eighteen. They were academically impressive and saw themselves as belonging, in many cases, to the Public School sector yet setting the pace for grammar schools as a whole.

Grammar schools separated themselves from Public Schools (although, more accurately, it was of course the other way round) by embedding themselves in the local provision for secondary education. They were the schools attended by the children of parents able to pay a modest but not negligible fee, together with the boys and girls who had by their own ability won a free or subsidized place. The abolition of fees, in all except the direct-grant schools, by the Act of 1944, sharpened the competitive and selective character of the schools. It also, of course, diminished their social selectiveness. Nevertheless, the schools remained conscious of their semi-independent past, of the closeness of their cultural alliance with the Public Schools, and (in consequence) attentive to traditional and ceremonious standards and to the preservation of an austerely academic curriculum.

For fifteen years after the 1944 Act the processes of selection for secondary education were refined. The assumption was that, with sufficient care, pupils could be selected at the age of eleven on the basis of a prediction of their success in pursuing an academic education. There was, in spite of the rhetoric, no attempt to identify aptitudes of a 'modern' or 'technical' character. The more able went to the grammar schools, and the rest did not: it was as simple as that. The proportions of each age group selected into grammar schools varied from as little as 15 per cent in some parts of the country to as much as 40 per cent in others. Selection was based upon written tests in English and mathematics, a report from a primary school, in some cases an interview, and—most important of all during the heyday of mental testing—an IQ score. Measurement of intelligence, relative to that of a pupil's contemporaries, promised the fairest and the simplest and (apparently) the most appropriate means for effecting selection of this kind. Most grammar schools were single sex; mixed schools were usually provided only where the sparseness of the population made it impracticable to provide separate schools for boys and girls. Most of the teachers in grammar schools were graduates of universities: many, but by no means all of them, had also taken a one-year course of teacher training after completing their undergraduate studies. The exceptions were the teachers in such subjects as physical education, art, and the crafts. The domination of the curriculum by subjects classically defined was, indeed, the most obvious feature of the grammar-school curriculum. That curriculum needed relatively little adjustment across the pre- and post-War years. The contrast for the eleven-year-old with the more informal and less specialist work of the primary school was sharp and abrupt. English, mathematics, a foreign language (usually French), Latin (often but not always), the sciences, history, geography, some art and crafts, but not too much, PE and games, the compulsory religious education: these were the invariable components of the first two or three years of a grammar-school education. In the 1950s, the decade on which this analysis is focused, timetables could have been translated from one county grammar school to another almost as readily as architects' plans. There was, and perhaps needed to be, very little variation from an understood pattern—which nobody needed to prescribe, simply because everybody agreed on what it should be.

After the second or third year the principle of choice, concentration, and specialization began to bite into the curriculum. The linguists were allowed to diminish or extinguish their study of the sciences: the scientists, if they were to maintain a full programme in three separate sciences, had no time to waste on languages. Those placed in an 'express' stream had even less reason for preserving a broad curriculum: like myself and my contemporaries in Cardiff High School they rattled along to their first public examination (O level after 1951) at the age of fifteen, and so secured the privilege of early entry—together with the possibility of some extra time—in the sixth form.

The concentration and academic character of that sixth form did not come under serious pressure before the 1960s, and even then remained a powerful influence upon those who taught and studied in grammar schools. A later chapter will examine the changes that had been introduced in the examination system, but for the dominant minority in grammar-school sixth forms very little had changed. Labels were shifted about, the Higher School Certificate became the General Certificate of Education at Advanced Level, but it was many years before new pressures distorted the ancient simplicities. Three subjects were taken at A level and they were usually taken as packages of closely related studies: physics, chemistry, and mathematics; French, German, and English; history, geography, and economics. Although the reality was, and always had been, very different the intention was to design and teach courses of study as a preliminary to an even more specialized university undergraduate course. Some space was made, but never very much and rarely very seriously, for general or liberal studies.

The decade closed with the publication in 1959 of the Crowther Report: the work of the Central Advisory Council established by the 1944 Act which endorsed the principle of specialization within the sixth form and related it to a high vision of what should be represented by that most English of institutions. Specialization of this kind was not, of course, the practice elsewhere in the civilized world 'but it is worth noting that the broad curriculum of Europe and America is almost equally under fire'. Specialization as an educational principle was, moreover, indissolubly linked with particular relationships between teacher and taught, characterized as discipleship, and a special responsibility towards younger and less mature pupils, epitomized in the prefect system. This was, indeed, a powerful and heady mixture.

Although there were some large and important exceptions, the population of most grammar schools fell within the range 550–750. Their organizational pattern was simple. Teaching by subject led naturally to organization by subjects, and to the almost baronial power of heads of department within the system. Given that membership of the school was universally perceived as a privilege, social and disciplinary problems were minimal and few special arrangements for pastoral care or counselling were thought to be necessary. For such happy negligence a price was paid, and especially by pupils from less-favoured backgrounds. Nevertheless, the prevalent mood was one of justified optimism. The grammar school paid little or no formal attention to the social origins of their pupils, and parents paid no fees. They offered a free and national alternative to the expensive Public School, yet occupied a confident place within the Establishment and in general esteem. They cultivated the virtues of hard work, celebrated the advantages of competition and the accessibility of success for any able and determined pupil, and efficiently pursued victory in the examination system. The vision of Tawney and the conservatism of Red Ellen had, it seemed, both been justified. The Crowther Report demonstrated that two-thirds of grammar-school pupils in the 1950s had parents both of whom had left school at the age of fourteen. The next decade should be one of consolidation and steady improvement. But it was not.

CHAPTER 3

Division

While I was teaching in London and Surrey, from 1954 to 1959, I completed a thesis for the degree of Ph.D. My subject was French history, and although my focus was on a relatively obscure piece of ecclesiastical history I had the good fortune to work with the most genial and scholarly of humanists, Professor Alfred Cobban of the University of London. At a time when it would have been altogether too easy to disappear into the exacting but ultimately limiting routine of grammar-school teaching, Alfred Cobban enlivened and enlarged my interest in scholarly work. Although that interest has been, in the course of my career, swept aside more than once by the demands of administration and politics, it will, I hope, never be finally submerged and killed.

Late one evening in 1958 Alfred Cobban telephoned me to see if I would consider going to Cumberland Lodge, in Windsor Great Park, to work there for three years as Director of Studies. Cumberland Lodge was and is a remarkable foundation: a grace-and-favour house belonging to the sovereign which, in the years after the War, had been set aside to serve as a meeting-place for university teachers and students. It was committed to the beliefs that specialization in higher education had been corrupted into narrowness, that scholars and students in sealed disciplines no longer communicated with one another, that values were neglected in a world of facts, that the lack of residence in many contemporary universities removed a deeply significant part of their traditional culture as institutions. These were the principles underlying the creation of the University of Keele (as it later became), whose founding Vice-Chancellor, A. D. Lindsay, had been Master of Balliol College, Oxford, and closely associated with the powerful group that promoted Cumberland Lodge. Another had been

William Temple, Butler's necessary ally in the passing of his Act.

The original model of the place had been one of an unintrusive liberal Christianity, and the first Principal was Sir Walter Moberly —a don and Vice-Chancellor who came from one of the great dynasties of bishops, scholars, and headmasters (of Public Schools, of course). His *Crisis in the University*, published during the Attlee government, was an influential analysis of the failures of the contemporary university. He was also Chairman of the University Grants Committee.

The late fifties and early sixties, when I lived in Windsor Great Park, were creative and critical in manner: the established order was questioned (sometimes cynically), but it was assumed that well-directed idealism could change human society. In 1959 the *Manchester Guardian* became the *Guardian* and C. P. Snow published his lecture on 'The Two Cultures'. His enemies attacked its vulgar over-simplification, but the lecture did bring near the centre of popular debate many of the problems which Moberly had analysed a decade before. What was new, of course, was the emphasis on the centrality of a scientific culture. What was mocked was the arrogant superiority of the traditionally educated arts man who knew nothing of the second law of thermodynamics.

The Russian Sputnik had been launched two years before, and produced in the United States a feverish alarm lest their Communist competitors should outstrip them in a world increasingly penetrated by science and technology. The consequences for education and schooling in the United States were dramatic. In September 1959, at Woods Hole on Cape Cod in Massachusetts, Professor Jerome Bruner presided over a meeting of influential scientists and afterwards wrote *The Process of Education*. Curriculum reform gathered momentum, and with it the confidence that—with the right intellectual and political support— teaching and learning could be revolutionized. In 1960 J. F. Kennedy became President of the United States, and in the following year the Peace Corps was established.

In the world of education and in the year of the Woods Hole conference, Britain had to content itself with the Crowther Report, which, even at the time of its publication and even more plainly in retrospect, reads more like an epitaph than a prophecy. Harold Macmillan spoke in Cape Town, in February 1960, of the 'wind of change' and directed the unwilling attention of his countrymen towards an Empire on which the sun was at last setting. In the following months he defeated Lord Franks in the election of a Chancellor for Oxford University: he was still in office in 1983, and still using in public ceremonies the Latin pronunciation he had learned at Eton in the last Edwardian days. The Labour party was changing too: Aneurin Bevan died at the age of 62 in July 1960, and with him much of the reforming passion which had created the Welfare State. In October, at the annual Party Conference, Harold Wilson unsuccessfully challenged Hugh Gaitskell for the leadership of the party.

The trial of the publishers of *Lady Chatterley's Lover* registered and accelerated a new tolerance in sexual behaviour and in published accounts of it. The innovation of *Private Eye* ensured that deference, if not quite dead, would henceforth have a hard time. Headmasters could take less for granted. Sussex University was born, with more glitter and publicity than had attended the more earnest first days of Keele, and with a declared mission to redraw the map of knowledge, to challenge the hegemony of the traditional subject, to celebrate a new scientific culture. The structure of DNA was determined by Sydney S. Bremner and Francis Crick, who came to Cumberland Lodge to talk about his work and to attack organized religion.

Innovatory places are, perhaps, never comfortable and the Lodge was never free from tensions. But there were always the acres of parkland, garden, and water, and always friends happy to come and stay.

We lived in a house at the end of an eighteenth-century mews, and my son Simon was born in November 1959, within a few months of our moving to Windsor. Koestler, Tillich, Montefiore passed by. So did many whose professional and intellectual concerns were with education, and who obliged me to reflect more on schools and on what, whether by intention or not, they did. Lord James of Rusholme (Eric James) irrupted, and I read in his *Education for Leadership* (1951) a robustly confident statement of what was best in grammar schools. At least three future members of the Public Schools Commission of the 1960s came to talk and walk—Bernard Williams, David Donnison, John Vaizey—and to challenge the assumptions of 1944 upon which British schooling reposed.

These particular circumstances, and the weekly necessity to define and defend rational positions, no doubt sharpened my own sense of the imminence of major educational change. But the growing pressure for such change can, of course, be illustrated more objectively by recalling some of the new evidence and arguments about education and social policy marshalled during these fruitful years. Even the Crowther Report was not wholly free from doubts and worries: it documented the waste of talent in the system, with only 12 per cent of each age group remaining in full-time education to the age of seventeen, and a meagre 6 per cent for a further year beyond that. Moreover, many of the more able pupils were leaking out of the system: even of the most able 10 per cent, two out of five had left before attaining their sixteenth birthday. Crowther looked back to the previous and deeply influential report, also by the Central Advisory Council, on *Early Leaving* (1954). This showed that of 16,000 children entering grammar schools in 1946 (the year when I left one), more than half failed to secure even three passes at O level, and almost a third left even before the end of their fifth year. As for the children of the unskilled workers, relatively few of them secured entry in the first place, and even those tended to do badly: only one in twenty survived to enter for two subjects at A level. After 1954, and however virtuously reassuring it had been to teach bright Battersea boys, it was impossible to ignore the influence of social class on educational achievement.

In the few years after 1958 a new word (and, underlying it, a new fear) took root: the meritocracy. Michael Young (now Lord Young of Dartington) published *The Rise of the Meritocracy*, a sparkling and satirical commentary on the ways in which secondary schools had developed and the futures to which they pointed. The form of the book, written from the imagined perspective of the year 2034, is a review of developments since 1870 and an

analysis of the surprising troubles of 2033 provoked by the populist movement—a 'strange blend of women in the lead and men in
the rank and file'.

'Until the Butler Act began to take effect in the 70's and 80's,
Britain was outstanding among industrial countries as the home
and fount of nepotism in a hundred subtle forms.' International
competition was the pace-maker for reform: reports like *Early
Leaving* demonstrated the extent of academic waste, and this the
country simply could not afford. Quality and not equality was the
dominant value propelling reform. Indeed, the proper development of the system—to make it more selective and more
efficient—required the defeat of the Labour party's sentimental
plans for comprehensive schools. Britain, which had been the
workshop of the world now had to become the grammar school of
the world.

Michael Young, in his paradoxically assumed role, quotes approvingly the strictures of Lord James on misguided attempts to
generalize an élite education:

The demand for such a common culture rests either on an altogether
over-optimistic belief in the educability of the majority that is certainly
not justified by experience or on a willingness to surrender the highest
standards of taste and judgement to the incessant demands of mediocrity.

Attention to the proper development of the grammar schools
required some surprising changes: the payment of pupils to defeat
the rival attractions of early employment, extra investment for
able pupils in primary schools, the conversion of Public Schools
into boarding grammar schools, more efficient testing and select-
ing, and (since some talent would still be missed at the age of
eleven, or developed later) continuous and lifelong selection.

Problems arise, of course, because every selection is a rejection
of many. The members of the new lower class, of those who are
not chosen for the meritocracy, not only are at the bottom but are
there because they both deserve to be and know it. This experience
is even more painful to those children of members of the meritocracy who are not bright and so move down the social and
economic scale. There is something, at least, to be said for the old

order: 'Educational injustice enabled people to preserve their illusions, inequality of opportunity fostered the myth of human equality.'

The roots of the current (AD 2033) discontents are complex. The feminists pursue a romantic attempt to disconnect schooling from economic competition, and to resist the 'intelligenic marriage', designed to ensure that the clever marry the clever to produce the clever. Now that, at last, in the twenty-first century, all selection can be accomplished before the child is three years old, later testing and reallocation can be discontinued: the escape routes from low status are blocked, and frustrated envy is nourished. The 'new conservatives' have made it worse by arguing, incorrectly as it happens, that since the children of the élite for the most part (and for both genetic and environmental reasons) become the élite, then the elaborate process of selection may as well be shortened and a plain hereditary principle reintroduced. The wheel has turned full circle.

The Rise of the Meritocracy was a brilliant fable, which offered no solutions. Its author was to have that opportunity later. Meanwhile, the probable and longer-term human consequences of a growing emphasis upon the efficient competitive selection and of a commitment to the formula (IQ + Effort = Merit) disconcerted those who had been content to march under the banners of equal educational opportunity, free access to grammar schools, and the end of nepotism.

Four years later, in 1962, Brian Jackson (who died while I was writing this book) and Dennis Marsden added their persuasive voices to the growing chorus of those who were aware of the weaknesses rather than the strengths of the grammar school. In *Education and the Working Class* they studied the attitudes and careers of eighty-eight working-class pupils in Huddersfield grammar schools: most of these had taken their A levels in the period 1949–52, and belonged therefore to the earliest generations of those who had been liberated from the payment of fees. They belonged without doubt to the successful minority, but a heavy price had been paid by most of them. Most of their working-class contemporaries, of course, did not even have the opportunity. For the middle-class child 'the prevailing grammar school tone was a natural extension of his home life'. When he did encounter problems, remedies were easily to hand.

The successful working-class children—that is, those who stayed the full seven-year course to Higher School Certificate or A levels—usually came from small families and often lived near to a primary school serving a predominantly middle-class area. They were, all in all, subject to considerable pressure to do well. For most of them the beginning of grammar school represented a sharp break from the familiarities of the neighbourhood primary school. Most of them adapted by distancing themselves from their homes, from the attitudes and habits of their parents. In adult life they were confident that the eleven-plus had separated them from 'the dim ones' and saw no reason to be troubled about the 'intellectually inferior' working-class boys and girls who had left school at the age of fifteen or sixteen.

Education and the Working Class, rooted in direct observation and rich reporting, raised 'the old dilemma: working class life— listen to the voices—has strengths we cannot afford to lose; middle class life transmits within it the high culture of one society, that must be opened freely to all. *That* is the problem the planners must solve.' It still is.

Behind such analyses lay Richard Hoggart's extensive and sensitive work in *The Uses of Literacy*, published in 1957 and documenting the assumptions, attitudes, and morals of working-class people in Northern England, together with the influence upon them of the magazines, books, and films which had been produced for a mass market. His theme is the exposition of the cultural dangers accompanying such valuable social changes as the achievement of literacy or the freeing of access to secondary education. Against such a background he perceives, in terms echoed a year later by Michael Young, that the eleven-plus is 'likely to cause the working-classes now to lose many of the critical tentacles which they would have retained years ago and that a new caste system might prove to be at least as rigid as the old'. The working-class boy who passes the eleven-plus is likely to come from an elementary or primary school from which only a few pupils each year penetrate the grammar-school world. He will do his homework in a cold and inhospitable bedroom, within a home marked by warm conviviality and sharing. The men and the boys have other and different interests, many of them outside the home, and he is a boy in a woman's world. Perceiving life as a series of hurdle jumps, 'he seems set to make an adequate, reliable and unjoyous type of clerk'. He sits, unhappy and proud, on the ladder of social promotion having lost the hold on one type of life, but failing to reach the one to which he aspires.

This for the majority. A few, of exceptional talent, will be able to make the great leap upward and outward in order to join the steadily growing group of 'declassed experts'. For the rest, there is alienation and loss. Much of this argument, even a quarter of a century later, remains powerful yet inconclusive, and provoked some irritable responses. Why should not 'middle-class values'— loosely articulated as industry, honesty, thrift, ambition, prudence, civility—be encouraged or even imposed more widely? And what, in any case, did these radical critics of social change in fact propose to offer? They were (like Tawney and Webb before them) clear about the injustices and the distortions in the contemporary system, but what kind of programme could be derived from their aching nostalgia for a working-class world that was slipping away?

But, without doubt, the inheritors of the grammar-school tradition were steadily pressed on to the defensive in the early sixties. A typical apologia was that offered in 1960 by Frances Stevens in *The Living Tradition*:

I believe that the maintained grammar school offers the best hope at present of making accessible to a larger population than ever before the best of the qualities and habits of which it somewhat accidentally finds itself the custodian: respect for learning, the encouragement of deep and strenuous thought, a regard for style, and the tacit assumption of contracts of mutual responsibility between individuals and between an individual and his society. The grammar school has its defects. But the petty snobbery and priggishness of which it is sometimes accused are in my view much less serious (and in any case demonstrably declining) than are two tendencies: the first, to make the curriculum and the public examination system a closed circuit; the second, to be increasingly concerned with training—in other words, to think of its pupil-product more and more as an instrument rather than as an end. Despite these defects, at its best it is a place of civilized relaxation, as well as hard work, and an unrivalled solvent of social prejudices and preparation for democratic living.

Perhaps. But to write as though the problem were one simply of petty snobbery and priggishness is, wilfully or not, to trivialize the argument, and not to hear the voices. The defence is still stout, but the manner less confident than that of Lord James ten years before, or of Goronwy Rees writing in 1971 about the 1920s.

Moreover, the social scientists now began to draw up alongside the social critics in throwing doubt upon the value and achievement of the grammar schools. (Nobody could find a good word to say for the secondary moderns, and that silence was eloquent and effective.) The alleged inadequacies would not just be described; they would be counted, as well. In 1957 Jean Floud, A. H. Halsey, and F. M. Martin in their *Social Class and Educational Opportunity* gave a new impetus both to the study of these themes and to action upon them. Their work returned afresh to the problem of social waste in education, and especially to its manifestation in the selective and divided system of secondary education.

Two contrasting parts of the country—south-west Hertfordshire and Middlesborough—yielded proof that if IQ was very reasonably taken as the key criterion, then there was no 'problem' associated with the access of bright working-class boys to grammar schools. The indignation of Tawney, confronting the massive injustices of 1922, was no longer appropriate. 'If by "ability" we mean "measured intelligence" and by "opportunity" access to grammar schools, then opportunity may be said to stand in close relationship with ability in both these areas to-day.' But, at the end of the 1950s, it was awkwardly clear that those were two big 'Ifs'. The number of working-class boys admitted to grammar schools was disproportionately small, and 'measured intelligence' could not—as had been conveniently assumed—be treated as though it were clearly independent of genetic endowment, or of environment. Equally, class was a powerful determinant of the progress and success of those boys who were admitted to grammar schools. In south-west Hertfordshire one in seven of the working-class boys secured entry to a grammar school, compared with one in two of the sons of clerks; the corresponding proportions in Middlesborough were one in eight and one in three.

During those same years J. W. B. Douglas was carrying forward into the secondary-school stage his massive study of a sample of 5,000 children born in 1946. *The Home and the School*, published in 1964, hammered home the message about selection at eleven-plus. Moreover, 70 per cent of those who had been admitted to grammar schools left school at the minimum permitted age, namely fifteen. There was only a thin trickle of transfers from secondary modern to grammar schools at the age of thirteen, but even this simply exaggerated the class differentials, giving an added advantage to the children of middle-class parents.

It was clear that the honest promises of 1944 had not been fulfilled: the secondary moderns had not secured parity of esteem, and never would. Parental and public anxiety grew, and especially as the size of the eleven-plus group expanded without any corre-sponding increase in grammar-school provision. The eleven-plus bulge was at its peak in the second half of the fifties. The system was, perhaps irreversibly, biased towards the selection of middle-class children. The accuracy of selection, if the system was to be maintained more or less intact, was of the highest importance. Unfortunately, a detailed and thorough piece of work (also under-taken in the 1950s) sapped confidence in the accuracy of that central process.

Alfred Yates and D. A. Pidgeon in *Admission to Grammar Schools* (1957) reviewed all the available evidence with scrupulous and objective care and concluded that the existing processes of selection could indeed be improved to yield more accurate results. Even then, of course, a problem would remain if Local Education Authorities continued to vary from one another in the proportion of all secondary-school places they reserved for grammar schools—from 10 to 45 per cent in this study. Moreover, there was considerable variation in the grammar-school provision in different areas within each Local Education Authority. But, when all had been done to make provision more level and selection more scientific, a stubborn error of 10 per cent would remain. 'Whether a 10% error for all the country at large', as Professor Ben Morris quietly observed in his preface, 'involving 60,000 children per annum, is to be regarded as reasonable or intolerable of course depends upon what particular educational values are regarded as most important.' The authors contented themselves with noting that things might be improved by more flexible and continuous transfer (and not only at age thirteen), by the introduction of General Certificate of Education courses in the secondary modern schools, and by the creation of comprehensive schools. After all, more than half the Local Education Authorities were initiating significant changes of one kind and another in the forms of secondary education.

The doubts and the arguments of critics undermined confidence in the system. They did so by highlighting the unlovely features of a meritocracy, by celebrating the virtues of a robust working-class culture now being absorbed into an imitative and shallow middle-class orthodoxy, by demonstrating that the eleven-plus examination unintentionally favoured children from the better-off families, by proving that measures of intelligence were not independent of social class or cultural background, by eroding confidence in the scientific accuracy of what needed to be an objective and reliable measure. Some of these arguments were presented with quiet, scientific calm, and others with prophetic zeal. They echoed and amplified the anxieties of parents, and not least middle-class parents, as their children approached the stage of selection for secondary schools. These anxieties were mercilessly sharpened by the popular press. The grammar school still had many powerful and eloquent friends; by 1960 the secondary moderns had none.

Nevertheless, the bipartite system remained in place and would be fundamentally modified only if a powerful political will to do so could be mobilized. Changes by either national or local government required the commitment of a major political party to the cause of wholesale reform. A later chapter will explore the process of conversion and persuasion which led to those structural changes which gathered momentum in the later 1960s.

But the 1950s did see the publication and extensive discussion of a key statement of political faith—*The Future of Socialism* (1956) by Anthony Crosland, who ten years later moved into the very centre of the educational stage. Tony Crosland had been a don at Oxford during my undergraduate years, and then spent five years in the House of Commons, to which he was to return in 1959. Meanwhile, reflecting upon the record of the Labour government of 1945–51 and on the policies which its successor should pursue, he argued for a coherent socialist policy which would be freshly committed to ideals and be capable of realization. On education his mind was severely clear.

The 1944 Act had, indeed, formally made secondary education universal and free. And yet proportionately more middle-class children enter grammar schools. Those from professional and managerial families account for 15 per cent of the total population, 25 per cent of the grammar-school population, and 44 per cent of the sixth-form population. Children in secondary modern schools are disadvantaged by working in bad and overcrowded buildings, and with not enough teachers. There is no particular logic in the tripartite system, and the eleven-plus is feared. Socialists must incline towards a comprehensive system of education 'under which all children would ideally share the same broad experience at least up to the school leaving age'. This is a condition of creating an equal and classless society. Moreover, we should concentrate less on the education of an élite, and more on the average standards of attainment. And yet a comprehensive system could not be rapidly imposed on the whole country. Only fourteen comprehensive schools existed at the time when Tony Crosland was writing: good grammar schools could not simply be swept away, nor the rights and duties of Local Education Authorities brushed aside. A Labour government, when it comes again, should explicitly state a preference for the comprehensive principle, and should actively encourage bold experiments by local authorities.

Meanwhile, the very best must be made of the existing system by providing new secondary modern schools and adding grammar-school streams to those which already exist, by encouraging late transfers, by improving standards in the State sector, and raising to sixteen the school-leaving age. Two other points, given their importance in later developments, must be abstracted from the argument. First, the independent schools. They must not be allowed to train a new and superior élite, and free places in them (when and where they are introduced) should go not only to the cleverest but to those who need a boarding education. Some of the schools will be converted to new uses: adult education centres, for example. In any case, for as long as they remain as powerful as they are and until the country is ready for a proper comprehensive system the grammar school should be preserved: 'It would, moreover, be absurd from a socialist point of view to close down the grammar school, while leaving the public schools still holding their present commanding position. This would simply intensify the class cleavage by removing the middle tier which now spans the gulf between top and bottom.'

That was to read oddly ten years later when Crosland was Secretary of State for Education and Science.

The second point on which Tony Crosland gives a rare hostage to the future relates to streaming and setting within the comprehensive school. On this matter he is surprisingly moderate, even conservative. Comprehensive schools should, in effect, preserve grammar-school streams, with (of course) easy transfer into and from them. The grading of pupils within a school is entirely justifiable, even necessary.

That was to read oddly twenty years later.

These, then, were the books that became required reading for those who came to Cumberland Lodge to debate such issues. Three years passed, and I had not lost my ambition to become the headmaster of a grammar school. I knew that informed public opinion might be shifting, but also that the school to which I hoped to return as head would not yet be very different from the one which I had left as a history teacher. That was still the kind of work that I wanted to do, and if I thought very much about comprehensive schools it was in a spirit of mild disquiet. There was, as Crosland knew well, too much to lose.

In July 1961 I was summoned to Banbury Grammar School for an interview for the headmastership. The interviewing panel was civil and included a peer of the realm, a major-General, and a gentleman farmer. This was very much the old Oxfordshire, in which the Earl of Macclesfield of Shirburn Castle was uninterrupted as chairman of the county council from 1937 until 1967. It was the month before my thirty-third birthday, and I was offered the appointment. The Director of Education for the county walked down the stairs with me after the decision had been made, and told me that (of course) I would be expected to pay early attention to the reorganization of the whole of secondary education in Banbury. Nothing had been said of such matters during the interview: that, too, was the old Oxfordshire.

The first section of the M1 had been opened in 1959, but the M4 did not yet exist. So I drove back across the whole of the county, from Banbury to Henley to return to Windsor, where my parents were spending the summer with us, and looked forward to telling them the news. My father's mother had been born in 1862 in Wroxton, three miles north of Banbury. For me, a century later, it was to be Oxfordshire again, and for a long time to come.

CHAPTER 4

Expansion

In January 1962 I drove to Banbury in the snow, a few days in advance of my family and the general removal. That gave me some time to take my new bearings, and I enjoyed sitting late in the evening in the warmth of the Headmaster's study thumbing through papers and timetables. One of these papers was a recent statement by the county education committee that no change in the status of the grammar school was contemplated: on that basis, I was able to reassure my anxious colleagues, when I met them on the first day of term, that abrupt change was not imminent.

The school had certainly not experienced any such dislocation over the past three-quarters of a century. Secondary, or higher, education in that corner of Oxfordshire had enjoyed an interesting but not untypical history. There had been a medieval hospital (in nature and purpose not unlike Emanuel in Westminister) from which had grown a grammar school. This school had enjoyed a brief period of success and national distinction in the first decade of the sixteenth century under the Mastership of John Stanbridge, who was well known when he migrated north from Oxford and whose *Grammar* was prescribed in the statutes of Manchester Grammar School. I later enjoyed reminding Eric James, who had been High Master of that school, of this proper dependence of Manchester upon Banbury. The school owed much at this time to the support of William Smyth, Bishop of Lincoln, who was one of the founders of Brasenose College in 1509. More threads were being drawn together. The school disappeared in the predatory years of the Reformation: otherwise, it might well have survived to offer an unbroken grammar-school education into the twentieth century. In the nearby town of Thame, Lord Williams (who did well from the pickings to be had in that century) founded his own grammar school: Oxfordshire lost one and gained one.

The provision of schools in Banbury remained patchy until the late nineteenth century. Some elementary provision was made, notably by the Church and the nonconformists early in the century, but of any more ambitious schooling there was none. A Mechanics Institute, mostly for adult education was provided in 1835, and—as public grants from London became available— alongside it grew the Banbury School of Science and Art. Banbury had long been a market town of importance, and acquired a modest industrial capacity in the nineteenth century. Many developments owed a great deal to the vigorous encouragement of the ironmaster and local MP, Sir Bernhard Samuelson, who was a patron of technical education and chairman of the Royal Commission on this subject appointed in 1882.

Eleven years later, Banbury Municipal School opened in Marlborough Road (where its buildings still stand) with forty-six boys on its books; the girls were added in 1900. Its history thereafter is even and steady, and part of the familiar national story. A fine example of local enterprise with modest financial support from direct government grants, it was drawn more fully into local provision by the Act of 1902. Thereafter, it received support not only from government grants, but also from the youthful Oxfordshire County Council. In 1923 (three years before the 1926 Circular) it passed into the control of that council, and became Banbury County School. It moved to new buildings in 1930 in Ruskin Road, where there was provision for 360 pupils. Shortly after that a headmaster's house was built, and that was where I lived with my family. The school had no boarders, but a resident headmaster somehow (I suppose) conferred upon the school something of the status of the independent boarding-school. We certainly enjoyed living there. Two daughters grew up there alongside Simon: Hilary was born in 1962 and Emma in 1966.

At the outbreak of the War in 1939 this was, then, a highly typical English grammar school. Fee-payers and scholarship holders existed happily together. Most, in both categories, left after taking the School Certificate (if not sooner), but a trickle went on into the sixth form and even to the universities. But not very many. Banbury in the 1960s was still full of professional and trades people who had been at the school before or immediately after the Second World War. In 1940, the school was badly damaged by fire—not by enemy action, but (it seems) by the carelessness of fire-watchers installed at night to forestall such action. This was in the year when, as a youthful and helmeted fire-watcher, I patrolled the streets at home in Cardiff.

The 1944 Act changed much for the school, but not everything and not all at once. Its name was changed, to make things clear to the outside world, from Banbury County School to Banbury Grammar School: in Surrey they had not bothered with such fine adjustments, although Wallington County School was unambiguously a grammar school. The fee-payers disappeared, and some of the older men were still lamenting this in 1962. A consequence had been the loss of some of the not-so-bright children of local tradespeople or farmers (who now looked to the independent schools), and some alleged decline in the social standing of the school within the town. Equally, it had made entry to the place academically more competitive.

My predecessor, who played the double-bass, had been appointed in 1935, and I was only the third headmaster to hold office since the death of Queen Victoria. (This is perhaps why those who appointed me enquired rather anxiously whether I, too, meant to enjoy the kingdom for thirty years.) When a colleague, or a former pupil, or a governor, wished to correct my waywardness he would refer approvingly to 'the old Headmaster'. They did not mean my predecessor, but his.

Oxfordshire, after 1944, was faced with a massive programme of building and reorganization, and (as its Development Plan makes clear) it would all take time. Secondary education had been provided only for a minority. Now, as Government Circulars from the hand of Ellen Wilkinson and John Maud insisted, it had to be provided for everybody—and that meant in the new secondary modern schools. Banbury was in one sense fortunate. When the County School had moved to the Oxford side of the town in 1930, generous provision of land had been made and that was prudently added to over the years. The Headmaster's House had stood in the middle of fields, but it was now to be surrounded by educational plant.

First, Easington Secondary Modern School for Boys was opened in 1952; the former elementary schools in and around Banbury gave up to the new campus their boys over the age of eleven. It was five years, and thirteen full years after the passing of the Act, before the same opportunity could be extended to the girls. In 1957 a girls' secondary modern was opened, sharing a large site but not much else either with the boys' secondary modern or (still less) with the Grammar School. The Roman Catholics had to wait another five years again, and I was already in Banbury when the Roman Catholic voluntary-aided secondary modern school was opened, in an odour of incense and the presence of an Archbishop. The last secondary modern school in Banbury, nearly twenty years after the Act, had been established just in time to be re-organized. All these schools were in Easington, and that left only a small but delightful anomaly on the other side of the town. There, a well-established elementary school was rapidly turned into a small secondary modern school under the same head (an old boy of Banbury County School, of course) and with three forms of entry for pupils at the age of eleven.

My predecessor viewed all these developments with some gloom. The Grammar School was, indubitably, still the best school in the town but all this change on his doorstep was unsettling. The view had been spoilt, and the drains became complicated. The latter (in which I took a great personal interest) required the installation of a special engine to pump up the Secondary Modern sewage into a tank, at the Grammar School level, from which it could then flow gently eastwards towards the Oxford Road. This machine would leap spontaneously and noisily into life at all hours of the day and night. My predecessor took me carefully aside to explain that this device was part of a plot by the Director of Education either to drive him from his place or to impose comprehensives on the whole campus. If it was, then it failed. He retired only after his sixty-fifth birthday, and it proved quite simple to reduce the engine to efficient silence.

Oxfordshire in 1962 still had ten years to wait before the reorganization of local government which followed the Royal Commission on that subject chaired by Lord Redcliffe-Maud (John Maud). This meant that, as a county, it was significantly smaller than it later became, and that (in particular) it did not include for local-government purposes the city of Oxford. It was a rural county with towns of modest size—Banbury (the largest, and growing), Bicester, Chipping Norton, Burford, Witney, Thame, and Henley. Each of these had its own grammar school, but (by a fine piece of local and ingenious conservatism) those at Chipping Norton and Burford were more or less comprehensive. This meant that in each case a secondary modern school which would have been too small to survive was absorbed quietly and without fuss into the grammar school, which did not bother to change its name. Comprehensive reorganization in the 1950s was therefore in Oxfordshire a pragmatic and local, and not yet a political, issue. Nevertheless, the grammar schools existing separately from secondary modern schools edgily defended their difference and their rights—even if one of them had only six pupils in the upper sixth. Their heads met regularly with the Director of Education and separately from the secondary-modern heads; they also belonged to their own professional association. Things would not move much further until they were given a determined push, and Mr Crosland was to do just that.

R. H. Tawney died in January 1962, and admirers of the grammar school (like myself) reflected on the contrasts between *Secondary Education for All* (1922) and *The Future of Socialism* (1957), and on the deep, underlying tensions in the growing debate on secondary education. David Eccles, the Minister of Education since 1959, registered a growing public concern with the content of education—what was to be taught, and how, and to whom—and a spreading belief that such questions could no longer be left to the professionals. In the debate on the Crowther Report he spoke critically of 'the secret garden of the curriculum', and in February 1962 established the Curriculum Steering Group. This was to be a body of experts—drawn from within the Ministry, HMI, the universities, and the schools—to advise the Minister, the examining bodies, and others concerned with curriculum change. Such changes, it was agreed, could not be allowed to run forward in an uncoordinated way. The orthodoxies honoured by my headmasterly predecessors in Banbury were no longer universally accepted. But what was to take their place? The asking of that question in 1962 brought problems about teaching and the curriculum into a sharper national focus, and into a context of Government and politics from which they have never since been dislodged. An unquestioning acceptance of the traditional academic curriculum, and vague aspirations about Mary Smith, would no longer do.

The Minister's initiative was deeply and immediately resented by those who saw it as an attack upon vested interests and professional autonomies: the teachers (and especially their unions), the Local Education Authorities (and especially the Association of Education Committees under its powerful Secretary, Sir William Alexander). The task of reconciling them to a diminution of their unexamined power fell to Sir Edward Boyle who became Minister in July 1962. Nobody could have been better qualified to construct a consensus, even if it had to be temporary, from the new and angular alternatives that were now being proposed for the future of secondary schooling.

Edward Boyle, whose thoughts and manner are finely captured in Maurice Kogan's *Politics of Education*, was educated at Eton and Christ Church and belonged to that distinguished generation of Oxford men who dominated so much of post-war politics: Dick Crossman, Tony Crosland, Denis Healey, Harold Wilson, Roy Jenkins, Reginald Maudling, Michael Stewart, Tony Benn, Patrick Gordon Walker. He represented Handsworth in the House of Commons from 1950 until 1970. After occupying junior ministerial office from his first year in Parliament, he became Economic Secretary to the Treasury in 1955. He resigned, on principle, over Eden's mismanagement of the Suez crisis, but quietly returned to office under Macmillan as Parliamentary Secretary to the Minister of Education (first Lord Hailsham, and then Geoffrey Lloyd). After three years as Financial Secretary to the Treasury he entered the Cabinet as Minister of Education, in July 1962. This was on 'the night of the long knives', when Macmillan dismissed seven of his Cabinet (including Eccles) and provoked the remark from Jeremy Thorpe: 'Greater love hath no man than this, that a man lay down his friends for his life.' Boyle had been, with one short break, continuously in Government office for eleven years and was to be the last Minister of Education, as Butler had been the first. In 1962 expenditure on education rose, for the first time, above one thousand million pounds.

In 1963 he called together a representative meeting to discuss plans to move forward from the Curriculum Steering Group and create a new and (of course) co-operative body which would assume responsibility for the national examination system, for giving advice on the school curriculum, and for relating the two. At a meeting in July a working party was appointed, with Sir John Lockwood as chairman. It was agreed that the growing diversity of pressures upon schools made it difficult for them to adapt intelligently and consistently. A worsening shortage of places in higher education, and especially the universities, generated greater competition and more rigorous demands mediated through the examination system. Employers, similarly, had expectations of schools and school-leavers but no national forum in which these could be articulated and discussed.

These were the tasks which the School Council, when it was finally constituted by Edward Boyle, was to assume. It was to be a 'free association of equal partners'—Local Education Authorities, teachers, employers, higher education—offering advice not only to Ministers but to all its member interests. It was to be autonomous, and to direct its own programme of work. Its dynamism and success in its early stages owed much to Derek Morrell, a civil servant in the effective reforming tradition of Morant, who died in 1969 with his life's work sadly incomplete. The Council was financed jointly by the Ministry and the Local Education Authorities and respected the principle that each school should be responsible for determining its own curricula and teaching methods. The early hope was that the Council would help this process by encouraging and disseminating good practice, and by providing a broad framework within which diversity would flourish.

The early opposition of teachers was muted by the agreement that they should be in a majority on the Governing Council, and on all the many committees of the Council. During the years of its active life (its decline and fall will be related later) it gave thrust and direction to the necessary attempts to develop curricula that would be appropriate to the diverse aptitudes and abilities now present in all secondary schools. Its fifteen subject committees usually met three times a year and contributed to the development of a long series of projects. Most of these were based upon university Departments of Education or Colleges of Education (as the teacher-training colleges were about to become). By the early 1970s, well over a hundred such projects had been completed or were in progress: the largest single number in the sciences, but with mathematics, English, and the humanities also scoring high. The Council became increasingly concerned with problems of dissemination and publication, as it became clear that much of its best work was unnoticed in schools. It had been too easily assumed that strong representation by teachers through their unions (which usually meant representation by powerful and semi-professional members who spent little time in class-rooms) would somehow guarantee the active interest and participation of large numbers of ordinary teachers. It did not.

One of the earliest preoccupations of the Council was with the implications, for the curriculum and for teaching, of the raising of the school-leaving age to sixteen, urged powerfully in the Crowther Report and now by its successor, the Newsom Report, published in 1963. After producing the Crowther Report, the Central Advisory Council was reconstituted under the chairmanship of John Newsom and set to work. It was obvious and natural that as the last report had dealt mostly with the more able pupils so its successor should focus upon the needs of the pupils of average and below-average ability—that 50 per cent of all pupils, in other words, who gave the Report its title, *Half Our Future*.

J. H. Newsom (later Sir John) was born in 1910 and educated at the Imperial Services College and Queen's College, Oxford. After an unorthodox early career—involving various forms of social work, including (so he was fond of saying) running a pub—he became in 1940 Chief Education Officer for Hertfordshire, where he remained for seventeen fruitful years. He therefore presided over the extension of secondary education throughout the county, and established new standards of school architecture and of taste. Around him clustered lively and innovatory young administrators, many of whom went on to be Directors of Education themselves —including Alan Chorlton, who spoke to me on the stairs after being totally silent throughout my Banbury interview. John Newsom, who later became my friend, endeared himself to head-masters by asserting the principle that as much freedom as possible in the running of schools should be delegated to heads—even although, or perhaps because, he well knew that many of them were rogues.

The Newsom Report provides a rich archive of information on the ways in which, by the early 1960s, the secondary moderns had developed. There were then 3,688 such schools in England alone, and their record was one of considerable achievement: the staying-on rate had doubled since 1958, and clear improvement could be noted—for example, in raising standards of reading. Nevertheless, lying beneath the humane optimism of the Report was a pattern of wasted opportunity. There was a deep reserve of ability to be tapped, and (whatever the improvement) only 45 per cent of all fifteen-year-olds—including, of course, those in grammar schools —stayed on at school for a fifth year or more. The Report, echoing the research of the previous decade and the confidence of Crowther, asserted that the 'Newsom Children' (as they were conveniently but inelegantly called) were held back more by social than by genetic factors. Links between home and school should be improved and narrow streaming by ability avoided. Pupils should be given as much choice as possible in the fourth and fifth years, with many courses marked by a vocational emphasis and a delib-erate relevance to the world outside school. The school day should be extended for older pupils, with many activities currently classed as voluntary or extra-curricular brought within the normal working framework of the school timetable.

The Report, to the surprise of some, was silent on the subject of secondary-school organization and on the strong differences of opinion then developing on whether secondary modern schools reserved by design for the less able could ever succeed. It made no reference to the possibility that schools for the less able might depress expectations and discourage the pupils in them, or make it difficult for such schools to attract an adequate share of available resources. It concentrated on the obvious truth that children of lower ability would have needs that should be met, whatever the organizational forms of schooling. The refusal of the members to commit themselves in controversial matters certainly made it possible to achieve uniformity, and to make a powerful contribution to the debate on curricular diversity.

More resources would, in any case, be needed. There were not enough teachers, and those who were in the schools moved too quickly from one to another. 80 per cent of the buildings were more or less seriously inadequate. Above all, the school-leaving age should be raised to sixteen, and this, if an early decision were taken by the Minister, could be achieved in the year 1969/70. The Minister (Sir Edward Boyle) announced that this would take place in 1970/1 and wrote a remarkable preface to the published text in which he stated that 'the essential point is that all children should have an equal opportunity of acquiring intelligence, and developing their talents and abilities to the full'. Ministerial blessing had been conveyed to the notion of 'acquiring' intelligence: the new sociology had triumphed. The surge of expansion and commitment to equality (in some of its many forms) which underlay this conviction sat uncomfortably with notions of selection at eleven-plus, but reinforced the rising demand for a huge expansion of higher education.

The force of this demand had already been recognized by Macmillan by the appointment at the end of 1960 of a Prime Minister's committee under the chairmanship of Lord Robbins. Within twenty-four hours of the publication of its report, also in 1963, the Government in a White Paper accepted all the basic recommendations on the enlargement of opportunities in higher education. My rose-growing Surrey headmaster (by now retired) came to Banbury for a weekend, and as we drove off to the Cotswolds he tried to persuade me that the implication of all this was that secondary schools would no longer be a worthwhile place for teachers with academic interests: all the good work would hereafter be done within an inflated system of higher education. He was not alone in his scepticism about the size of the pool of ability, the optimism of 1963, or the soundness of a Conservative Minister with whom the Labour party found it difficult to quarrel.

Numbers and commentaries upon them lay at the heart of the Robbins Report, although there was much else besides: the scale of research undertaken for the Report and the quality of the statistical analyses were unprecedented. Arguments about the untapped pool of ability were not only restated, this time with impressive statistical tables, but enlarged with a new confidence. Not only was there unrealized potential, but it would become (so to speak) self-accelerating. 'If there is to be talk of a pool of ability, it must be a pool which surpasses the widow's cruse in the Old Testament, in that when more is taken for higher education in one generation more will tend to be available in the next.' Girls were, at the time, seriously underrepresented in higher education as, yet again, were the children of the working classes: only 4 per cent of the skilled manual classes, against 45 per cent of the higher professional.

There was, too, some interesting evidence affecting secondary education and consolidating the probability that a restrictive eleven-plus throttled back talent. Given that (irrationally and indefensibly, the reader must conclude) Local Education Authorities varied wildly among themselves and within themselves in the scale of grammar-school provision, that variation had a powerful effect upon the preparation of the whole age group staying on at school to the age of seventeen. The staying-on rate varied from 7 per cent, in the authorities with low grammar-school provision, to 12 per cent. Even without assumptions about the scale of future demand, the pressure on places in higher education was already severe. The post-war bulge, which had exacerbated discontent with the procedure for allocation to secondary schools in the late fifties, had now arrived at the gates of higher education.

The Robbins 'principle', not to be seriously challenged for

twenty years, was a simple one: every qualified school-leaver (qualified, that is, in terms of his A-level passes) who wished to enter higher education was entitled to a place. Moreover, and although certain persuasive remarks were made about the desirability of shifting the balance towards science and technology, no sustained attempt at manpower planning was to be made. The place was, again in principle, to be provided in the subject of the candidate's choice. National provision would therefore represent a reflection of such cumulative choices, and not a theoretical view of what the needs of the economy or of society might be. The implications of applying such broad principles were breathtaking in their scale. The 216,000 places already available should be enlarged to 560,000 in 1980/1, which would in turn require 390,000 by 1973/4.

These places would be divided, within a better co-ordinated system, among universities, Colleges of Education (the proposed new title for the teacher-training colleges), and the Colleges of Further Education. The Colleges of Education should be drawn fully into university Schools of Education and receive their funds from them. The Colleges of Advanced Technology should become technological universities—so becoming, like the former teacher-training colleges, free of the Local Education Authorities—and a new Grants Commission should be established to distribute funds within this enlarged 'autonomous' field of higher education. With one exception, no new categories of institution were to be created: the Regional Colleges of Education would provide opportunities for higher education and provide 'the seedbed for some further growth of institutions to university status'. Degree courses were also to be provided in some Area Colleges, to ensure a fair geographical distribution of opportunities. The Council for National Academic Awards was to be established to validate degrees in this rich variety of institutions within the public (that is, the Local Education Authority-controlled) sector.

The university share of higher-education students should rise from 55 per cent to 60 per cent; existing universities should therefore be enlarged, six new universities created, and ten existing institutions (or federations) within the public sector promoted to university status. The age participation rate (roughly, the proportion of eighteen-year-olds going on into full-time higher education) would advance from 8 to 17 per cent. Five new high-powered centres of scientific and technological education and research (on the model of the Massachusetts Institute of Technology) should be created. There should be more graduate work generally, and an increase in the number of undergraduate courses covering wider fields of study. A new Ministry of Arts and Sciences should be created to superintend this new empire, separated from the Ministry of Education and assuming that Ministry's current responsibilities for the research councils, the Arts Council, and similar bodies.

Many, but by no means all, of these proposals were accepted. Within twenty-four hours of the publication of the Report, Boyle rose in the House of Commons to announce that its recommendations on the scale of necessary expansion were accepted by the Government, that funds were being made available to cover the next ten years, including £650,000,000 for capital expenditure on building by universities. These dramatic proposals and responses threw the Newsom Report into an undeserved shadow. Even a brief recital of them does, however, illustrate well the confident expansionism of 1963 and makes it, in my view, the pivotal year in an examination of the development of secondary schools since the war. It gave them a new sense of opening opportunity, a new reason for raising standards and expectations, new cause to doubt the wisdom of a system which excluded many children from the chance of a full academic education from the age of eleven, and a new hope.

A few miles north of Banbury, in the village of Cropredy, Prescote Manor dominates the meadows of the Cherwell River. R. H. S. Crossman lived there with his family, combining an interest in farming and neighbours with a passion for politics and contention. He enjoyed finding people to argue with and, recently arrived as the headmaster of the local grammar school, I was one of them. In January 1963 Hugh Gaitskell, the leader of the Labour party, died at the age of fifty-six and within a month was succeeded by Harold Wilson. Dick Crossman had been kept out of office or the expectation of it by both Attlee, who could not forgive him for resisting Bevin's policy towards Palestine, and his successor. In 1963, everything changed and Crossman became the Shadow Minister for Higher Education. Even a man dedicated to constructive yet volatile disagreement could find little wrong, as he turned his mind towards the probability of power in the near future, with the proposed reforms.

The year 1963 was eventful in other ways, and the Great Train Robbery filled the newspapers and the media in August. A month later, as the conventional headmaster of a county grammar school I put on my gown and hood to play the appointed part in the annual school prize-giving. The guest of honour was Lord Denning, who had just completed his report into the Profumo scandal of that year. The report was due for publication and the text was placed in the school safe. The words of the, hardly original, school song filled the Hall:

> And when the trumpet-call in after years,
> 'Lift up your hearts' rings pealing in our ears
>
> Still may our hearts respond with one accord—
> We lift them up, we lift them to the Lord.

'That Was The Week That Was' moved into its second year, and nothing was safe.

CHAPTER 5

Comprehension

In 1963 the Peerage Bill became law and members of the House of Lords could now renounce their titles and preserve their political careers in the Commons. In October Macmillan went into hospital and resigned as Prime Minister; the implausible Lord Home, incorporating the highest virtues of the traditional Tory, succeeded him (becoming plain Sir Alec in the process) but no changes were made at the Ministry of Education. The Tories had been in power for twelve years already, and a general election could not be more than a year away. President J. F. Kennedy was assassinated on 22 November, when he was forty-six years old, and the world was numb.

But it continued. I was busy trying to set a grammar school on a new course, meeting the heads of the other secondary schools for a long and sticky evening in the north Oxfordshire village of Adderbury, and experiencing some of the excitements and discomforts involved in shuffling and reorganization: it was the year in which C. P. Snow published his *Corridors of Power*. The first imperative was, nevertheless, to strengthen the Grammar School itself. Bright pupils should be encouraged towards Oxford (or Cambridge) and a steady stream began to flow. If maintained schools failed (and fail) to scale those commanding heights it is because they have not wished to. The sixth form grew, and deserved more stimulus. In May 1964 I travelled by coach with a couple of willing colleagues and a score or more of sixth-formers to spend a week reading, arguing, and welcoming visitors to a refreshing house on the Gower Peninsular in Wales.

The coach drove back through Cardiff, and past the High School—which looked, and was, much as it had been. We did not stop, and when I got home to Banbury it was to hear that my mother had died that day in Cardiff. She had been ill for some time and, driving back again to Cardiff to join my father, I reflected on the sadness that parents can never know what their children owe them. The balancing truth is that children can never know what parents owe to them. Simon started to go to school in the same year. Hilary was too young for that, and sat instead on a swing in the front garden of the Headmaster's House, watching the secondary-modern-school pupils flock by to their separate schools.

On 27 July Churchill made his last appearance in the House of Commons (his first had been when my father was head boy at Thame), and after the summer the country accelerated into a general-election campaign. This time, the Labour party had smoothed most of the inconsistencies and hesitations from its policies for secondary schools: thirteen years of loyal opposition had given them plenty of time and motivation to do that. The essence of pristine Labour policy had of course, and largely through the influence of Tawney, found its way into the official Hadow Report of 1926: 'Selection by differentiation takes the place of selection by elimination.' The attack on free and special places in the 1930s had driven the party into an inflexible defence of grammar schools and access to them. This, as has been shown, was the background to the development of policy under Attlee, although critical voices and advocates of a more unified form of secondary education began to be heard. After all, the National Association of Labour Teachers had been pressing for Common Schools since 1930. The spectre of comprehensive schools nevertheless remained an alarming one, and not least to those who taught in the secure and effective world of grammar schools. The buildings of these vast new schools will 'dwarf the countryside and be visible for miles around . . . It will have its own aerodrome and pupils will arrive by commercial transport plane . . . From an eyrie in its control tower the supreme headmaster will be able to tune in by television and telephone to any classroom' (AMA, Annual Conference, 1945). There would be no place there for a rose-growing headmaster.

Secondary-school organization was not an issue in the general election of 1950 or 1951. But the defeat of Labour in the latter year led, as usual, to a critical examination of conscience and record. Henceforth, the Labour party (or some parts of it) would be less concerned with nationalization and more preoccupied with the reshaping of society and the improvement of the quality of life. *The Future of Socialism* made, of course, a significant contribution to this shift of emphasis. By 1953 there was a general but vague commitment to comprehensive schools—sometimes, in some places, and provided the grammar schools could be kept as well! Ellen Wilkinson's old ally, Herbert Morrison, was not prepared to 'say that the comprehensive schools should wipe the other schools out of existence'. Omelettes were to be made without the breaking of eggs.

Emanuel Shinwell, who has never changed his mind on this issue, was clear in 1958 about the wrong-headedness of destroying the people's grammar schools while leaving unscathed the privileged Public Schools: 'We were afraid to tackle the public schools to which the wealthy people send their sons, but at the same time are ready to throw overboard the grammar schools which are for many working-class boys the stepping-stone to the universities and a useful career. I would rather abandon Eton, Winchester, Harrow and all the rest of them than sacrifice the advantage of the grammar school.'

By 1963, under the pressure of opinion already analysed and the genial leadership of Boyle, the rationale of any rigorous Conservative case for selection at eleven-plus had been fatally undermined. Moreover, the proportion of the secondary-school population staying on beyond the minimum school-leaving age was steadily rising from 29.2 per cent in 1959 to 51.3 per cent in 1964, and by 1969 it would be 61.5 per cent. In the election campaign of 1964 Harold Wilson, the new leader of the Labour party, adroitly integrated two themes: the surge towards equality (and, more specifically, the end of the eleven-plus) represented by comprehensive schools, and the national need to embark upon a 'white hot technological revolution'. Both presupposed open policies in secondary education and the active pursuit of talents. This was a skilful vulgarization of the statistics of Robbins and the persuasiveness of Crowther and Newsom. Wilson was, as ever, careful to hedge his bets: grammar schools would disappear, he asserted, over his dead body and the fundamental purpose of the reform was represented as the extension to all of the opportunities of a grammar-school education. The Labour party might be looking to a new future, but it was not going to forget its ancient roots.

Education was probably a larger issue in the 1964 general election than ever before (or, it need hardly be added, since): the national opinion polls placed it second only to the cost of living. 317 Labour candidates were elected, against 304 Conservative and 9 Liberals. For eighteen months the Government lived on a wafer-thin majority which was shaved down to two seats, and in economic circumstances of exceptional difficulty. There was no reference to the key educational issue in the Queen's speech, and Michael Stewart (the new Secretary of State) was obviously playing for time: 'I would rather wait a bit for a good comprehensive system than try to push a sham version in its place.'

But others were pushing—notably such local authorities as Liverpool and Bristol who wanted from London a strong lead (and money) in pressing forward their plans for comprehensives. The Opposition was also anxious to embarrass the Government, and to trap it within its own latent inconsistencies. They secured a debate, which led to the adoption on 21 January 1965 of a Resolution noting 'with approval the efforts of local authorities to reorganise secondary education on comprehensive lines which will preserve all that is valuable in grammar school education for those children who now receive it and make it available to more children'. It also agreed that the time was ripe for a declaration of national policy.

On the following day, and to his surprise, Tony Crosland succeeded Michael Stewart as Secretary of State for Education and Science. Michael Stewart moved to take the place of Patrick Gordon Walker, Wilson's choice as Foreign Secretary, who had twice failed to secure the necessary seat in the House of Commons.

Crosland, born in 1918, was educated at Highgate School and Trinity College, Oxford. After the War, he was Fellow and Tutor in Economics at that college, deserting Oxford for a political career when he became an MP in 1950. 'I wanted to be involved in the actual process of taking decisions and making policies. This seemed to me, and still seems to me, more satisfactory than writing books from an Oxford chair.' He lost his seat in the election of 1955, and then completed his *The Future of Socialism*, which I read at Windsor. He returned to the Commons in 1959 as MP for Grimsby, a seat which he held until his death. Unlike Dick Crossman, he was a close ally and friend of Hugh Gaitskell, and worked unsuccessfully against Wilson in the dispute over the succession to the leadership in 1963. After the Labour victory of October 1964, he held a ministerial post under the ebullient George Brown at the newly created Department of Economic Affairs until his abrupt transfer to Education and Science at the beginning of 1964. Like Edward Boyle, but for very different reasons, he refused to take the oath but chose simply to affirm on being admitted to the Privy Council. Boyle was one of the few Tories for whom Crosland had any time. Both of them were successful in squeezing money for Education out of the Treasury, although Crosland was forced to do so in a very much more bleak economic climate. The balance-of-payments deficit rose to £278,000,000 in 1965, and pressure on the pound hardened. The Prime Minister and his immediate allies had rejected the possibility of devaluation—the 'unmentionable' solution to which Crosland was committed, but which was not faced until 1967. By that time he had left the Department of Education and Science for the Board of Trade. But also by 1967, expenditure on education had for the first time in history equalled that on defence.

His first task was to drive forward the strong but uncertain movement towards comprehensive schools. Toby Weaver, Deputy Secretary at the Department of Education and Science and a merciless private critic of successive Ministers, found in him 'the first person to stop talking about comprehensive reorganisation and to do something about it'.

A Circular on this subject (to appear in July 1965 as 10/65, probably the best known of a long series of Ministry and Department of Education and Science circulars) was already in draft, but Tony Crosland was anxious to improve it.

Its central purpose was to ensure that all Local Education

Authorities should prepare and submit, within twelve months, plans for comprehensive reorganization throughout the territory for which they were responsible. Some Labour politicians, including Reg Prentice as a junior minister, wished them to be 'required' to do this; Crosland preferred that they should be 'requested', determined that empty threats should not be issued or implied and to go forward as fast as he could by agreement and persuasion. After all, most Local Education Authorities were Labour controlled, and remained so until the landslide local elections of 1968 and 1969. But the Secretary of State was not prepared to wait until research demonstrated, if it could, that common schools were better than a divided system; such divisions were, in his view, matters of value rather than of fact and related to a vision of the nature of a social democracy.

It is in some ways surprising that, even in 1965, the idea of a comprehensive school should still seem novel, and in many ways startling. When such a school was opened by the Queen in November, the *Sun* could observe sententiously and without intended humour that, naturally, 'the word "comprehensive" was not mentioned in Her Majesty's presence'. Part of the difficulty with the image came from the noisy fears of the critics, especially those who insisted that comprehensive schools would, if they were to be as good as grammar schools, have to be huge. But part of it arose from some of the exaggerated enthusiasms of their advocates.

The growth of comprehensive schools had been firm but gentle since the 1944 Act and, provided that no abolition of a grammar school was involved, relatively uncontroversial. In 1950 there were ten such schools, embracing 0.3 per cent of the secondary-school population; in 1960, there were 130 with 4.7 per cent of the pupils; by 1965, there were 262 with 8.5 per cent. The impetus of 10/65 brought 35 per cent of pupils into them by 1971, and within ten years that was to become 85 per cent.

There is no clear, positive, and agreed definition of what a comprehensive school is. Some wish it to be, and therefore are disposed to describe it as being, a school which serves the neighbourhood, and acts as a focus for its life. In a properly shaped world, all the pupils could walk there and home again. But others (or, paradoxically, the same people deploying a different argument) wish it to be perceived as a microcosm for the whole of society—a school, therefore, in which all groups and classes mingle freely and naturally, whatever their economic position or home background. In a world in which, for the most part, neighbourhood and class are largely coincident, the two definitions are of course at war with another.

The only safe definition is negative: it is a school which admits pupils of all academic standards and without a test or assessment of ability (save in so far as that may be used to secure what came to be known as 'a balanced intake'). Certainly there was no hint of dogmatism in Circular 10/65. Local Education Authorities were jealous of the autonomy that they had enjoyed since 1902, and which had been consolidated in 1944: they would not take kindly to being told precisely what to do, and even a persuasive circular about the organization of secondary education was too much for some of them. Moreover, an attempt to require (or even request) a uniform organizational pattern throughout England and Wales would certainly fail. School buildings, built for other purposes, existed, and the best possible use must be made of them: money for replacements did not exist.

The Circular therefore offered six possible patterns of reorganization 'on comprehensive lines', and Local Education Authorities were free to choose from them and (of course) to make different choices in different places. Two of the schemes were paraded somewhat grudgingly, and only on an interim basis, because they involved preserving a measure of selection at the age of thirteen or fourteen. They never in any case became a significant part of the newly emerging pattern, whereas the other four did. The first, and most orthodox, of these was the 11–18 comprehensive school. Where at least six forms of entry (i.e. 180 pupils a year) could be secured, and where the right buildings were available, this solution was the 'simplest and best'. But the Circular also approved two-tier systems, where all pupils would transfer without selection or choice from a junior to a senior comprehensive school at the age of thirteen or fourteen. Middle schools (for pupils from eight to twelve, or nine to thirteen) would also be acceptable, but only in 'a very small number' of cases. The Plowden Report on primary schools was awaited, and a wholesale tinkering with the age of transfer from primary to secondary school would obviously be unwelcome. Sixth-form colleges did not arouse enthusiasm in the Department of Education and Science of 1965. Such a college would admit students at about the age of sixteen, but there are risks attendant upon such a scheme and only 'a limited number of experiments' would be approved.

No uniform pattern could or did emerge, and by the 1980s the diversity had grown. But in 1968, Brian Simon and Caroline Benn (in *Half-Way There*, first published in 1970) were able to review the changes which had taken place, and to raise important questions about the pace and nature of that change. Most children were, of course, still in grammar or secondary modern schools, and in most cases the comprehensive schools (new or old) were in competition with local grammar schools for the 'better' pupils at the age of eleven-plus. Without these pupils, the new schools could not of course demonstrate whether or not they could provide for them as well as the grammar schools had. This simple fact was studiously ignored by ill-disposed critics, then and since.

The comprehensive schools, in a perfectly adjusted system, should have had 20 per cent of their pupils in the top 20 per cent of the ability range: in fact, they had only 15 per cent and one-quarter of the schools had less than 5 per cent. More than half of the comprehensive schools in existence by 1968 were of the orthodox 11–18 variety, and most arrangements were crystallizing around the approved versions of 10/65. The number of 11–16 schools (without sixth forms in them, that is) was growing—from 9 per cent in 1965 to 21 per cent in 1968. This means that a growing number of pupils would transfer from their comprehensive secondary schools at the age of sixteen: the implications of this change will be explored when the whole question of the changing education of the 16–19 age group is raised in Chapter 8.

Schools, in many cases with little preparation or warning, now had to redesign their curricula for the 11–16 age group. For some, it was simply a case of combining the orthodox grammar-school curriculum with the much less precise curriculum of the secondary modern school, and hoping for the best. If, however, the unpopular rigidities of the eleven-plus selection system were to be avoided then it was plainly necessary to avoid too much differentiation (at least on the surface) in the early years of secondary schooling. By the end of the 1960s, most comprehensive schools were offering at least the core of a common curriculum to most of the pupils in Year One. About half the schools surveyed in 1968 succeeded in maintaining this policy for three full years. There was, however, disturbing evidence that in a large number of cases—almost half —the teaching of a foreign language was not included in the programme open to all.

From the beginning of the fourth year, and especially for as long as pupils were legally free to leave school at the end of that year, very much more definite choices were made: 'Newsom' courses for those who were to leave, examination courses for most of the rest, with many decisions then to be taken about which subjects to drop, and which to pursue. The tendency of the later 1960s was to move away from packaged courses towards 'options' in the hope that many pupils would be able to choose from a wide range of subjects and so assemble a programme best fitted to their own interests and abilities. This was to be preferred to the more rigid prescriptions of schools like the large 11–18 Welsh comprehensive which allocated young pupils to sharply divided courses within the school: one group advancing fast to O level in four years, four groups in five years, the next four to CSE (for which see Chapter 7) in five years, four groups following special technical courses, two following general technical courses, two or three on commercial courses, and finally two groups for 'low ability' pupils.

Such arrangements tended, and tend, to perpetuate grammar schools within comprehensive schools. They were disliked by those whose ideal was a more flexible school, even if they were unclear about the means of attaining it, and that dislike extended to arrangements which classified children by ability, placing the more and the less able in separate streams. There never has been one simple view of what a comprehensive school is or should be, nor was there any single ideological thrust behind even the rapid development of the 1960s. Even Crosland took it for granted, in trying to disarm those critics who argued that comprehensives would damage standards, that pupils who would have gone to grammar schools would of course still be taught with those of their contemporaries who would also have gone to grammar schools. Similar assumptions were made by those authorities, like the London County Council, which had for some years been committed to the development of comprehension.

There were at least three overlapping sets of arguments under-lying the drive away from segregation at eleven-plus: each repre-sents an advance upon its predecessor and towards some pure ideal of comprehensiveness. The first, simplest, and strongest argument was that it was wrong and unnecessary to place eleven-year-olds in separate schools. They should all be 'under one roof': that was what mattered, and what they did when they got there was an issue of relative indifference. The second position was that (as in the Welsh school cited above) simply changing the name and use of buildings altered very little: a common curriculum was what mattered and all pupils should be given the same opportuni-ties of learning the same subjects. They might still, for their own sakes, be taught in groups segregated according to ability, and that did not matter. Those who adopted the third and final position—although the arguments were rarely in practice as clear as this—went further still to argue that pupils should be brought together not only under one roof, not only studying one curricu-lum, but also within mixed-ability groups. Separating sheep from goats within a school was little better than separating them into different schools.

More will be said later about the development of this argument. It is, in some ways, unfortunate that the massive structural re-organization that was required could not have been completed before being complicated by even more difficult and contentious issues. A price was certainly to be paid later, when criticisms that grammar-school standards had been destroyed gained momentum and credibility. Some of those arguing for mixed-ability teaching did so on the narrowest professional grounds that it would im-prove teaching and learning, obliging teachers to treat pupils as individuals each proceeding at a different pace and in a different manner. But some of the more outspoken advocates—like Brian Jackson and Albert Rowe—implied that the real priority lay in the pursuit of a society in which classes and divisions would fade away.

Most practising teachers tried to effect compromises, and developed no small ingenuity in doing so. 'Fine streaming'—the allocation of pupils, according to their general ability, to classes in which they remained for all subjects—declined in favour. This had been the method of Cardiff, Emanuel, Wallington—and, I suspect, most places besides. It made the life of the timetabler blissfully simple. 'Setting' now became more popular—the allocation of pupils to subject sets, having regard to their ability in each subject. So did 'broad banding'—the division of a whole year-group into broad bands of ability (sometimes unsuccessfully disguised with implausible labels), often with subject setting within them. Full mixed-ability teaching, especially if it reached into the middle and later years of secondary schooling, was comparatively rare. It probably still is.

The volatile nature of teaching groups, and the associated difficulties of teachers getting to know their pupils, emphasized a new problem within the enlarging schools. The schools, because of their size and because of the problems presented by pupils of all abilities coming from all kinds of backgrounds, needed to pay attention to problems of 'pastoral care'. They could not assume, as most grammar schools and some secondary modern schools complacently had, that the problems of pupils and the needs of counselling would be met by teachers in the normal course of their teaching responsibilities. Existing comprehensive schools in Coventry, for example, had successfully developed forms of organization based upon the 'house'—a unit in which a pupil would remain throughout his school career, and to which also belonged a group of teachers.

Between 1965 and 1968 there was a shift away from this system, to some extent because its success depended in part upon the availability of purpose-built accommodation. Alongside it grew other patterns of pastoral care and supervision, based upon organization by years, with year-tutors often moving up through the school with the pupils, at least some of whom they could teach on a regular basis. The growing complexity of the tasks under-taken by the schools produced a new emphasis on careers guidance and upon counselling, for both of which staffing provision now had to be made.

Nor could the academic organization of the schools remain as rudimentary as it had been: communication and management would not just 'happen' in schools of a thousand pupils or more, and the stream of curriculum innovation needed to be carefully channelled—especially in a system where each school enjoyed considerable freedom in choosing patterns of study and teaching methods. Heads of department acquired heavier responsibilities, but were at the same time often grouped in wider partnerships—often known, somewhat grandly, as faculties—to encourage more interdisciplinary work and greater flexibility in the use of resources. The development, not always as carefully planned as it might have been, of two sets of responsibilities—pastoral and academic—obviously needed to be integrated if confusion and conflict were to be avoided. Methods of co-ordination and formal consultation were needed; deputy heads acquired a new signifi-cance, and their number increased; headship itself changed in character, more rapidly than in any of the last four centuries, and the language of management science supplanted simpler models of leadership or autonomy.

In the early summer of 1965, in the short lull between the Commons debate and the issuing of Circular 10/65, I enjoyed an hour in the early evening drinking a pint of beer alongside the Thames with one of the senior educational administrators of Oxfordshire, who later became a Chief Education Officer himself. We outlined the various alternatives that were emerging in Banbury. Discussion of them since 1962 had been frequent but hesitant: teachers, governors, parents in the various schools were apprehensive of large-scale and unpredictable change, and no firm decision was emerging. Successful efforts had been made to bring the work of the schools for pupils aged between eleven and thirteen closer together, and to encourage co-operation among the various subject specialists—most of whom eyed one another warily, hedging their bets until decisions were taken. There had been inconclusive talk of establishing middle schools, or a peculiar 11–13 school with a chain of upper schools thereafter, but nothing was settled. My companion put it to me that an initiative must now be taken, and reminded me of the unrecorded conversation at the time of my appointment.

I had been hesitant. Without the authority to initiate change, more harm than good would be done by reforms which may get stuck half-way, and which would be resented by heads and teachers in all the schools. Moreover, I was (and am) conscious of the strengths of a grammar-school tradition, and was enjoying the work of building on these foundations within a relatively secure system. But when I got home, I spent an hour simply looking out of the window of my home at the campus, and speculating on its future. I was convinced, and did not afterwards look back, that the only solution would be a bold one. Unless one school was created as rapidly as it honestly could be, then the corrosive uncertainty would spread, tentative plans would proliferate but never come to fruition. Since one certainty had already been destroyed, another would have to be built.

A few months later the Oxfordshire Education Committee responded to 10/65 by appointing me as co-ordinator for the Banbury reorganization, and commissioned me to submit plans: the noisy sewage pump had done its work.

The general election of 31 March 1966 gave the Labour party a comfortable working majority and removed any uncertainty about the movement towards comprehensive education. On the following day, I formally became co-ordinator, although a good deal of preliminary negotiation had been completed. A month later, our daughter Emma was born. By September, I had been joined by a director of studies and in November the first draft of a Development Plan for Banbury was published.

It proved to be a surprisingly accurate account of what in the event did happen, and is outlined here to illustrate the way in which, in one corner of Oxfordshire, changes which had been argued over for a decade could be effected in a relatively short time. The campus, it may be remembered, was the setting for three schools: Banbury Grammar School (with 634 pupils in 1966), Easington Boys (with 547), and Easington Girls (with 517). Moreover, and as a result of growing numbers in the town and in the school, a building programme had been approved to provide about 600 new places: no decision had been taken about how or where they should be deployed. Grimsbury Secondary Modern was on the other side of the town, and had to be accommodated— I believe it was, successfully—within the plans, but only for a transitional period. The following months were very busy, and included extensive individual consultations with all members of staff.

Parents were anxious, especially those with present or hopeful grammar-school children, and public meetings were packed.

What emerged was a scheme which struggled to combine the advantages of size with the effective intimacy of small communities, in which each pupil would be known and would count. Each of the three existing sets of buildings was renamed a Hall, and every year each would admit 120 pupils of all abilities. They remained as members of that Hall for four years, taking no public examinations, and being taught predominantly but not exclusively by teachers attached to the Hall. Each of these communities had its own head, who assumed most of the duties and rights of the head of an orthodox and separate school.

At the end of the fourth year, pupils moved to the Upper School—provided out of the building programme, and having associated with it certain specific areas (science and mathematics, for example, or modern languages), which were also available for planned uses by some of the pupils in the Halls. The Upper School also had its own head—the former deputy head of the Grammar School, who by his quality and determination guaranteed that nothing of value was lost in this elaborate and dangerous transition. The Upper School was linked closely with the Technical College, one mile away: common programmes and a common timetable were developed. At the other end of the school, in the first year of the Halls, close links were established with the many primary schools (some of them tiny) which sent eleven-year-olds to the school, and the style of teaching for that first year was aligned as closely as possible with the more effective primary-school practices.

Heads of department, and (most important) of subject groups, exercised their responsibilities throughout all four parts of the school; a teacher therefore belonged to two professional teams—Hall, and department. The centralizing pressures of the whole school were kept at the lowest level compatible with the necessary coherence of the enterprise. There was, I thought then and believe now, much to be learnt in secondary schools from some of the more flexible forms of collegiate organization to be found in higher education.

I have cast this account in the past tense in order to relate it to the developments of the late 1960s, although I know that much of this shape and many of these assumptions have survived. I have also made the exercise sound blissfully simple and free of controversy: it was not. But my strongest surviving impression is of a large team of teachers, several of them coming specifically to Banbury to undertake this work and now scattered in headships across the country, determined to carry change through—not because it was imposed by politicians or bureaucrats, but because they believed it to be right and wanted it to work well.

In 1967 I was appointed as Principal of the new school, which was to open in September. On the coast of North Cornwall, tucked into the estuary of the Camel River, is the old fishing port of Padstow. At Easter we went there for a holiday, and often have since. It is one of those places in which perspectives are restored, and anxieties erased. It is also a fine place for walking along the cliff-tops, inventing stories for your children (or yourself), and watching the changing moods of an ocean. One of those walks stretches alongside the estuary, and at one point it is possible to look back to the solidity and placidity of the harbour and out, across Doom Bar, to an unpredictable sea. The change through which schools moved in those years was no less dramatic than that.

Banbury School opened its doors on 1 September 1967, but not very much changed on that day. The two youngest classes in the single-sex secondary moderns were mixed, and for many that was the most disturbing change of all. In the following year, all the Halls admitted pupils comprehensively and the planned movement began in earnest. The builders marshalled their machinery, but it was 1970 before the Upper School was genuinely open. Already, in that year, there were 1,145 comprehensive schools, and 32 per cent of all secondary pupils were in such schools. The tide would not stop there.

CHAPTER 6

Privilege

Banbury offered a bright and clear window through which to view national developments across the 1960s, and into the 1970s. Neil Marten (now Sir Neil Marten) was an active local MP, and a Conservative who took a characteristically independent and critical line in the apparently endless debates about Britain's entry to the Common Market. The farmers listened to him, and he was no great admirer of Edward Heath, who replaced Home as leader of the Conservatives in the summer of 1965. Angus Maude, who had written about *The Middle Classes* and in 1983 was to become a life peer, lived in a nearby village, sent his children (or at least his daughters) to Banbury Grammar School and was an incisive critic of the contemporary changes in educational policy. He had succeeded Profumo as MP for Stratford-upon-Avon in 1963. But, most of all, there was Dick Crossman.

R. H. S. Crossman was born in 1907, and was the ambivalent recipient of the best education that could then be provided for the son of a professional family: Winchester and New College. He was a Fellow of New College from 1930 to 1937, when the Warden was H. A. L. Fisher who had been President of the Board of Education under Lloyd George during and after the First World War (and who deserves a book to himself). He deserted the safe cloisters of that college in order to teach for the Workers' Educational Association: he had been leader of the Labour group on Oxford City Council since 1934. During the war he worked in psychological warfare, and doubtless learnt many of his more infuriating tricks of debating and persuasion. He rarely seemed happier than when intolerantly defending propositions in which he did not believe. In 1945 he became MP for Coventry East, and nine years later married Anne McDougall, the daughter of a senior manager of the aluminium company whose arrival in Banbury had brought a measure of prosperity to the town in the years of the Depression. He therefore settled in her family house at Cropredy, where his children, Patrick and Virginia, grew up. It lay conveniently between London and his Coventry constituency. Dick had been assistant editor of the *New Statesman* from 1938 to 1955 and, as has already been explained, was no friend of the leading men of the Labour party in the years after the War. His support of Wilson in 1963, and the Labour victory of 1964, brought him in one leap to the Cabinet and to the summit of his career. When we first began to meet and talk in 1963, he was expecting to be offered a Cabinet post in education if Labour won and he could keep in step for long enough. Instead, and to his surprise, he was in October 1964 given the Ministry of Housing and Local Government, in which both Chamberlain and Macmillan had made their considerable reputations. Two years later he became Leader of the House of Commons, and for the last two years of the Labour government presided over the empire of the Department of Health and Social Services. He became passionate about pensions.

His *Diary*, one of the most incisive and entertaining accounts of the workings of government and the foibles of politicians, is a rich illumination of national history and institutions. But, as he always found room in his life for north Oxfordshire and his family, he also enjoyed setting down some of his local preoccupations and irritations. Like many socialists and intellectuals educated in the traditions of the high establishment, he fussed about the education of his own children and about the schools to which they might go. The primary schools of Oxfordshire, with their occasionally romantic commitments to open learning and creativity, more than once felt the lash of his tongue. He certainly had no patience with the teaching of italic handwriting.

As a Cabinet minister, taking an impish pleasure in his red boxes, he was entitled to a specially reserved first-class compartment on the London train. He enjoyed the fury, not always speechless, of the good Conservatives who occasionally had to stand in the corridor, popping their eyes at this spectacle of enthroned privilege. He would, as the *Diary* records, sometimes enliven the journey by opening the door for the local MP, or for the headmaster of the Grammar School. There were often sharp exchanges. On other occasions, we would spend time together at the weekends. Before 10/65 was published there was a sequence of proposals for secondary-school reorganization in Banbury. Dick had persuaded himself (and so had I) that a good solution would be a middle school for 9–13-year-olds, and an informed choice of a variety of upper schools thereafter: this would open up a rigid system and preserve the best in the grammar-school tradition, as a counterpoise to the strengths of the Public Schools. Dick was very annoyed when his own party ruled out this solution as being insufficiently comprehensive.

The 1960s were marked by a strong interest in the relationship between primary and secondary education, and in possible changes in the age of transfer from one to the other. After completing its work on the Newsom Report, the Central Advisory Council was reconstituted under the chairmanship of Lady Plowden, and turned its attention to primary schools. The question of the proper age of transfer was referred to it, as the West Riding was making plans for a series of middle schools spanning the age range nine to thirteen. Under the 1944 and 1948 Education Acts such schools would have been illegal: pupils must be transferred from primary to secondary between the ages of ten and a half and twelve. Edward Boyle had secured the passage of the 1964 Education Act in a characteristic effort to introduce more flexibility and loosen the grip of selection at eleven-plus. The first middle schools were opened in 1968, and by 1980 there were 1,700 of them.

The categories of 'primary' and 'secondary' were not, however, abolished, and a Local Education Authority had to decide whether it wished a middle school to be 'deemed' to be primary or secondary. The middle-school initiative, as it gathered momentum in the 1960s, was concerned with a great deal more than legalistic terminology. Those who argued its virtues saw in this new kind of school an opportunity to blend the best in primary and secondary habits and, in particular, to extend for two extra years some of the freedom associated with good primary-school practice. Subject specialization and formal teaching would be undermined.

The Plowden Report, which was published in January 1967, took a cheerful view of good primary-school practice, and many of its paragraphs are a celebration of liberal ideals of teaching and learning. 'Finding out' was better than 'being told'. For this reason, and at a time of less genial moods, the Report was to come under severe criticism. In the event, it recommended that the age of transfer should be raised to twelve, with the first school (5–8) followed by middle schools (8–12). It also urged a move away from the practice of streaming—which, given the importance after 1944 of the universal competitive examination at eleven-plus, had tended to increase in the years after the War. The Plowden Report was a national corollary to contemporary changes in assumptions about secondary education and the structures which embody those assumptions.

The Report was not, however, flattering in its description of the material basis for primary education, which was marked by deficiencies common to many secondary schools as well. It is only through the most tinted of retrospective spectacles that the 1960s can appear as a golden age, and least of all in the deprived areas to which the Report correctly gave so much attention:

We noted the grim approaches; incessant traffic noise in narrow streets; parked vehicles hemming in the pavement; rubbish dumps on waste land nearby; the absence of green playing spaces on or near the school sites; tiny playgrounds; gaunt looking buildings; often poor decorative conditions inside; narrow passages; dark rooms; unheated and cramped cloakrooms; unroofed outside lavatories; tiny staff rooms; inadequate storage space with consequent restrictions on teaching materials and therefore methods; inadequate space for movement and P.E.; meals in classroom; art on desks; music only to the discomfort of others in an echoing building; non-soundproof partitions between classes; lack of smaller rooms for group work; lack of spare room for tuition of small groups; insufficient display space; attractive books kept unseen in cupboards for lack of space to lay them out; no privacy for parents wishing to see the head; sometimes the head and his secretary sharing the same room; and, sometimes all around, the ingrained grime of generations.

You can almost smell them now. John Newsom was vice-chairman of the Council, and David Donnison and Michael Young among its members. Michael Young came specially to Banbury to talk about the age of transfer, and many things besides. I was able to try out on the author of *The Rise of the Meritocracy* some local antidotes to the disease he had diagnosed a decade before. The influence of such men assured that the Report would be tough, as well as humane, and that it would apply sociological insights to the analysis of the conditions of schooling. Most striking of all, and having relevance far beyond primary schools themselves, was the emphasis on the correlation of social disadvantage and educational achievement. It also made respectable the unfamiliar doctrine of 'positive discrimination'—going beyond weak doctrines of equality (perceived as the removal of artificial obstacles), to strong doctrines (based on the conviction that the socially disadvantaged should receive more than, not the same as, their more fortunate contemporaries). This, however, must be achieved by an increase in total resources and not simply by a redistribution of those already available. More provision should be made for the under-fives; teachers' aides should be recruited and trained; problem areas should get extra teachers; home–school relations should be improved, and a triangular partnership of home–school–child established. Most children simply did not have a fair chance: two-thirds of the homes in the unskilled-worker category had five *or fewer* books in them, compared with one-twentieth of the professional homes.

Most important of all, educational priority areas should be formally designated, and teachers paid more for working in them. Crosland's response to Plowden was as positive as that of Boyle to Robbins. By the summer of 1967, when he left the Department of Education and Science for the Board of Trade, £16m. had been made available for a building programme over the next two years, with a further £18m. to follow in 1971/2. The Educational Priority Areas were, indeed, constituted and Crosland agreed with Maurice Kogan that he had 'legitimised the radical sociology of the 1950's and 1960's'. Moreover, the impetus had been given to the establishment—under the direction, for England, of A. H. Halsey

—of five action research programmes, to be initiated in 1968 and completed within three years. Halsey wrote the first volume of the Report on these programmes, published in 1972. It pointed towards the possibility of achievements that have not yet been actively pursued. The creation of the Educational Priority Areas was one of the last things which Tony Crosland accomplished at the Department of Education and Science, and one of those that gave him the greatest pleasure.

It was, of course, far from being his only achievement. He had already, in April 1965, made a speech in Woolwich on plans for the development of higher education. It was, as he readily acknowledged, in many ways an unfortunate statement into which he had been pushed by his officials before he had fully mastered the intricacies of the problem. The Robbins Report, and its acceptance in broad terms by the Conservative government of the day, marked the beginning of a period of rapid expansion. Not all its proposals were, however, given effect: after a debate in 1964, in which Lord James was particularly influential, it was decided to have one overall Minister for Education, and not two. The Department of Education and Science therefore took over the enlarged responsibilities of the Ministry created by Butler in 1944, and Quintin Hogg (who had divested himself of his peerage in the hope of succeeding Macmillan as Prime Minister) became the first Secretary of State. Robbins had seen the universities as dominant within higher education: they were to have most of the extra numbers and to provide the model of perfection. Other institutions which grew in stature might aspire, one day and if they behaved, to become universities themselves.

Some were critical of this orthodoxy and—behind the scenes— nobody more effectively so than Toby Weaver, the most powerful civil servant of his generation in the formulation of educational policies. He has not concealed—still, in retirement, does not conceal—his scepticism about a worship of universities marked by prejudices about the superiority of the academic over the practical, of the pure over the applied, of the traditional over the innovatory. In Tony Crosland he found a ready listener, and the Woolwich speech marked a sharp redirection of policy in higher education. It was to have considerable effects upon the earlier stages of education.

Crosland told his audience that whereas higher education must indeed be developed systematically, it should not be represented as a unitary or hierarchical system, with the universities sitting at the top. On the contrary, it should be a dual system based upon the twin tradition of universities (the so-called autonomous sector) and of the public sector (further education and other colleges maintained by Local Education Authorities). The one should not imitate the other, and the public sector should be 'under social control, directly responsive to social needs'. For that reason, it should remain in the hands of local government. It should emphasize the value of professional, vocational, and technical courses and of links with industry. 'Let us move away', he appealed, 'from our snobbish caste-ridden hierarchical obsessions with university status.' The colleges should not be the poor relations of the universities, trying to become more like them. Teacher training should be expanded, but the Colleges of Education should not (as Robbins proposed) become part of the university system. No more universities would be created, either as new foundations or as promotions from the public sector. The technological universities, as the former Colleges of Advanced Technology, would be the last such redesignations, so there would be no point in joining the queue. The 'binary policy' had taken shape, and in 1966 the White Paper *A Plan for Polytechnics and Other Colleges* filled in the details. A new category of institution, the polytechnic, would be created—mostly by mergers of existing colleges—to serve as the flagship of the public-sector fleet and in which would be concentrated most of the advanced work of that sector. Their degrees would be validated by the Council for National Academic Awards. By 1973, all thirty polytechnics had been established. Critics have since commented on the paradox offered by a Secretary of State sharply defining two categories of higher education —the one more theoretical and academic than the other—in the same year as he was energetically destroying similar categories in secondary education. But he had good reasons.

The most urgent need of the mid-1960s was for teachers, and

the Secretary of State in a speech to the annual conference of the National Union of Teachers earlier in April 1965, outlined new policies. He made fourteen suggestions related to the recruitment and deployment of teachers. Colleges were encouraged to introduce a four-term year, to make full use of their accommodation and to establish 'outposts'. Four or five more day-colleges were to be established. There was to be a drive to recruit married women who had left teaching, and to make part-time teaching more attractive. This, observed Crosland, 'was perhaps the greatest achievement of those years—to bring the problem of teacher supply within sight of solution.'

Crosland, like Boyle, was a Minister with a policy. He gave himself time to think, and to argue with his friends. A. H. Halsey, David Donnison, John Vaizey, Noel Annan, and Michael Young were among those whom he invited to his home to argue about the strategies and, but only after they had worked, to enjoy his hospitality: 'People become much too talkative if you give them something to drink.' He was certainly talkative enough over the November weekend which he spent with the Crossmans in north Oxfordshire. The *Diary* for 7 November 1965 reads:

A perfect day out on the hills behind Boddington watching the hunt career around us while we were exploring Hobbit country with Patrick. Anthony Crosland and his wife Susan arrived at 5.30 and we gave a dinner party for them with Harry and Mary Judge from Banbury Grammar School and Richard and Ann Hartree ... [The] Headmaster and the Secretary of State got on very well, and I was impressed by Tony's proficiency in explaining his plans.

The plans in which he was most interested were those for teacher supply and (even more) comprehensive reorganization. But, late in the evening, he enquired without ceremony 'What *am* I going to do about the direct-grant schools?' This problem overlapped with that of the Public Schools generally, and he had already in the summer secured Cabinet approval for setting up a Public Schools Commission. A few weeks after our meeting I accepted his invitation to become a member of that Commission, which also included David Donnison, Noel Annan (Lord Annan),

John Vaizey (now Lord Vaizey), and Bernard Williams (then married to Shirley Williams). John Dancy, the Master of Marlborough, represented the reformers among the Public School headmasters, and Tom Howarth, the High Master of St Paul's, did not. The secretary of the Commission was Geoffrey Cockerill, who had been Private Secretary to Boyle and, for a short while, Crosland.

The chairman was Sir John Newsom, and in 1966 we set to work. John Newsom brought to that task an intimate knowledge of the workings of the Establishment, a rich store of anecdote (much of it scurrilous), a delight in getting to know his fellow members and in entertaining them in princely style, and a huge sense of fun. I learnt more from him that I can ever acknowledge. The Public Schools, as the Secretary of State well knew, represented an intricate puzzle and their power seriously undermined national efforts to generate a comprehensive system. More particularly, those who owed their careers and their satisfactions to grammar schools, or were headmasters of them, feared that the progressive elimination of those schools might make it more difficult for the maintained sector to compete effectively with the independent schools. Emanuel Shinwell's rhetoric, and the arguments which Crosland himself had developed in his writing, could not be brushed aside.

In the event, of course, nothing was or could be done. Nor had any effective measures been taken after the Fleming Report was submitted to Butler in 1944. The Fleming committee had been set up in response to pressure from the independent schools themselves: their heads and governors had been worried by the drop in enrolments and income in the 1930s, and many hoped to share in the growing national investment that would follow the War. Some of them, like Sir Robert Birley, the headmaster of Eton and a member of the Fleming Committee, disliked the social selectiveness of the schools and the dependence of admission upon the ability to pay fees, and hoped to see the schools brought fully into the mainstream of national life. Butler was anxious that the implications of the abolition of fees in maintained secondary schools should be studied and, ever prudent, hoped to avoid polemics by keeping 'the public school question' out of the Act and out of debates. The Committee noted that 'the trend of social development is leaving the public schools out of alignment with the world in which they exist'. They proposed a scheme to replace the existing direct-grant scheme, but the Ministry preferred plans of its own and, as has already been explained, gave effect to them. They survived until 1976.

Proposals for the future of the Public Schools, mostly boarding, were made in 1944, against a background of assumptions no longer valid in 1966. It was known that fees in secondary schools would shortly be abolished, that grammar-school education would be developed for about 20 per cent of the population, and assumed that secondary modern schools would be provided for the rest. The Committee recommended that bursaries should be provided for pupils who had attended maintained primary schools and that any independent schools participating in the scheme should admit at least 25 per cent of its pupils in this way. Interviewing for places would be conducted on a regional basis, and fees paid by the LEAs (who would receive government grants).

What, then, should be the principles of such selection? Obviously, the pupils would want or need a boarding education, and the reasons for that preference would have to be stated—on all this, the Report was embarrassingly vague. But, more important, the participating schools should not take only the very clever. Nevertheless, there is an unquestioned assumption that the pupils selected would have no difficulty in following a grammar-school course. The affinity between Public School and grammar school was still very close. 'It can never be satisfactory for a child to be educated in a school in which the standard of work is above his powers, or the curriculum not suited to his particular aptitudes.' Underlying the 1944 Report are assumptions both about the moral advantages of boarding and about the centrality of the grammar school and its curriculum.

Those assumptions could no longer be made by Mr Crosland's Commission, although one or two members of it plainly wished that they could. As a result of Circular 10/65, and the more general movement of opinion and policy associated with it, the two sectors of secondary education were diverging. The Public Schools which we visited and enjoyed had already changed a great deal since the War. Just as, in the previous century, they had modified their style from that of the Christian gentleman into that of the muscular Christian, so now they were completing a transition towards becoming highly competitive academic schools. Royston Lambert, who undertook a great deal of research for the Commission, recorded the prayer of a twelve-year-old boy:

> Dear Lord
> You know that I have not worked as hard as I ought.
> I have shirked my work.
> And now, during this exam I deserve to fail.
> But forgive me
> and let me succeed.   Amen.

Although the size of the independent sector had been shrinking, its reputation and power had not. In 1947 it accounted for 9 per cent of the secondary-school population, but in 1967 for only 5.5 per cent—made up by 1.4 per cent in Public Schools narrowly defined, and 3.9 per cent in other independent schools. Direct-grant schools, formally independent but associated with the maintained system, accounted for a further 1.5 per cent. But higher staying-on rates amplified these figures: 3 per cent of boys in Public Schools at age 14, but 12 per cent at age 17. It is not surprising that a high proportion of A level candidates came and come from such schools. The Commission reported that although 9.3 per cent of all seventeen-year-olds (boys and girls) were in independent schools of all kinds, boys from boarding Public Schools were statistically overrepresented in many careers: 49.3 per cent among the heads of colleges and professors at Oxford and Cambridge, 42 per cent in the Labour Cabinet of the day and 90.9 per cent in its Conservative predecessor (things are no different now), 75 per cent among Church of England bishops, 79.2 per cent among judges and QCs, and 43 per cent among successful applicants to the Administrative Civil Service (in the years 1963–7). Doubtless, given the backgrounds from which they came and the support they received, many of these dis-

tinguished citizens would have done well, whatever school they
had attended. But the Commission concluded that this measure of
institutional concentration was unhealthy, and related it in part to
the surviving power of snobbery in English society. But it was
even more clear that the Public Schools had adapted themselves
rapidly and skilfully to the demands for a meritocracy as identified
by Michael Young. John Newsom knew that, in his two Reports,
he was moving nimbly between two worlds that had nothing in
common. As, on many visits to the schools, we argued far into the
evening, several Commissioners and their hosts became unclear as
to whether Public Schools should be abolished because they were
very good or because they were very bad.

Of the fathers of the boarders in these schools, 92 per cent were
in the Registrar-General's Class I or II, and 52 per cent had been to
Public Schools themselves. This kind of concentration could still
produce a narrowness of horizon, or a confident self-satisfaction.
Royston Lambert captured this mood in a seventeen-year-old boy
talking about his family and school: 'They have been coming here
since the seventeenth century, I think, although what they did
before that I can't imagine, had Tutors I suppose. You even used
to be able to bring them here with you. Everyone I know at home
is either here, or has been here. Yorkshire is such a small place
really.'

The quality of the staff was impressive, and many of them in
those days were among the most adventurous of professionals in
introducing new teaching methods and new curricula. The teacher–
pupil ratio was 1:11.6, compared with 1:16.8 in contemporary
grammar schools. Graduates of Oxford and Cambridge predominated, and over 70 per cent of all masters had themselves attended
HMC (Headmasters' Conference) schools. Most HMC schools
covered the age range 13–18 (although the education offered in
preparatory schools for pupils to the age of thirteen would not
have won the approval of the Plowden Committee). Very few
pupils left before completing a full five-year course, and 40 per
cent of the total pupil population of all the schools were in the
sixth form. The standards and ideals of the sixth form, as the
Crowther Report had epitomized them, dominated the school.

The pace of work was always high, and sometimes ferocious. Many sixth-formers, of course, left a maintained school to go on to universities, but only 10 per cent of these went to Oxford or Cambridge, compared with nearly half of the university-bound sixth-formers from the Public Schools. Of all pupils 9 per cent had an IQ of 130 or more, compared with 4.5 per cent in the population as a whole.

Very few had an IQ below 100: the lower half of the ability range was simply not represented in these schools. Some three-quarters of all the pupils in them had the necessary ability for admission to grammar schools. Although the classics were still important, their grip was slackening in a competitive and utilitarian age. The most popular A level subjects today in such schools are engineering, law, economics. All these comments apply to boys' schools: the girls' schools represented a much wider variation in style, and in many cases offered (deliberately) only a modestly academic education.

The endowments of the schools were rarely lavish, and they depended on fees which necessarily remained high. 42,000 pupils in independent schools were assisted from public funds, amounting in all to some £11m. each year. Rate relief came to another £1m., and various forms of tax relief to a considerable sum, which could not be accurately assessed. The schools were expensive, and necessarily exclusive, in part because of the considerable burdens of providing boarding education. It was boarding that gave solidity to the schools, turning them into total societies—often in rural and inaccessible surroundings—and reinforcing both achievement and a potent sense of cohesion. If they are somewhat more relaxed today, it would be a mistake to exaggerate the contrasts. They certainly preserve a dominance within the system generally.

The Labour party had an unsurprising and intuitive dislike of the Public School, but very few ideas about what might be done. Even members of the Commission who, like myself, were not members of the Labour party, hoped that their social exclusiveness could be softened, and that they would follow the lines of development then visible in Oxford and Cambridge. But those universities moved very largely into the public domain without sacrificing too much of their independence, and by improving the standard of their entry. How could relatively small and expensive boarding-schools move in a similar direction within a system explicitly dedicated to comprehensiveness?

They could not, and many of them regretted it. It would have been wrong to propose that subsidized admission to such schools should be offered to very bright pupils, at the same time that comprehension was being commended (sometimes forcefully so) to grammar schools. It would have been wrong to propose abolition, and in any case no member of the Commission in fact believed that it should be illegal for a parent to spend money on a child's education. History, in the shape of the tardiness of public authorities in setting up a proper system of secondary schooling, was responsible for the 'Public School problem'—which is, in my view, both real and insoluble. But the Commission did assemble a mass of fact and opinion about the schools and, with little confidence in the outcome, proposed a compromise solution.

This turned upon the provision of boarding. The schools were rightly proud of the contribution made by boarding to the lives of pupils, and especially those from homes which could not provide a stable background. At the same time, it was clear there was a substantial need for boarding education throughout the country, and that this need was not being met. A limited number of boarding-schools should therefore be drawn into a partnership with the State, by agreeing to give at least 50 per cent of their places to pupils formally assessed as having a boarding need. The presence of a significant number of such pupils in the 'integrated' schools would ensure that the manner and style of those places would change: there would be no risk of new pupils simply being absorbed into the mores of the upper classes, or of a repetition of the kind of conflict from which a working-class minority had suffered in grammar schools. The academic range of the schools would become wider, to include some three-quarters of the full ability range. A minority of us thought that some schools should be integrated as sixth-form colleges, or centres, to which entry might properly be academically competitive.

We signed the Report in April, and I went away to Padstow. It was published on 22 July, and it soon became clear that the schools were not interested. Neither, to be fair, was the Government. Things might have been a little different if Tony Crosland had still been at the Department of Education and Science, but I doubt it. In any case, the Government was in trouble. It had done very badly in the 1967 local elections, and in November Wilson at last devalued the pound—assuring a somewhat puzzled nation that 'the pound in your pocket' would somehow not be affected. Integrating some of the Public Schools in the way proposed would eventually cost about £12m. each year, and £6.1m. in the short term: these plans would now be in open competition with the proposals of the Newsom and Plowden Reports, at a time when severe economies were being applied to public expenditure. In 1968, the raising to sixteen of the school-leaving age was postponed. Crosland opposed this, and thought Crossman 'crazy' for not doing so as well. For my part, I welcomed the temporary relief from an added pressure of numbers and new problems at a time when Banbury School was in its infancy. Expansion in education became suddenly less attractive, as well as being less affordable: in New York the Columbia University sit-in began in April, Paris flared into disorder in May, and in January 1969 trouble was to spread to the London School of Economics, where David Donnison had his chair.

Meanwhile, the Commission had been reconstituted under David Donnison and addressed the question of the direct-grant and independent day-schools. Throughout 1969 I spent some time each month visiting schools, and attending yet more meetings in Curzon Street. Dick Crossman was still on the train each day. Crossman had, in May 1966, appointed a Commission under the chairmanship of Lord Redcliffe-Maud (formerly Sir John Maud) to report on the reorganization of local government. It reported in June 1969 and it became clear that even Oxfordshire would change its size and shape. On 1 July Prince Charles was invested the Prince of Wales at Caernarfon Castle and I bought a large Welsh flag to cheer the many Welsh, or half-Welsh, teachers in the school. A small English patriot tried to haul it down, but was apprehended; I bought a St George's flag as well, to demonstrate impartiality.

The direct-grant schools, more than the independent schools, represented a real and local problem for the emerging comprehensive system. For as long as the most able pupils were, with the support of public money, taken from the comprehensive schools, the development of comprehensives with high academic standards would be frustrated. The main virtue of the Donnison Report (eventually published in 1970) lay in its cool and thorough analysis of the nature and pace of the movement towards more openness in secondary education. It made it clear that, whatever their achievements in the past, the direct-grant schools could not look towards a stable future within the national system of education. They were of course no different from good maintained grammar schools and owed their survival after 10/65 only to the anomaly created in 1926 and perpetuated in 1944. They valued their independence, and one of the persuasive recommendations of the Report was that all schools should—as John Newsom had secured in Hertfordshire—be given as much freedom as possible in determining their priorities and policies. It was not a coincidence that Tom Taylor, later to become a Labour peer and the principal author of another report, was one of the newly appointed members of the Commission. The Report suggested two ways in which direct-grant and other schools might be drawn into patterns of local provision: either as full-grant schools (a new category), or as voluntary-aided or controlled schools along the well-established lines defined in 1944. In either case, fees would be abolished along with the principle of selection. A minority of the Commission argued for a small number of super-selective schools, for the most able 2 per cent of each age group. I was not of that minority, but the argument sharpened my concern for the education of the most-talented pupils—a concern that was to run through my last years in Banbury and into my work in Oxford.

The direct-grant schools did not like these proposals, and had little to gain from them. By the time action was taken, by the Labour government in 1975, school rolls were already falling and there was little interest in the forging of any new partnership. What little opportunity there might have been for careful integration, had been lost.

When we signed the Report, on 29 January 1970, I was in my first few weeks of a sabbatical term at Merton College, Oxford, and in need of a short rest from the work and vocabulary of education. I turned back to seventeenth-century France. In January, too, the leading figures of the Conservative party met at Selsdon in order to hammer out new policies. Margaret Thatcher had already replaced Edward Boyle as their Education spokesman, and the sixties had indeed finished. The general election was held on 18 June, and election and examination fever coincided for the first time since 1945. The Conservatives won 330 seats, against 287 for Labour, and an overall majority of 30. Mr Heath moved into Number Ten, Sir Keith Joseph succeeded Dick Crossman at the Department of Health and Social Security (as Crossman had succeeded Joseph at Housing and Local Government in 1964), and Mrs Thatcher became the third woman since 1944 to assume responsibility for education. She was to keep it for the next three and a half years. The first 'Black Paper', attacking many recent trends in education, had been published the year before. Its title was *Fight for Education*.

CHAPTER 7

Examinations

In the summer of 1970 the Schools Council made two important decisions (if that is not too emphatic a word) about the secondary-school examination system. The first, which related to sixth-form examinations, was negative and will be commented upon later. The second represented a commitment to develop a new and single system for examining pupils at the age of sixteen-plus. The debate about examinations was to continue unresolved throughout the 1970s and into the 1980s, and reflected profound dilemmas about the nature and purpose of secondary education as it had developed since 1944.

Examinations occupy a uniquely important place in English secondary schools. They raise questions about the relationship between education and employment, about the control of the curriculum, about the maintenance and improvement of standards, about the nature of meritocracy, about the purposes of comprehensive reorganization. By 1970 such questions came painfully to the surface, and were to prove even more visible and demanding when the minimum school-leaving age was raised to sixteen in 1973. The year 1970 was, moreover, the centenary not only of Forster's Education Act—the first systematic intervention by the State in the provision of publicly funded education—but also of the imposition of the principle that entry to the British Civil Service should be by competitive examination. That principle was embedded in the development of schooling and examinations, and explains much of the tangle into which the examination system had fallen a century later.

Examinations, as administrative and educational devices, were a central part of the response of nineteenth-century Britain to the twin imperatives of efficiency and fairness: the analogies and links with the development of secondary education are therefore very close, since examinations came to be integral both to questions of access to secondary grammar schools (the examination at eleven-plus) and to exit from them (at sixteen-plus or eighteen-plus). Efficiency required that an increasingly bureaucratic and imperialist State should be served by men of competence and intelligence, and that the needs of a complex industrial and commercial sector should be adequately met. Fairness required that access to favoured positions, conferring status and security, should not depend entirely upon patronage and nepotism. Examinations were designed to meet both these sets of requirements.

These points need to be made and developed further, as a preliminary to an analysis of the proposed changes in the 1970s, not only because the only explanation of these changes is a historical one, but also because the later complications and distortions of the system were the direct consequence of an honest and increasingly elaborate attempt to respect the virtuous requirements of efficiency and fairness. The surge towards comprehensiveness represented a public wish to extend more widely, even universally, the right of access to a grammar-school education. As a corollary, more pupils must have the right of access to an examination at sixteen-plus, and—paradoxically, if competitive standards were at the same time to be preserved—must as a consequence be in many ways exposed to the certainty of failure and disappointment.

No such paradoxes surrounded the origins of public examinations. Oxford University in 1800 reformed its examinations in an earnest attempt to raise its own low academic standards and to make the honours system, in which candidates are carefully graded, central to the identification and stimulation of talent. The reforms, first of the Indian and then of the Home Civil Service, were designed to eliminate corruption and to raise administrative and clerical competence. As more public grants for elementary schooling became available, so it became necessary to introduce rational principles of distribution and accountability. Elementary schools and the teachers in them should therefore be paid in proportion to the results achieved, and the most reliable way of measuring those results was by examining the performance of the pupils. The Revised Code of 1861 was designed for that purpose, by specifying the standards to be measured and so providing a yardstick for the distribution of cash.

The development of examinations in secondary schools is less easily explained. Given the persistent reluctance of government (whether central or local) to make any adequate provision of such schools, everything was left to private enterprise and imagination. Independent schools flourished, as has been explained, and decayed grammar schools were revived. But how could the anxious parent choose among such schools, or discover anything about their quality? In 1857 a group of public-spirited men in the South-West of England persuaded the University of Oxford to conduct an examination of pupils, in order to provide some reliable measure of quality and achievement and to provoke emulation. An enlightened university reformer rejoiced that 'Oxford has opened a locomotive department'—and this was thirty years before the opening of the Severn Tunnel. In the following year, the Oxford Delegacy of Examinations was established to plan this work upon a more permanent basis. Cambridge and other universities followed Oxford into the examination enterprise, and the foundations of the contemporary system were laid.

Several motives therefore underpinned the development of examinations—the raising of academic standards (inside and outside the universities), payment by results, the selection of appropriate candidates for employment, the testing of the quality of schools. For the Victorians it was plain common sense that examinations should be used as a basis for distributing opportunity, at every stage of education and employment. The village schoolmaster at Kidlington prepared my father for a highly competitive examination for a scholarship place at Thame, and that examination was the precursor of the eleven-plus. At Thame, he took the Junior and Senior examinations of the Oxford Delegacy of Local Examinations and framed the certificate—signed in 1903 by the Vice-Chancellor, and bordered with yellowing photographs of the towers and spires of Oxford—which conferred on him the title of Associate in Arts. Entry to the salaried branch of the Great Western Railway—like the Civil Service, or the Army—similarly depended upon performance in an examination, as did the earlier stages of subsequent promotion. The system was in place, and grew with reckless abandon.

By 1914, something like one hundred different examinations provided by a wide variety of different organizations were available in secondary schools. There had been, from the beginning, a deeply rooted hostility to any kind of centralized or government control of the examinations or of the schools, but the confusing dangers of anarchy were now equally clear. A report in 1911 by the Consultative Committee (the precursor of the Central Advisory Councils of the 1944 Act) offered a classic defence of the virtues of examinations and pointed towards the need for some rational co-ordination. In 1917, H. A. L. Fisher (as President of the Board of Education) established the Secondary Schools Examination Council (SSEC), to supervise the introduction of the School Certificate and the Higher School Certificate. These were designed to absorb many of the *ad hoc* arrangements and were, with some minor modifications, the examinations which my contemporaries and I sat at Cardiff High School.

They are the direct precursors of the O and A levels introduced after the Second World War, but differ in important respects from them. Responsibility for the examinations rested with boards constituted by universities, but national currency was secured by the approval of the SSEC and of the Minister—whose interference was minimal, and remained so until very recent times. Nevertheless, the examination system was used—by an early consensus of the academic and political establishments—to shape and control the secondary-school curriculum. This influence remained direct and unchallenged for as long as secondary schools all remained academic in character, and for as long as effective competition for university places remained low. From 1917 until the early 1950s, the examination system reinforced doctrines of a balanced curriculum and a broad, general education. It has, of course, long ceased to do so.

These doctrines were given shape in a requirement that a School

Certificate (designed for pupils at about the age of sixteen) could be awarded only to a candidate who secured passes in five subjects, which had to be drawn from three different groups. One group included such subjects as English, history and geography; a second comprised foreign languages, ancient and modern; a third was made up of mathematics and scientific subjects. A candidate could be awarded a Certificate only if he secured these necessary passes in the same examination. It followed that schools and pupils were not free to abandon core subjects before completing the full secondary course, in order to concentrate upon a narrower and more specialized curriculum. A success in any subject could be recorded as a pass or as a credit, and a sufficient number of credits in specified subjects secured exemption from matriculation—the examination, previously conducted separately for universities, which was the qualifying test for admission.

The Higher School Certificate marked the terminus of sixth-form studies, at the age of eighteen or thereabouts, and its evolution will be discussed when the development of post-sixteen education in secondary schools is outlined below. The modest growth of other, and less precisely academic, forms of secondary schooling in the years between the wars led to criticism of the rigidity of the School Certificate system at sixteen-plus: the Hadow Report of 1926 recommended a new examination under different control for the projected 'Modern' schools (which did not materialize until after 1944), and the Spens Report of 1938 was critical of the pressure on schools of the matriculation requirement. The Norwood Report, timed to coincide with the discussions leading to the 1944 Act, optimistically believed that a formal, external examination at sixteen-plus would soon wither away, was strongly critical of the group requirements in the existing School Certificate, and wished to make a general school report an important part of any school-leaving certificate. The Norwood Report not only accepted but fiercely emphasized the concept of a divided system of secondary schooling and its necessary relationship to different mental characteristics served by appropriately adapted curricula. The assumption that public examinations would be confined to the grammar-school sector was carried forward by the SSEC with its 1947 recommendations that the present system of O and A levels should replace the old School Certificate and Higher School Certificate. The new secondary modern, the Ministry was fruitlessly to insist, should not be embraced or limited by these new examinations, which were taken for the first time in 1951.

Although, in practice and for many years, the new system proved to be suspiciously close to the old, that was far from the intention of those who designed it. Most important of all, it was to be a single-subject examination, and not one based upon groups: candidates should take subjects at the appropriate level, and their performance in each subject should be recorded. O levels should, indeed, be taken at the age of sixteen and A level at eighteen, but there was no reason why any subject should be taken at both levels: a candidate going on to take A-level French, for example, would not waste time first taking the same subject at O level, and the pressure of formal examinations would be reduced. The grammar-school course was perceived as a full seven-year course, starting at the age of eleven-plus, and pupils embarked upon it should not be expected to leave prematurely at sixteen.

The reality, as has been shown, was very different, and the O level became, and has remained, as clearly marked a stage as its School Certificate predecessor. The bypassing of subjects never became general, and university entrance requirements (cast in terms of satisfactory performance in specified subjects) had much the same effect as the old group requirements. The necessity to repeat the whole examination in order to redeem a failure in one subject, was, however, eliminated. This new flexibility made it impossible in practical terms rigidly to exclude secondary modern schools from the examination network.

The examination remained in the hands of the university boards, of which there are now eight (two of them in a somewhat special constitutional position). The O-level system was at first designed on a simple pass/fail basis, and no other information was given on the certificate. A pass was related to the existing credit standard in the School Certificate, and the pass rate has remained surprisingly (some would say, suspiciously) constant in most subjects at about 60 per cent. Grades, numbering from one to nine were nevertheless given (1–6 being various levels of 'Pass'), and these results made available to schools. Inevitably, information of this more detailed kind was sought by employers and others, and soon became generally available. In 1975 the system was rationalized; grades are now recorded on the certificates, with A to C corresponding to the old grades one to six: the absolute pass/fail distortion has been removed, although most of the world has failed to notice this. The number and proportion of school-leavers attempting O levels rose steadily towards 1970, and has continued to rise since. 23.6 per cent of all school-leavers attempted the former School Certificate in 1948; by 1962, when I went to Banbury Grammar School, the national figure was 39.3 per cent, and by 1970 (when Mr Heath won the general election and the Schools Council bravely tried to adapt a system which was under strain), that figure was 42.2 per cent.

Why, in 1970, was a well-tried system under strain? The fundamental cause of this stress, which survives into the 1980s, is that the system introduced in 1951 could not appropriately meet the needs of the growing number of pupils who were, for a variety of reasons, pressing to become candidates for public examinations. It was at this point that the virtues of the classical system began to be distorted into vices. The Ministry of Education and HMI had, of course, tried to stem this flood, to promote a concept of the secondary modern school as something different in kind from the academically competitive grammar school, and to discourage attempts to enter secondary-modern candidates from taking public examinations. After all, the O level had been designed (like its School Certificate predecessor) for pupils of grammar-school ability and with matching intentions. But the market forces were too strong for enlightened educational theory. Already, in 1954, 357 secondary modern schools were entering a total of 5,500 candidates for the General Certificate of Education; within three short years that figure had been trebled.

There was something restrictive and unjust in the attempts to exclude secondary-modern pupils from the benefits of public examinations. The steady erosion of public confidence in the accuracy and reliability of selection at eleven-plus served only to highlight this injustice. Experience in Banbury was only too typical. When the boys' secondary modern was established there at the beginning of the 1950s, its headmaster and several of the senior staff came from a background of grammar-school teaching, and had all been pupils in grammar schools themselves. They were well aware of the imperfections of selection at eleven-plus, and knew that they had in their care boys who, in other parts of the country, would in any case have been given grammar-school places. They also knew that ability and promise are (fortunately) not frozen at the age of eleven, and that late developers could often achieve surprising results.

The option of proposing transfer to the grammar school at the age of thirteen was, save where parents proved particularly determined or even aggressive, rarely viewed with any favour. The practical problems were not trivial, for it was not until the 1960s in Banbury that any effort was made to align the curricula and objectives across the 11–13 age range within the separate schools. Even more to the point, teachers who had worked hard to eliminate the sense of failure among some of the 80 per cent of all pupils allocated to secondary modern schools at the age of eleven were understandably reluctant to see their successes 'elevated' to the grammar school at the age of thirteen. These were the very pupils who could help to improve the standards of secondary modern schools. It was also perfectly clear that, in considerable measure, schools would be and are judged by parents and employers on the basis of their success in improving the prospects of their pupils. It would be surprising if it were otherwise, and this kind of success depended in large measure upon performance in examinations. That is why secondary modern schools began to develop O-level streams. The girls' secondary modern school in Banbury was, at least in this sense, less competitive. Its teachers were content that girls should take a four-year secondary-school course (for the school-leaving age was still set at fifteen) and then, if they wished, follow self-contained O-level courses at the local College of Further Education. The 1950s were not, in any case, a decade when the ambitions and potentialities of girls were taken as seriously as they should have been.

The pressure on the O-level system was, therefore, sustained. By 1964 there were 1,264,259 subject-passes at O level, compared with an estimated equivalent of 423,070 in 1948, when people of my generation began their university careers. A new examining board—the Associated Examinations Board—came into business in 1955 in order to increase the capacity of the system, and in particular to meet the needs of secondary modern schools and Colleges of Further Education. Other unofficial and semi-official bodies offered examinations at fifteen-plus or sixteen-plus: pupils could not be sent into a competitive world naked of formal qualifications. But the O levels continued to represent the gold standard within this bewilderingly diverse set of currencies.

Doubts and criticism began to grow. Hard-pressed secondary modern schools were, it was alleged, directing too much of their energy and resources to securing O-level passes for the minority of their more able pupils. Many such schools were becoming pale imitations of diluted grammar schools, just as within higher education (so Tony Crosland was soon to assert) all ambitious colleges were aping the traditionally prestigious universities. Examinations, and especially O levels, were being used to coax pupils with little chance of real success into staying on at secondary school for an extra year. Too many teachers saw work of this kind as conferring extra prestige and extra pay. Employers, parents, and the schools themselves were confused by the many different examinations now on offer, and uncertain about their value and comparability.

There was, then, a real danger that some of the problems of the pre-1914 grammar schools would now be reborn in the secondary modern school, and in 1958 the SSEC set up a committee under the chairmanship of Sir Robert Beloe (then Chief Education Officer for Surrey) to review present arrangements and to make recommendations. The Beloe Report was published in 1960, and the new examinations were approved in 1963, when Edward Boyle was Minister of Education, and taken for the first time in 1965, when Tony Crosland was Secretary of State. One problem had, perhaps, been solved: but only at the expense of creating new complications —many of which came to the surface only in the 1970s.

The Beloe Report recommended the introduction of a Certificate of Secondary Education, to be awarded to pupils at the age of sixteen who had completed a five-year course of secondary education—who had, that is, remained at school one year longer than was required by law. The Certificate of Secondary Education is, like its O-level cousin, a single-subject examination with no group requirements. But, in important respects, it differs from the General Certificate of Education. Its administration and control are in the hands not of the Universities but of fourteen regional Boards, on all of which practising teachers are powerfully represented. The priority of the curriculum over examinations is strongly asserted, and this principle is related to teacher control, which (in its turn) is linked to regional organization. The contrast with the free market of the GCE boards, where each school is free to make its own choice and even to use different boards for different subjects, is obvious.

The CSE examination is designed for the 20 per cent of the ability range immediately below the 20 per cent for whom the GCE is appropriate. But there is considerable overlapping, subject by subject, and many pupils outside the 'top' 40 per cent take particular subjects in the CSE. In 1965, however, it was assumed that a very large number of pupils would fall outside even the enlarged scope of public examinations. The grading of results in the CSE is, at least in principle, relatively simple: a Grade 1 'corresponds' to an O-level pass, and a Grade 4 is used appropriately to record a performance of an average pupil who had worked steadily at the subject in question. Grades 2 and 3 fall between these two marks, whereas a 5 records simply that it was not inappropriate for the candidate to take the examination—a 'near miss', in other words. An 'unclassified' result is self-explanatory.

There are three Modes of examination. Mode I is the closest to traditional GCE examinations, in that the syllabus is prescribed by the board, the papers set by the board, and the scripts marked by examiners appointed by it. In Mode II the school itself or a group of schools may design the syllabus, but the rest of the process is external to the school. Mode III maximizes the contribution of the responsible teachers within the school, who not only design the syllabus but also assess the work (often undertaken during the course rather than examined at the end of it)—subject, of course, to the controls and checks of external moderators. Early reformers hoped that Mode III would become the central element in the CSE process. In general terms, all forms of CSE marking and assessment are more flexible (and therefore, some critics argue, less objectively reliable) than their more traditional GCE counterparts.

In terms of the general response to its availability, the new examination was a success: 21.2 per cent of school-leavers entered for it in 1967, and 32.9 per cent in 1970; in 1975, by which time the school-leaving age had of course been raised, the figure was 65.4 per cent. Many of these pupils also attempted a number of O-level subjects—some of them entering in both examinations for the same subject. Overlap has always been considerable, and this has been one of the problems—albeit a minor one—associated with the operation of a dual system of examining at sixteen-plus.

The major problems arose as a result of later, but not unforesee-able, developments. It is plain that the new system of 1965 was neatly adapted to an educational world in which pupils were conveniently divided between grammar schools (about 20 per cent, of course) and the rest, and when the school-leaving age was still fifteen. But it was in 1965, the first CSE year, that Tony Crosland accelerated the destruction of the divided system of schooling. And it was clear that the raising of the school-leaving age, although it might be delayed by economic pressure for a year or two, could not be indefinitely postponed. These developments —more comprehensive schools, and a school-leaving age of six-teen—made the new dual system obsolescent almost as soon as the ink was dry on the 1965 examination scripts.

For a few years yet the new arrangements seemed simple and appropriate, and the principal task was that of persuading a sceptical public that the new examination was a real and useful test. In Banbury Grammar School, then in the last few years of its life, nothing needed to change very much. In the secondary modern schools there was great concern lest the innovation should divert quite able and promising pupils (mostly boys) from GCE to CSE; it became a nice point whether it was better to fail an O level altogether, or to get (say) a Grade 2 in CSE. For such reasons, the practice of double entry grew and with it the overall weight of the growing examination system. Nevertheless, the CSE and its rewards were a powerful incentive for pupils to remain at school an 'extra' year and significantly improve their prospects.

But by 1970 this relatively comfortable position was seriously threatened, and was to become more so in the following decade. The GCE + CSE = Grammar + Modern equation made little sense, when most secondary schools were comprehensive. Decisions about allocation to GCE and CSE teaching-groups became increasingly sensitive and difficult, and the greater the uncertainties about subsequent employment the stronger the pressure from parents or pupils. Nor could problems be solved by teaching GCE and CSE groups together into the fifth, or even the fourth, year: syllabuses diverged, and the level of ability to be covered in the teaching was often embarrassingly wide.

In 1964, one year before the CSE examination was taken for the first time, the Schools Council inherited the responsibilities of the SSEC for the general co-ordination and oversight of the national system of examinations. In 1966 the Council was still understandably vague about the future of the system: it was against episodic change, recognized the incipient problems in the dual system, played for time, and devoted most of its energy to the reform of the post-sixteen examination system. Nobody was, in any case, clear about how the two systems might be better co-ordinated, and experience of the CSE was inevitably slight and recent. The organizational problems of merging two very different families of examination boards—one regional and the other not, one directly linked to universities and the other closely engaged with Local Education Authorities, teachers, and their unions—were daunting.

It was easier to rest upon general propositions than to make precise recommendations. Moreover, it was obvious that the existing systems were only for 'volunteers' (who stayed on at school by choice) and not intended or readily adaptable for the whole ability range. Blending systems that covered 40–60 per

cent of that ability range would be difficult, but beyond that . . .
The paradox slowly clarified itself. In England and Wales an
examination system had developed within a set of assumptions
about meritocracy and, for all its faults, had served society and the
schools well. But there proved to be no way in which its advantages
could be confined to a minority selected for grammar schools.
Examinations grew in importance in secondary modern schools,
for which the GCE remained too narrow in range. The CSE was
invented, essentially for secondary modern schools and (even
then) only for that more able and better motivated minority which
did not leave school at the age of 15. The coexistence of GCE and
CSE raised problems of principle, but its practical difficulties were
at first modest. Comprehensive reorganization amplified these
difficulties by bringing GCE and CSE examinations together in
the same school, but still only for those who 'stayed on'.

Although the raising of the school-leaving age had been postponed from 1970/1 to 1972/3, its implications could no longer be
ignored. An examination system designed for two (but only two)
sections of the ability range might—just possibly—be run as one
system, rather than as two. But what then? If any standards or
sense of reality were to be maintained, then concepts of failure or
(to be more subtle but no more convincing) of levels of success
would persist. And yet, after the requirement that all pupils
should spend the fifth year in school, that could only mean that
many would be excluded from the 'benefits' of examination or the
prospects of success. The examination system was, and is, out of
line with the pattern of schooling, and yet very few critics were
prepared to argue for distancing an examination system from the
last year of compulsory schooling. For historical reasons, and for
no other, it was assumed that this is where it had to be.

The Schools Council therefore found it relatively easy to agree
in the summer of 1970, having just failed for neither the first nor
the last time to reform sixth-form examinations, 'that there should
be a single examination system at the age of 16+ and that this
should be under the Schools Council'. Since no one knew quite
what that meant, a brief postscript to the events of 1970 must be
added. In the following year the Council proposed a joint examin-

ation system for the 'top' 60 per cent of the ability range; the 'bottom' 40 per cent were effectively excluded, with dangerous educational and social consequences, although some of the pupils in this group might take examinations in isolated subjects. More detailed work was undertaken, a firmer recommendation made in 1976, and a report to the Government made by a special committee (the Waddell Report) in 1978. A White Paper, produced by a Labour government later in that year, proposed a single examination—to be called the CGSE (the Certificate of General Secondary Education, an eirenic anagram)—with seven point gradings, to be managed by amalgamated groups of examining boards. A general election followed and, since more even of those who had followed the debate so far were now lost in the woods, the new Conservative government decided to think again. The Secretary of State would first wish to know in detail the 'criteria' with reference to which new syllabuses would be constructed, subject by subject. In August 1983 he announced himself unable yet to make a decision, but promised one for the second quarter of 1984.

This postscript lay, in 1970, far in the future. Meanwhile, schools had to manage as well as they could within the system. The future of examinations became entangled with anxious arguments about standards, national control, accountability, the nature of the curriculum—and in those contexts will reappear later in this story. Similar arguments run through the attempts (so far, equally unsuccessful) to develop new examinations for the sixth form, reflecting equally fundamental changes within that institution. What is, in both contexts, striking is the centrality in educational debate of the issue of examinations, and this chapter has attempted an explanation of the peculiar Englishness of these questions.

In 1975, when the debate was still hot, David Lodge published his novel, *Changing Places*, describing the adventures of an English and an American academic who switched jobs (and much else besides). The novel is set in 1969, when students were troublesome and education declined in public esteem, and allows its author to make many penetrating comments on contrasting educational systems at that time.

Under the British system, competition begins and ends much earlier. Four times, under our educational rules, the human pack is shuffled and cut—at eleven-plus, sixteen-plus, eighteen-plus and twenty-plus—and happy is he who comes top of the deck on each occasion, but especially the last. This is called Finals, the very name of which implies that nothing of importance can happen after it . . .

Philip Swallow had been made and unmade by the system in precisely this way. He liked examinations, always did well in them. Finals had been, in many ways, the supreme moment of his life. He frequently dreamed that he was taking the examinations again, and these were happy dreams. Awake, he could without difficulty remember the questions he had elected to answer on every paper that hot, distant June. In the preceding months he had prepared himself with meticulous care, filling his mind with distilled knowledge, drop by drop, until, on the eve of the first paper (Old English Set Texts) it was almost brimming over. Each morning for the next ten days he bore this precious vessel to the examination halls and poured a measured quantity of the contents on the pages of ruled quarto. Day by day the level fell, until on the tenth day the vessel was empty, the cup was drained, the cupboard was bare. In the years that followed he set about replenishing his mind, but it was never quite the same. The sense of purpose was lacking—there was no great Reckoning against which he could hoard his knowledge, so that it tended to leak away as fast as he acquired it.

That for the successful. When John Newsom came to Banbury in this same year of 1969, he repeated advice attributed to one of his tutors at Oxford: 'Mr Newsom, it is important to remember that the Final Honour School of this University and the Last Day of Judgement are *not* the same examination.' We agreed that the same message was even more important to give to the boys and girls about whom he had written his report. But, inevitably, the system seemed to say otherwise, and they got and get a different message.

CHAPTER 8

Tradition

On 7 July 1970 the Schools Council then agreed that a single examination system for pupils at the age of sixteen-plus should be introduced. It was a hot day, and that may have contributed to the decisive if somewhat imprecise enthusiasm for change. The year 1970 was not revolutionary in other ways: the Tories had just won the general election, and in December the House of Commons voted for a return to Greenwich Mean Time. The experience of fiddling with the clocks was to end, and the evenings thereafter became darker. At its July meeting, the Schools Council voted against the currently proposed reforms in sixth-form examinations. The effort to find an acceptable formula was to continue. In 1970, the first purpose-built sixth-form college opened at Stoke-on-Trent, and Exeter formally became the country's first tertiary college. On the Banbury landscape, the new Upper School appeared. Pressure for change in the teaching, examining, and organization of the 16–19 age group had become intense.

In the mid-1960s I spent a good deal of time, at meetings for teachers and other conferences, arguing that the sixth form as we knew it was bound to disappear, or at least be subjected to profound modification. It was, as an institution and as a set of educational and social values, indissolubly linked with the ideals of the Public and grammar schools, with the principles implicit in the 1944 Act, with a concept of secondary education as being limited to a minority. As these ideals changed under the pressure of events and arguments, so would the sixth form.

Thomas Arnold made the rhetoric of the sixth form central to the practice of secondary education. The sixth was to be composed of 'those who, having risen to the highest form in the school, will probably be at once the oldest, and the strongest and the cleverest' and who 'should feel like officers in the army or navy'. Chapter 21 of the Crowther Report (1959) has already been cited as evidence of the persistence of such attitudes deep into the twentieth century, with a characterization of the marks of the sixth form as preparation for a university, study in depth, independent work, intellectual discipleship, and the acceptance of social responsibility —traditionally, through the prefect system—for younger pupils. The Ministry pamphlet of 1951, with its unfulfilled hope that O levels as a distinct educational stage would disappear, enjoyed the significant title of *The Road to the Sixth Form*: that was the purpose which the earlier years of the grammar school should properly serve. More surprisingly, the Crowther Report explicitly rejected the probability that even the advent of comprehensive schools would make any significant difference: 'As far as we can foresee development, what is true of Sixth Forms in grammar schools will be true of the comprehensive schools, and the view we hold about the one, we should expect to hold about the other.' The Report made the parallel assumption that the sixth form would be an élite generated within the school, and therefore very large secondary comprehensive schools would be required as the basis for such sixth forms.

In such confident beliefs there had long been contradictions. In grammar schools as a whole in the 1920s or 1930s only half the products of the sixth forms went on to universities. Between 1950 and 1970, when total sixth-form numbers (spread over two years or more) rose from 100,000 to 250,000, the number securing two or more A levels rose from 34,000 to 77,000, and those securing university admission from 15,000 to 53,000. In other ways, too, the pace of change remained surprisingly slow: it was 1965 before the number (but not, of course, the proportion) of A-level candidates in Latin reached its peak. Crowther anticipated that each year there would be 40,000 sixth-formers with two or more A levels, but only 24,000 going on to university. But the prevalent assumption remained that the sixth form was essentially a stage of academic *preparation*, in which a high degree of specialization would be appropriate and necessary.

By 1970 noisy doubts were being raised about the appropriateness of the three-A-level pattern even for those (never the over-whelming majority) who were going on to universities, which epitomized 'the best' in the higher education system. Unflattering comparisons were made with the broader education enjoyed at this stage by Continental Europeans or with the wider and more relaxed pre-college education of young Americans. High-minded attempts were made to introduce general studies into the work of the sixth form, and in 1961 360 heads of schools signed the Agreement to Broaden the Curriculum, undertaking to reserve at least one-third of each student's time in class from the persistent invasion of specialized A-level studies. But realists acknowledged, and especially at a time of growing competition by large age groups for scarce university places, that nothing much would happen until the examination system was changed. Nevertheless, successive efforts to achieve just that ran repeatedly on to the rocks.

Sober appraisals of the needs of a modern and technological society linked Britain's economic failures with the inability of the educational system to accord sufficient importance to a broad education in sciences and mathematics—a failure which would in turn be attributed to habits of early specialization. It was, and is, too easy for an English boy or girl to give up subjects found difficult or unpalatable. The Dainton Report of 1968 confirmed that there was indeed a 'swing' away from science in sixth forms, that this was dangerously out of line with an expansion of science and technology within the universities, and that the actual numbers of sixth-form science students (not, that is, simply the propor-tions) were about to fall. As a secondary-school head with a firm base in the arts subjects, I had made no friends when arguing at a lecture to the Royal Society of Arts in March 1969 that specializ-ation in sixth forms had some share of the responsibility for the decline in our national fortunes. In the county as a whole between 1962 and 1967, the years when I was the headmaster of a relatively uncomplicated grammar school, the number of sixth-form stu-dents reading science dropped from 32,700 to 31,700, while the number in the non-science group doubled from 38,300 to 76,100. Figures gave substance to the polemics of C. P. Snow, in his denunciation of the weakness of an English world unhelpfully and snobbishly divided into two cultures.

Many sixth-formers, then, were following courses designed in principle for those going on to university, but were nevertheless completing their full-time education at the age of eighteen. Many teachers believed that the traditional programme of studies was inappropriate to the needs, and in some cases the abilities, of the rapidly growing number of sixth formers. Even for the more able, there were doubts about the suitability for the late twentieth century of a pattern of studies which allowed the study of science, or mathematics, or the humanities, to be finally discontinued at or before the age of sixteen. That choice, moreover, was starving the country of the scientific and mathematical manpower which it needed, as a result of the 'swing' away from the sciences. The 'bulge' (the larger birth-rate in the post-war years) and the 'trend' (to stay on at school longer) were not sufficient even to mask this dangerous tendency.

Here were sufficient reasons for concern, and under their weight confidence in the traditional sixth form began to crumble. Even more important were the effects of a growth in numbers, undermining élitist notions of the sixth form, and in the diversity of courses and objectives. The percentage of school-leavers attempting A-level examinations rose from 2.5 per cent in 1938 to 6.2 per cent in 1948 (in both these years, of course, the reference is to the Higher School Certificate) through 9 per cent in 1962 to 17.9 per cent in 1970. By 1972, the total number of A-level subject-passes was 341,297: the corresponding Higher School Certificate figure for 1938 had been under 10,000. No traditional institution could survive change on this scale, especially since alongside this growth was a smaller but qualitatively significant increase in the number of sixth-formers who were not taking A levels at all.

These were, and fifteen years later still are, 'the new sixth-formers'. In 1970/1, of nearly a quarter of a million students in sixth forms, just over 200,000 were following courses leading to one or more A levels, and the remainder were following other courses—in many cases repeating O-level or CSE courses, and often spending only one extra year in school. By 1976 these new sixth-formers amounted to 7.3 per cent of the whole national age group. Their presence disturbed traditionalists, and led to some tortured arguments with metaphysical overtones. When was a sixth-former a sixth-former? The orthodox view, rooted in Arnold's innovations, had been that a sixth-former was distinguished by his cleverness, by having earned the right to join an exclusive club. At first, and in many places, pupils who stayed on beyond a fifth year of secondary education, but not to take A levels, were excluded from the privileges and title of sixth-formers. They were not 'real', but ghostly and rather elderly fifth-formers. A statement by the Inner London Education Authority in 1966 reflects this muddle, and now reads oddly as an attempt to preserve the distinctiveness of a sixth-former, while at the same time robbing the concept of anything except a bare chronological meaning. 'It is a characteristic of the approach of the comprehensive school . . . that it should quite naturally be prepared to regard all boys and girls in their sixth year or upwards as "sixth formers", recognising that they are maturing together, that socially they are alongside one another and equally recognising that their varied intellectual ability will result in some of them having more advanced objectives than others.' That sentence deserves to be read twice.

The Upper School in Banbury reflected many of these changes, and its organization raised many critical questions about the education of the older secondary-school pupil. Some of those questions were made more manageable by the federal structure of Banbury School as a whole. In this regard the school was unique, and is still unusual. It surprises and saddens me that the rush of development and adaptation in the late 1960s produced so few organizational innovations: it was assumed that each relatively small school would need to enjoy a large measure of autonomy, and many opportunities for effective co-operation were sacrificed. In Banbury, the attempt was made to combine the advantages of a larger school, in terms of quality and effectiveness, with those of a small school, in terms of human scale and personal relations. This is why each of the 360 pupils admitted each year at the age of eleven spent four full years in one of the Halls, each with its own head and own staff, but already enjoying the advantages of involvement with the life of a larger school. The larger unit was especially important in terms of science and modern languages, and in providing strong professional support for all teachers.

The most obvious peculiarity of the Upper School—marking it off from other developments in the upper-secondary and sixth-form range—was that it took pupils (thereafter dignified as students) from all the Halls and admitted them to the Upper School at the beginning of their fifth year of secondary education. This was the doctrine of *The Road to the Sixth Form*, expressed anew in a comprehensive context. The coexistence of CSE and O level was a manageable problem, since large numbers allowed a flexible and diverse arrangement of teaching-groups. The distinction between 'fifth form' and 'sixth form', which, as has been shown, had deep historical roots but produced strange contemporary anomalies, disappeared. All students, before the raising of the school-leaving age, were volunteers. They were following a variety of courses, involving combinations of O levels and A levels. Stage was more important than age. By no means all of them were 'academic'. But a rapidly growing minority of them stayed in the Upper School for a full three years, and went on to A levels, and higher education. I had not forgotten the parents who, when the school was being planned and community interest was at its most intense, lent out of the gallery at public meetings and with an accusing finger claimed that the abolition of selection at eleven and the death of the sixth form would bring standards tumbling down. They had been promised that one result of the reorganization was to be a planned and assertive raising of academic standards, in the most conventional of senses. It is a pity that some prophets of reorganization were less emphatic on such matters, and continued to suggest that comprehension meant accepting (in the name of equality) the standards of the lowest. That uncertainty of purpose explains much of the anger and confusion which surrounds the 'Fight for Education', as it began to rumble in 1969 and 1970.

The improvement of traditional sixth-form standards was not, however, to be the only objective of the emerging Upper School. A mile away (or a few minutes' cycling distance, in the metric of a seaside landlady) stands the North Oxfordshire Technical College and School of Art: a College of Further Education (CFE). The CFE represented a very different tradition in the training and education of young people beyond the age of fifteen. Its roots in Banbury went back as far as those of the Grammar School, which inherited the functions of the County School and, before that, the Municipal School. It enjoyed close links with local industry and commerce and provided a wide range of vocational and pro- fessional courses in engineering, agriculture, catering, commerce, building, and so on. It provided, with a flexibility which schools might admire but could not emulate, part-time courses both in the evening and during the day for those released from full-time employment. The CFE, like its equivalents up and down the country, also offered GCE courses, many of them full time, to those who left school early or who—in many cases—had been robbed by the eleven-plus of the opportunity of even trying for such courses. Already in 1970, further education was making a massive and often undervalued contribution to the education of the 16–19 age group: for every two seventeen-year-olds in school sixth forms there was one following a *full-time* course in a CFE. Grammar schools generally regarded the CFE as a second-class organization, and nourished their prejudice by a rigid commitment to the historic sixth form (of the Arnold-to-Crowther model) and relating it to a deep-seated reverence for the pure, rather than the applied. These were the harmful prejudices which in his Woolwich speech Crosland had attacked, in the shape which they assumed in the field of higher education.

They made no sense in 1970—which has not prevented their surviving into 1984. In Banbury the opportunity of reorganization was seized in order to forge a close working relationship between the CFE and the Upper School. Joint appointments were made, all students were made aware of the opportunities available within the combined programme. Most important (and difficult) of all, a single timetable was planned to allow students to combine courses and subjects in both establishments: choice was improved, and waste reduced. Within a few years, and in anticipation of the raising of the school-leaving age, it was even possible to open a physically distinct school unit on the CFE site, so that linked courses could be preserved for those below the age of sixteen as well as those above. Purists could argue that the needs of Banbury might have been even better served by the creation of a unitary college to serve all the students beyond the age of sixteen, but such a development would have been at the expense of cutting off the links between the upper and lower stages of secondary education. It was discussed only behind closed doors, and usually late at night.

Such possibilities became more real in other places, and the development nationally of institutions providing only for students beyond the age of sixteen has become one of the most distinctive elements in the system which has now developed. Such institutions, which have a deep if indirect influence upon the earlier stages of secondary education, can take various forms. The Banbury version, encouraged in various forms within Oxfordshire, is one. At Mexborough and at the Rosebery School in Epsom (two very different parts of the world) an 11–18 school worked alongside a group of 11–16 schools, with pupils transferring to a central sixth form: the so-called sixth-form centre, or 'mushroom', which may become more widely favoured in the later 1980s, and as numbers fall.

The virtues of simpler forms of unitary 16–19 organization had long been expounded. At Croydon, only a few miles from Wallington in Surrey where I was teaching at the time, the five grammar schools of the early 1950s produced a *total* enrolment of only 269 sixth-formers, and three of the schools had sixth forms with fewer than 50 members. This did not inhibit a passionate defence of the view that each school must have its own sixth form, and the visionary plan of the Chief Education Officer to produce one junior college of quality was soon reduced to rubble. Crowther himself later admitted that although he personally (and not only as an economist) found such an idea attractive, only one other member of the Central Advisory Council could be persuaded to show even a mild interest. Eric James was there to keep his eye on things.

But by 1966, the defences had cracked and the first sixth-form college (SFC) was opened in Luton: it was based on the buildings of the old grammar school, which, over the next few years, therefore lost all its younger pupils. The arguments for the SFC are not complex. It permits economies of scale, by concentrating higher-level provision in one place, keeping teaching-groups at a reasonable size and enlarging the choice of subjects. The SFC, within a comprehensive sector, can concentrate attention upon preparation for higher education, and develop a particular expertise in that field. It 'liberates' its students from the sometimes inhibiting social restrictions of the all-age school, and encourages the development of greater independence and more mature social attitudes.

The arguments against the SFC were and remain equally simple. A break at sixteen-plus is disadvantageous, and many pupils will leave school rather than go to an unfamiliar college. (For this proposition, unlike most of the assertions on either side, there is not a shred of evidence.) The 11–16 schools without sixth forms will suffer, certainly in esteem and probably in the quality of their staffing. Both they, and the SFC, will be impoverished by the destruction of the opportunity for the older sixth-form pupils to take responsibility for younger pupils, and to help in instilling high standards of work and behaviour. Although some useful research has been undertaken into such assertions, it is plain that many of them are qualitative, if not ideological. (For that reason, more will have to be said later about the 16–19 age group at a time of diminishing employment.) For many, the sixth form within the school is a necessary guarantee of stability, even of continuity with the tradition of Public Schools and grammar schools. In 1981 Sir Keith Joseph, as Secretary of State for Education and Science, rejected proposals for SFCs in Manchester on the grounds 'that only in very exceptional circumstances can it be right to reduce the age range from 11–18 to 11–16 of secondary schools of proven quality which continue to demonstrate their success in the provision they make for sixth-form education'. In November of the same year, the Labour party adopted a policy obligingly placed at the other extreme of possible opinions: *no* schools should keep sixth forms.

In all this, there is a curious paradox, which expresses itself in the variety of styles adopted by the SFCs. Some, like Luton in the earliest days, saw the college as the guarantor of high standards across a period of perilous reorganization: it was to be the ghost of the grammar school 'sitting crowned upon the grave thereof'. The imposition of a competitive bar—a stated number of O levels —was also adopted at Stoke-on-Trent, the first SFC to open (in 1970, the pivotal year for this chapter) in buildings specially designed for the purpose. Other colleges, like the group opened in Southampton from 1967, prided themselves upon being 'open access'. Although the precise distinction between 'open' and 'closed' can no longer be maintained, it is obvious that some colleges are, and are glad to be, 'selective'. One even has a Head Master (not even a headmaster, still less a principal) to show that nothing has changed very much. Gowns are still worn by staff, and uniform by pupils. But that undoubtedly represents one extreme.

The bumper years for the foundation of new SFCs were 1973 and 1974: fifteen and twenty-one respectively. By the end of the decade there were 102 colleges, with 60,000 students, representing 18 per cent of all sixth-formers in England and Wales. The average size of the colleges was then 569, with variations from an implausibly small 109 to 1,200. Very few of them provided only A-level courses, and recent years have seen a rapid development not only of O-level, CSE, and non-examination work, but also of courses with a more overtly vocational bias or technical element. The figure for SFCs as a whole of 21 per cent of all students on non-A-level courses is very close to the national average for all schools and colleges. As for A levels themselves, the colleges are generous in the provision of choice of subjects: a national average of twenty-seven, with variations from about eighteen to a massive total of forty-five. The SFCs can, for good reasons, generally offer a wider choice of languages than most schools.

The purpose-built sixth-form college was not the only institutional innovation of 1970. In the same year, Exeter College became the country's first tertiary college: with some 1,600 full-time students, it is still the largest, although it now has about a score of companions. A tertiary college differs from an SFC in being established upon a further-education and not a school base. The teachers in it work under different conditions of service and have often followed different patterns of training. It would be simple, but wrong, to represent a tertiary college as no more than a CFE (like the one in Banbury) expanded in order to include the work of the traditional sixth form. But a tertiary college does offer full-time courses drawn from both sectors, together with the opportunity of combining elements from both traditions. The tertiary college is, in one sense, the offspring of the idea of a sixth-form college. When reorganization in Exeter was under debate, the first and simpler proposal was that an SFC should be created to coexist with the CFE which was already in place. But that CFE had almost as many GCE students as did the existing sixth forms in the schools and, given the restraints of finance and the building programme, it seemed more sensible to manufacture the unitary tertiary college.

The long-term effects of that decision will prove momentous. Even in the short term, the progress and demonstrable success of the tertiary college raises doubts about whether, in the longer term, SFCs can survive. The pressure to include a growing variety of courses for the 16–19 age group, the necessity to co-operate with the further-education sector, the implications of a decline in employment for the 16–19 age group, the links between school-based activities and those sponsored by the Manpower Services Commission—all these will contrive to make the tertiary college an increasingly attractive solution in those areas where demography and the distribution of buildings make it accessible. Those tertiary colleges which already exist have been ingenious in designing new patterns of organization and curriculum. The strength of the CFE has traditionally lain in its responsiveness to the needs of local employers, in its business-like approach to providing marketable courses, and in the confidence and autonomy of its various and powerful departments. Becoming a tertiary college involves a significant change of emphasis, and an attention both to groups of students who would (under different arrangements) have been in school sixth forms, and to other groups whose needs cannot be neatly classified as A-level or 'vocational'. It is, moreover, often forgotten that in addition even to these larger groups of full-time students, the typical tertiary college has to honour its further-education commitments to part-time students. Exeter, for example, makes provision for some 3,000 part-time daytime students, and a further 2,500 on evening courses.

The work of the full-time students—in school sixth forms, in SFCs, in CFEs, and in tertiary colleges—has to be contained within the framework of a national examination system. The attempts to modify that framework, in the decades before and after 1970, mirror the difficulties of adapting the strong and consensual arrangements embodied in the settlement after 1944 to the very different needs of contemporary society. An A-level system corresponded to and sustained a pattern of schooling in which grammar was divided from modern, most secondary pupils left at the age of fifteen, the more able (or some of them) went on to sixteen, and the most able or determined advanced into the sixth form and to specialized study. How might such a system be adapted?

This was one of the earliest tasks which the Schools Council set itself after its creation in 1964. The A-level system had much, but by no means everything, in common with the Higher School Certificate which it replaced, when the GCE was introduced in 1951. One important difference was that the Higher School Certificate had to be taken in a number of subjects at the same time: either three principal subjects, or two principal and two subsidiary. The A level, like the O level, was and is a single-subject examination. Nevertheless, most candidates attempted three subjects in the old Higher School Certificate tradition, although some offered less. Three subjects certainly became the norm for those aiming towards higher education. As the sixth form became more diverse, so it became more usual for candidates to take only one or two A levels, often with O levels (which might be completed in the first year). Although this was more flexible than the old Higher School Certificate arrangements it could not taken by itself be defended as a satisfactory educational programme, and for many of the 'new sixth-formers' even one A level was often inaccessible. Nor were any satisfactory examinations available for the growing number of young people who wished, or were able, to spend only one year in the sixth.

These factors—the unsuitability of the A-level pattern for many sixth-formers staying on for two years, the patchiness of a programme of study made up of one A level and other bits and pieces, the lack of any clear objectives for those staying on for less than two years—combined with some dissatisfaction with A-level studies to produce a strong movement towards reform in the 1960s. The dominance of examinations at both sixteen and eighteen made it unrealistic to suppose that work without examinations would be taken seriously in secondary schools, so that even those who disliked the existing pressure of examinations on the system found themselves arguing for the introduction of more (if better) examinations. The movement for change was defeated not only by ambivalences of this kind, but also by a brave if misguided attempt to produce one pattern of examination suitable for all candidates in schools. For a number of years little serious thought was given to provision in further education—just as the scantiest of references to that sector was thought to be sufficient in Circular 10/65.

The first substantial proposal was made within the Schools Council as early as 1966, and it was for a major/minor pattern. The more able pupil would offer two major and two minor subjects, but less demanding combinations would be available. All courses, however, would be for a full two years and this pattern had nothing to offer the newest type of student. In the following year, 'electives' had a brief period of serious discussion. These would be one-year courses (of an unspecified character) alongside the traditional two-year courses, designed to reflect the particular interests of staff in each school, and available to sixth-formers of all (or most) levels of ability. Meanwhile, the Schools Council and the universities (through the Standing Conference on University Entry) had agreed on three general principles. Reform of sixth-form examinations was needed, to reflect the changing nature of the students and their needs. Less specialization should become the order of the day. Subject choices should always be made as late as possible.

The joint working party struggled to make sense of these principles and of their application to students aiming at higher education. If all problems could not be solved by one examination structure, then perhaps some could, and perhaps there would have to be a new examination to deal with candidates outside the pale. The irony of the attempt to develop two types of examination for sixth-formers at the same time as the effort to amalgamate the two separate examinations at sixteen-plus did not pass unremarked. Nor did the oddity of establishing alongside the working party (in effect, on traditional sixth-formers) a second working party (to deal with those without ambitions for higher education). The internal contradictions soon fractured all the plans, and seriously weakened the Schools Council.

In 1969, both working parties came together to propose a 'Q and F' pattern. The Qualifying examination, taken in about five subjects (by most candidates) in one year, would be followed by a Further examination one year later, in about three. Thus was the circle to be squared. Nobody was satisfied—traditional A-level virtues would be at risk, pupils (many of them) would be examined publicly every year for three years, the needs of one-year sixth-formers would be sacrificed to the ambitions of their more academic contemporaries. These were the proposals which the Governing Council of the Schools Council rejected at its July meeting in 1970.

The rest of the story may be briefly told. The Schools Council battled on, still with two working parties, and on the same day in 1973 produced two sets of proposals. One paper, significantly called 'Preparation for Degree Courses' proposed the N-and-F pattern: five subjects to be taken over two years, probably three of them (but who could tell?) to Normal level and the remainder to Further level. The second set of proposals dealt essentially with those on one-year courses, and for them advised a Certificate of Extended Education, to record study in a balanced group of five subjects. This examination, which survived a short and shadowy life under the aegis of the CSE Boards, had enjoyed the dubious status of a pilot scheme since 1972. It reflected the will of the schools to develop a concept of an extended secondary education which would be at once general (like A levels, unlike further education) and demanding (yet, plainly, easier and shorter than an A-level programme). It perished in the more utilitarian, or more realistic, weather of the 1980s. The N-and-F proposals met a similar fate. They were agitated until 1979, when the Conservatives won the general election. Within weeks the Secretary of State wrote to the Chairman of the Schools Council ruling that it would be wrong to replace A levels with N and F, or anything of a similar character, within the foreseeable future.

This brief account of attempts to reform examinations for sixth-formers illustrates the tenacity of certain principles—a commitment to the idea of the sixth form, an addiction to examinations, an attempt to become more comprehensive or open—and the (perhaps inevitable) failure of a body like the Schools Council to resolve the contradictions. The rejection of the N-and-F proposals in July 1970 was not the only misfortune into which the Schools Council had fallen in that year. It also wished, as a modest reform within the current A-level system, to introduce a twenty-point grading scheme to replace the grading of A–E (for passes), and the two lower grades. But Mrs Thatcher was by then Secretary of State, and she rejected this recommendation. Those who thought then that the days of the Schools Council were numbered took note.

These things lay, in 1970, in the future—and no one supposed that, even in 1984, A levels would still be in their dominant position. In the months before the summer of 1970, and for reasons obviously connected with the evolution of Banbury School, I had been increasingly concerned with problems of teacher training. Whatever happened to intricate national arguments about examinations, pupils would still need to be taught and—now that the problems of supply which had so preoccupied Tony Crosland had been largely solved—better teachers were urgently needed. The teacher-training system, like the examination system, had not yet caught up with the realities of comprehensive reform. I had been chairman of a group of headmasters arguing for particular changes, and in October 1970 was summoned to the Department of Education and Science (still in the Curzon Street fortress) to explain the proposals to one of Mrs Thatcher's ministers.

A few weeks later, Toby Weaver (to whom John Newsom had first introduced me) came to Banbury with a question and an invitation. Would I join a Committee of Inquiry into Teacher Training to be set up by Mrs Thatcher under the chairmanship of Lord James of Rusholme? We were to work full-time, and for a year. A new style in Government had arrived, and it was to make secondary schools very different places.

CHAPTER 9

Teachers

The Secretary of State for Education and Science, Mrs Margaret Thatcher, was determined that the Committee of Inquiry should report within a year, that it should be small, that its members should effectively be full-time, and that it should work from within the Department of Education and Science. The exercise was to be very different from the leisurely, consensual proceedings of bodies like the Central Advisory Councils. Indeed, after Plowden the Councils were not reconstituted, although Tony Crosland remarked that, if they had been, their next task would have been a short, sharp inquiry into teacher training. In open defiance of the requirement of the Act of 1944 the Central Advisory Councils have simply been allowed to wither.

In January 1971 the seven members of the Committee had lunch with Mrs Thatcher in the House of Commons, and, fortified with that encouragement, set to work. The unions and associations, who had been so powerful in determining the agenda and membership of the Schools Council, had no say in arranging either the terms of reference or the composition of this Committee, and uttered their ritual grumbles. The seven members included a Chief Education Officer, a former Senior Chief Inspector (HMI), a professor of education, the principal of a College of Education, a primary-school headmistress, and myself.

Presiding over us was Lord James of Rusholme. Eric James brought to the business in hand an absolute refusal to be bamboozled by defensive jargon, an incisive mind and caustic wit, a commitment to quality in schools, the powers of a mimic, and a smoking pipe. He was born in 1909, and educated at Taunton's School, Southampton (a grammar school whose transformation into a sixth-form college in the 1960s produced strong local opposition), and Queen's College, Oxford. After taking his D.Phil. in Chemistry, he was for twelve years an assistant master at Winchester, of all the Public Schools probably the one with the clearest commitment to the highest academic standards. From the year after Butler's Act (which he welcomed) until 1962 he was headmaster of Manchester Grammar School, one of that small group of internationally respected direct-grant grammar schools offering a rigorous academic education to able pupils, regardless (unlike Winchester) of their parents' ability to pay. I took pleasure, and so I believe did he, in reflecting that my headmastership began in the year in which his ended. For in 1962 he became the first (and profoundly influential) Vice-Chancellor of the University of York, one of the universities founded in the period of expansion surrounding the Robbins Report. He had been a member of the University Grants Committee, of the Crowther Committee, and the chairman of the Headmasters' Conference. His book on *Education and Leadership* remains the classical exposition of grammar-school virtues and, although he came to Banbury and said pleasant things, he remained sceptical about comprehensives (especially in large cities) and contemptuous of some of the wilder claims that were then made for them. He was knighted in 1956, and became a member of the House of Lords in 1959, where a few years later he made a decisive contribution to the debate on the Robbins Report.

He wasted no time, once turning up for an early meeting of the Committee in his carpet slippers: traditionalist that he was, he had left his shoes outside a hotel bedroom door to be cleaned, and they had disappeared overnight. He could stop even the most garrulous of witnesses with a sharp rap of the pipe, or eloquent movement of the face. A sense of attack and amusement was certainly needed if the Committee was to find its way through the jungle of teacher training. The system, as it was in the early 1970s, had been evolved to deal with patterns of schooling very different from those then developing, and was groaning under the strains of a rapid and recent expansion. Its origins had much in common with the beginning in this country of elementary and secondary education. Neither central nor local government played any significant part, and it was left to the Churches to make some modest provision. Most teachers were hardly trained at all, and certainly not in institutions providing full-time courses: apprenticeships, or pupil-teaching, offered the main route into teaching for much of the nineteenth century.

Nevertheless, by 1900 sixty-two voluntary colleges did exist, and the Act of 1902, which allowed the newly constituted Local Education Authorities to support grammar schools, also permitted them to establish training-colleges. Nevertheless only eighty-three colleges—voluntary and maintained—were active in 1939, and of those sixty-four had less than 150 students. Most of them were residential, many of them in rural areas and with custodial regimes, few of them had any pretensions to academic standards. The universities came late and hesitantly upon this scene, and many of them are still hesitant. The first university enterprises—the so-called day training-colleges—were established before the 1902 Act, simply to provide on a very small scale some secular alternative to the voluntary denominational colleges. They were not otherwise different in nature or purpose from those colleges, and were at first equally concerned with elementary-school teachers. The growth of maintained grammar schools after 1902 extended the scope of teacher training into secondary schools, and by 1939 the teacher-training system very largely reflected the sharp divisions of the public schooling system. Most secondary schools were grammar schools, most grammar-school teachers were university graduates, and those of them who bothered with training at all (for it was not compulsory for them) naturally remained at a university to take, when they had completed a first degree, a one-year course leading to the Postgraduate Certificate in Education (the PGCE). Other intending teachers, those bound for elementary schools, followed a two-year course at a training-college leading, not to a graduate award, but to a Certificate in Education.

The 1944 Act made surprisingly little difference to this basic pattern, although it naturally led to a considerable enlargement of the scale of the operation. Primary-school teachers came almost entirely through the College of Education route; grammar-school teachers followed the road through the university, in growing numbers taking in the Postgraduate Certificate of Education on the way; secondary-modern-school teachers could follow either path, although most of them (given the laws of supply and demand) were trained in the colleges. In the same year as the 1944 Act, the McNair Report had reviewed teacher training and, although the members of the Committee were equally divided on this issue, this led to the creation of loose links between the two sectors. The Area Training Organizations (ATOs) were established under university auspices to associate the colleges with one another and with a 'parent' university. These were the bodies that would, it was hoped, bring university standards into teacher education and a new dignity to the teaching profession. They were loose federations, with very little real power.

In 1960 the two-year course was lengthened by one further year, and this long-awaited improvement significantly increased the size of the training-college population. In 1936 there had been 10,000 teachers in training; by 1957 there were 28,000, and by 1964 63,000. The Robbins Report of 1963 made a number of recommendations. A proposal that all the colleges should be drawn within the limits of the universities by forming, with the university Departments of Education (UDEs), new and integrated Schools of Education was rejected by the Government. The binary policy, as Tony Crosland and his advisers developed it from 1965, required that the colleges should remain in the public sector, under the control of the Local Education Authorities (or the voluntary bodies) and the Department of Education and Science, and responsive to the very rapid adaptations that the school system required. The Robbins suggestion that training-colleges should be renamed Colleges of Education was, however, accepted: it cost nothing, and sounded better. More controversial was the proposal, also accepted, that the degree of Bachelor of Education (B.Ed.) should be developed. This, for a minority of the more able students in the colleges, would require an extra year of study. The hope was that this measure would, in an increasingly comprehensive world, soften the harsh distinction between the university-trained graduate and the college-trained non-graduate. In the event, it increased the tensions within the system and (in the early years, at least) elevated the 'academic' at the expense of the 'professional' in the education and training of teachers. The 'untrained' graduate came under growing criticism and, from the early 1970s, the successful pursuit of a Postgraduate Certificate in Education became for graduates a necessary condition of qualified-teacher status.

The achievement of Crosland in securing the necessary expansion of numbers in teacher training has already been celebrated. The 63,000 of 1964 had become 105,000 in 1968, and by 1972 (the year from which decline began) it was 130,407—with a further 5,281 in the universities. I do not believe (although many in the early 1970s did) that it is possible to prove that this increase in numbers was associated with a decline in the quality of candidates being admitted. On the contrary, if the figures for 1960 are compared with those of 1971 (when the James Committee was deliberating), they show that, of those admitted to colleges, the 25.3 per cent which had achieved a maximum of one A level rose to 26 per cent, two A levels from 10.6 to 12.1 per cent, and (even) more than three from 0.6 to 1.4 per cent. Entrants with one A level or more therefore represented 59.5 per cent in 1960, and 65.3 per cent in 1971. In the mean time, the number of entrants had shot upwards from 14,200 to 25,700. Of course, there were weaknesses: the number with O-level mathematics had increased from 57.2 to only 58.9 per cent, although the number with O-level English remained at over 97 per cent. Nor, as will appear, were these figures as good as they are now, in 1984. The point is not that the standard had 'fallen', nor even that it was not good enough in the first place, but that the overriding importance to secure more teachers pressed selectors into admitting many unimpressive candidates, and that the frenzied expansion of the system overstrained its capacity to work well.

This is one of the reasons why the James Committee was appointed. Another, surely, was the conviction that a system rigidly divided on the premise that there were academic pupils (in grammar schools), and non-academic (in secondary moderns) and younger pupils (in primaries) no longer matched the realities of schooling. It is no accident that comprehensive reorganization coincided with a rising wave of criticism of teacher training: too many comfortable teachers were being exposed, and those who were involved in opening up secondary education were sometimes ferocious in their comments upon teacher trainers who were remote from such pressures. Underlying these concerns—the obsolescence of a divided system, the strains of expansion, a perennial concern with standards, doubts about the relevance of theoretical training, the pressures of comprehensive change—was the reality of imminent contraction. The country, soon, would not need so many teachers and yet the massive teacher-training system was geared to produce nothing but teachers. The James Committee knew this, but failed to make this point with sufficient emphasis. The numbers were then speculative, and nobody in 1971 was disposed to believe them. They soon did.

Four days each week were spent in London, or visiting colleges and universities up and down the country. The Department of Education and Science had by now moved to Elizabeth House, entangled with Waterloo Station, from which the Chairman led us to eat mammoth sausages in a noisy pub. It was also near the Festival Hall, and organ recitals at 5.55 p.m. One of the visits in March took me back to Cardiff, where the smoke was still drifting across the comprehensive battlefield and the school which Goronwy Rees had admired was disappearing. Most of the Committee members tried to maintain contact with their normal work, and I tried to persuade governors and the parent–teacher association that two things could be done at once. The arguments about mixed-ability teaching remained as inconclusive as ever, and my colleagues in Banbury as divided as usual. We decided that each of the Halls should choose its preferred method of setting and grouping, so that teachers would have confidence in what they were doing. Moreover, the Department of Education and Science was persuaded to fund a significant research project based upon a study of these emerging difficulties, and a school-based research officer was appointed, to work in the school but under the aegis of the Oxford University Department of Educational Studies. I had my first experience of putting to the test a deeply held conviction that educational research should spring from the needs of schools, and engage the interests of scholars. Freddy Yates, whose book on grammar-school selection now belonged to a remote but real past, became the director of the project, which proved to be the first of a series.

The school also appointed its first, and indeed the first, professional tutor, whose task was to link practising teachers in classrooms with teacher training, and with the induction and probation of new teachers. The arguments of Banbury were carried back to Elizabeth House, for the Department of Education and Science provided financial support for this scheme, and echoed in the James Committee. A decade later, developments of this primitive scheme were adopted more widely in Oxfordshire.

Dick Crossman lost political office, of course, in the general election which had brought Mrs Thatcher to Elizabeth House, and for two years after 1970 he was editor of the *New Statesman*. They seem, in retrospect, years of transition and paradox— ending with the publication at Christmas 1972 of the Conservative plans for education from then until now, *A Framework for Expansion*. 200,000 demonstrators marched on Washington, to protest against the Vietnam War, *The Greening of America* (an optimistic and romantic account of changing attitudes) pointed towards the mirage of a gentler and more convivial world, and Britain decided to enter the Common Market. Sixty-nine Labour members and thirty-nine Conservatives voted against their own parties, and Parliament Square was packed with people waiting for the results. I was there with other members of the Committee. In a contrary spirit, the constituent nations of the United Kingdom —notably the Scots and the Welsh—revived their antagonisms to Westminister and Whitehall, and urgent talk about devolution became fashionable.

Butler published *The Art of the Possible*, and gave some account of his part in framing the Education Act of 1944. John Newsom died on 23 May 1971.

In the summer, now that Britain was to be European, we enjoyed a family holiday in Brittany, and I invented new songs to sing as the sun went down on the cliffs. In September, we bought our first (very small) canal boat, and called it *Marly* after the house to which Louis XIV occasionally retired from the business of Versailles. The canals became for me, as for a growing number of people, a seductive way in which to be temporarily removed from the pressures of everyday work, and from inappropriate hurry. Simon and I brought *Marly* down the Oxford Canal as the summer of 1971 began to tilt towards the winter.

The James Report was signed on 14 December, just before my father came to spend Christmas with us. What were its recommendations intended to achieve? I put the question this way (rather than, 'What were the recommendations?') for one good reason. Although, formally, most of the recommendations were not implemented by Government, they had a profound effect on policy and action, and reflected important changes of mood related to teacher education, and to secondary education as well. An underlying intention was to draw teacher education, and the institutions within which it was contained, more fully into the enlarging family of higher education. There was a visibly growing concern with the evolution of higher education—the *Times Higher Education Supplement* was launched in 1971. It was argued that monotechnic institutions (that is, those offering only one type of course with one type of career outlet, namely into teaching) would not attract a fair share of the abler eighteen-year-olds embarking upon higher education. Certificates and baccalaureates in education alone were too narrow. The first cycle of teacher education should therefore be non-professional, and non-specific, and should embody no commitment to teaching. The universal model, adapted and improved, should be that of the first university degree. It followed that those who might become teachers would be educated for a few years after the age of eighteen alongside contemporaries with many different career objectives. From this, all would gain. An important and necessary change would be the introduction of a two-year Diploma of Higher Education, alongside the more conventional three-year degree.

Graduates and diplomates wishing, now in their early twenties, to become teachers would then apply for admission to the second cycle, a two-year phase for all. The first year would be based in a university or college, and would represent an enriched version of the existing and growing Postgraduate Certificate in Education. At the end of it, successful candidates would become 'licensed teachers' and move into the world of schools—rather like house-men, or interns, in medical education. During that year they would, of course, continue to receive a great deal of support, and the emphasis would be upon the successful development of good practice. At the end of this, the professional stage of teacher training, the professional degree of BA (Ed.) would be awarded, and the status of 'registered teacher' conferred. A year of induction would follow, in which the novice teacher would be released for further professional development for one day a week. Each school was to have a professional tutor.

These proposals were an attempt to disentangle the 'general' from the 'professional' education of the teacher, to disperse some of the fog surrounding a B.Ed. which attempted to do everything, to substitute a consecutive for a concurrent style of teacher edu-cation, and to place a central responsibility for teacher training upon schools and the teachers in them. Their full implementation depended upon the creation of a new national framework of committees and other professional bodies, and it was this necessary suggestion which drew a great deal of fire from miscellaneous critics. It was wrongly supposed that the tasks of validation and recognition could be undertaken by universities and the Council for National Academic Awards, and/or by the Area Training Organizations (which soon disappeared into the twilight). Thirteen years later another Secretary of State is at last taking steps to fill the gap that was already there in 1971, and became painfully visible as the decade advanced.

Although the proposals for a formal separation of the first and second cycles were not accepted, and those for the BA (Education) were somewhat cursorily dismissed, the pressure of events and a toughening of attitudes have changed the system in many of the ways which James commended. In 1972, for every four students accepted for training through the concurrent method (Certificate or B.Ed.), one was accepted for the consecutive style (PGCE). In 1982, more students were accepted for the consecutive than for the concurrent—although the absolute numbers had, of course, declined across the decade. There are those, including myself, who do not believe that the concurrent mode will survive this century, and wish that a firmer and earlier decision had been taken ten years ago.

The shift towards an emphasis upon the professional relevance of teacher training, itself related to the growing complexity of teaching in secondary schools, also had significant effects upon the B.Ed. Although the degree has survived as an 'integrated' programme across a three- or four-year course of study, there is in a growing number of instances an informal division within it— with the emphasis shifting from the academic to the professional in a way expressed (perhaps too harshly) in the formal separation of cycles. Meanwhile, of course, the Certificate in Education has disappeared and all entrants to teaching are now graduates.

The urge towards professionalism has also, in the spirit although not by the methods for which James argued, stimulated the growth of a new partnership between training institutions and schools. Pioneer schemes existed already in the 1960s, of course, but the decline in numbers coupled with a change in attitudes has multiplied schemes in which practising teachers are involved in training, and in which the training itself has shifted from a college or university towards a school base. Such schemes, actively encouraged by the Government, are likely to develop further in the 1980s.

But, back in 1971, the most important single imperative of the James Report was to raise to its proper priority the in-service training of teachers. It was here, rather than in initial training, that teachers would be most effectively helped to meet the needs of all secondary schools, and especially of comprehensive schools. Although the recommendation that there should be an entitlement to a specific amount of in-service training was not accepted, the expansion of opportunities since 1971 has been impressive. A fall in pupil numbers has, again, made possible a new and welcome emphasis upon quality. What this has meant in practice will be discussed later.

On 24 January 1972 Mrs Thatcher, with those senior civil

servants who had been most active in supporting or opposing the work of the James Committee, summoned the members of that Committee to a dinner at the Dorchester. It was just over a year since they had been bundled into taxis after a morning's work to cross the Thames to the House of Commons, and nearly twenty-seven years since Butler, Mrs Thatcher's predecessor, had celebrated in the same hotel the return of Emanuel School from its wartime exile. The following months were busy, not only in Banbury but with meetings and conferences in every spare moment. The Government had announced a period of consultation before any decisions were taken on the James Report, and was obviously intending to link those decisions with a wider statement of its educational policies. On 8 March, a few members of the now discharged Committee had lunch at the House of Lords and listened to the inconclusive debate which followed. Lord Beaumont found the Report a pleasure to read, but to Lady Gaitskell the prose was opaque.

Discussions in 1972 took place under darkening skies. The year began with a national coal strike, which lasted for seven weeks, and by the end of January the total of unemployed had risen to the (then) alarming figure of one million. Many took refuge in nostalgia or wondered at a remoter past in the Tutankhamun Exhibition. In April, Roy Jenkins resigned from the Labour Shadow Cabinet, and a work-to-rule began on British Rail which lasted until 12 June. Five dockers were sent to gaol under the new industrial-relations legislation, but the courts ordered their release a few days later. The dockers were on strike in August. Reginald Maudling resigned from the Cabinet because of his association with the Poulson scandal, and in November President Nixon was elected for a second term (which scandal did not allow him to complete). The school-leaving age was raised, so in the summer of 1972 pupils could for the last time leave after only four years of secondary school. Corelli Barnett published *The Collapse of British Power* and, on 6 December 1972, the Government published *Education: a Framework for Expansion*.

For expansion was still to be the order of the day, albeit with some rearrangement of priorities. The focus was to shift from secondary schools (with which this book has been exclusively concerned, and which had been the cause of so much contention) to the earlier stages of schooling. In particular, provision was to be made for the under-fives on the generous scale recommended by the Plowden Report, to meet an estimated demand of 90 per cent of all four-year-olds, and 50 per cent of all three-year-olds. Particular attention would be given to deprived areas and dis-advantaged children: a powerful lobby had done its work well. A special building programme was to be launched. Unsatisfactory secondary- and primary-school buildings were to be replaced. A teaching force for 1981 was promised which would be 10 per cent above the number required to maintain the staffing standards already reached in 1971.

As for the James Report, its objectives (but by no means all its methods) were welcomed. Moreover, greatly improved arrange-ments were to be made for the induction of new teachers, the Diploma of Higher Education was launched, and, most important of all, generous policies for in-service training proclaimed. Expansion should begin in 1974, to reach by 1981 the target of 3 per cent of all teachers being on secondment at any one time. Although a target of 510,000 teachers (since abandoned) for 1981 was adopted, the teaching force would not need to maintain its present rate of growth, and by no means so many new teachers would in future be required. Perhaps only 60,000–70,000 initial training places would be needed, of the 120,000 then available. The long agony of the colleges was about to begin.

Some of these colleges might, of course, hope to find an oppor-tunity within that expansion of higher education which was also a marked feature of the White Paper. The 463,000 places in higher education then available should grow by 1981 to a total of 750,000, of which half should be in universities, and the remainder in the public sector. These projections will be of interest when the actual position in 1984 is reviewed, but for the moment at least the message was clear. Public expenditure on nursery, primary, and secondary schools would rise from £1,475m. to £2,000m. by 1981/2, and on higher education from £687m. to £1,120m. (all at 1971 prices). Expansion was not yet dead.

Neither were schools, although criticisms and doubts were growing, and in the summer of 1972—with my mind still very much upon the particularities of Banbury and the reorganization which had just been completed—I wrote a short book (published in 1974) with the title *School is Not Yet Dead*. Its title, and some parts of its argument, were provoked by the appearance in 1971 of *School is Dead* (by Everett Reimer), as well as Ivan Illich's *Deschooling Society*. The deschoolers, looking to the Third World and disillusioned with developed societies, argued that school reform had now defeated its own purposes. Education was consuming wealth rather than creating it. The myth of certification did not create jobs, but simply rearranged their distribution. Schools did not promote equality, and the main function of a compulsory and highly bureaucratic schooling system was to provide occupation and money for those who taught and administered within it.

The polemic was more persuasive than the tentative alternatives proposed, but did have the effect of undermining the confidence of many committed to educational causes, and of many teachers. However different in style, the deschoolers amplified the more conventional doubts of those whose attacks on the education establishment were to reach a climax in the later 1970s. Meanwhile, I felt compelled to argue from within the framework of what had been achieved in Britain since 1944. Much of the criticism of schooling—then and now—draws strength from the exaggerated claims made for the potentialities of educational reform. It was, indeed, dangerous to suppose that an extension of educational provision was always and everywhere necessarily benign. The raising of the school-leaving age should not have been regarded as a self-justifying dogma, and a further expansion of higher education (of the kind then enthusiastically proposed) might not represent the wisest use of resources.

Progressives of a different kind were having by 1972 too easy a time in their attacks on vocationalism. The sixth-form tradition, I argued then, had been extended far beyond its appropriate frame of reference, and attempts to develop a Certificate of Extended Education—and thereby devalue vocational training after the age of sixteen—were profoundly misguided. So was the preoccupation with examinations at sixteen-plus, and the fanciful mission to develop a universal and common system of examinations at that age.

Within the 11–16 sector the reputation of traditional 'subjects' had suffered in a way that was unhelpful to teachers, leaving them uncertain about what to teach, or how. Similarly, a growing and not wholly rational preoccupation with a so-called common curriculum undervalued the importance of a diversity of educational experiences, and might lead towards wholly undesirable attempts to define nationally what such a curriculum might be. Such efforts would, I thought, be offensive—whether undertaken by a Schools Council, a Government, HMI, or anyone else. If schools were mistaken (and would in consequence be demoralized) in believing they could offer secular salvation, or prescribe the necessary education for all pupils, they would be equally wrong in diluting their strictly pedagogic functions. Contemporary talk about community schools (not all of which has evaporated) distracted teachers from those very functions which parents understandably insisted were central to the schools. Schools needed, then as for the future, to act constructively within the limitations imposed upon them.

I had not intended *School is Not Yet Dead* to be an informal postscript to my twelve years in Banbury, but it proved to be so. On 26 October 1972, I was appointed Director of the University of Oxford Department of Educational Studies and, in the following summer, followed in reverse the journey which Stanbridge had made from Oxford to Banbury School in 1501.

Sorting through my papers before that removal, I came across a copy of Matthew Arnold's 'The Last Word', which Eric James had handed to me the year before. He had added a note of his own: 'As promised. *Not* a good poem—but we both know what it's about.'

> Creep into thy narrow bed,
> Creep, and let no more be said!
> Vain thy onset! all stands fast.
> Thou thyself must break at last.

Let the long contention cease!
Geese are swans and swans are geese.
Let them have it how they will!
Thou art tired; best be still.

They out-talked thee, hissed thee, tore thee?
Better men fared thus before thee;
Fired their ringing shot and passed,
Hotly charged—and sank at last.

Charge once more, then, and be dumb!
Let the victors, when they come,
When the forts of folly fall,
Find thy body by the wall!

Good or bad, I began to read more of the poems of Matthew Arnold, sometime HMI, and when we decided that a longer canal boat was needed, it was to be called *Scholar Gypsy*.

CHAPTER 10

Influence

Moving to Oxford in 1973 carried me into the heart of a group of men who, although none of them had ever taught in secondary schools, were deeply concerned with the state of public education, and with the contribution which a university could make to its continuing improvement. One of the first to welcome me was Lord Redcliffe-Maud, Master of University College since 1963. John Primatt Redcliffe Redcliffe-Maud was knighted in 1946, and raised to the peerage in 1967: his very name, and successive titles, read as an epitome of the influence on English education, across most of the forty years with which this book is concerned, of an upper-class/conservative/progressive Establishment.

He was born, the son of a bishop, in 1906 and educated at Eton, and New College, Oxford, and (more surprisingly) Harvard. At the age of twenty-three he returned to Oxford as a Junior Research Fellow at University College, and in 1930 was elected to Oxford City Council, where he was joined by Dick Crossman, his junior by some eighteen months. He taught John Newsom, who always referred to him as 'my old Tutor', and was the first Oxford man to be a full-time tutor in politics. From the beginning of his career, his strongest interest was in local government and (unsurprisingly) its relationship to public education. For a few years after 1939 he was Master of Birkbeck College, London, but was drawn more directly into the public service by becoming a civil servant, first at the Ministry of Food, and then in Reconstruction.

When Ellen Wilkinson became Minister of Education after the general election of 1944, she asked for a Permanent Secretary who would be 'a good administrator and not establishment minded'. The partnership of John Maud with her, and subsequently with George Tomlinson, gave administrative substance to the Act of

1944 and built Britain's system of post-war education. In 1952
John Maud became Permanent Secretary at the Ministry of Fuel
and Power, when his first task was to supervise a great shift from
coal to oil, and his second, after Suez, to do the opposite. Seven
years later, in 1959, he became High Commissioner in South
Africa, and the first British ambassador there when that country
left the Commonwealth. He is believed to have played a major
part in the drafting of Macmillan's 'wind of change' speech at
Cape Town in 1960—a fine example of his commitment to the
effort to adapt powerful institutions to new conditions and new
purposes.

Sir John Maud returned from South Africa to become Master of
the College in which he had been a Fellow, and three years later in
1966 was appointed chairman of the Royal Commission on Local
Government. One of his earliest books had been published in
1932 on the subject of *English Local Government* and he had
already chaired a committee on the management of local government. The Report of the Commission in 1969 led, although not at
all in the way its authors had intended, to the Local Government
Act of 1972, and to the reshaping of the whole system from
1 April 1974. Dick Crossman used to growl that he would have
had me as an education member of the Royal Commission, if
Tony Crosland was not already (as he put it) wasting my time on
the Public Schools Commission. At two significant stages in his
career—Permanent Secretary in central government, Chairman of
the Royal Commission—John Maud changed the terms of reference within which education was governed. The ways in which
that map of power and influence was redrawn directly affected the
patterns of secondary schooling across the years 1944 to 1984.

The Royal Commission had been established by the Labour
government of 1964–70 in an attempt to confer both a rational
shape and greater significance upon the activities of local government. Prominent among these activities was the provision of
education, although it is often forgotten that this need not and
might not have been so. Nor will it necessarily be so at the end of
this century. The first publicly constituted local authorities for
education in this country were single purpose, and *ad hoc*: the

school-boards for elementary education were, under the 1870 Act, elected solely for the provision of schools and were empowered to levy rates for that purpose only. This was a familiar contemporary model, as it is still the prevailing pattern in the United States, and the concept of a unitary local authority—one which would combine responsibility for such diverse activities as roads, lighting, sewage, police—would have seemed peculiar. When the county councils and county boroughs were established in 1888, the position of the existing school-boards (as of the voluntary societies) was not touched, although the new councils did begin to acquire some powers to spend rates and grants on secondary schools—this is how my father got to Thame.

The great argument at the turn of the century revolved around the virtues of unification against those of fragmentation. Should schools be controlled by democratically elected all-purpose local governments, as constituted by the Act of 1888? Should elementary and secondary schools be controlled by the same authorities? Should the denominational schools also be in some sense controlled and financed by those same local authorities? The Education Act of 1902 gave an unambiguous answer. Local councils should be all-purpose, and all public schooling should be under their control. Central government would provide some supplementary funds and the necessary legislative framework, as it would also authorize a national examination system, but further than that it should not go. The implications of the settlement of 1902 remain potent in 1984, with still unresolved ambiguities about where the springs of influence should lie.

Nor was the framework of that settlement fundamentally altered in 1944. Some anomalies were, to be sure, erased, and the so-called Part Three authorities, which had responsibility in some urban areas for elementary but not secondary schools, disappeared. Banbury Borough Council had, for example, been responsible until then for elementary education in the town, but Oxfordshire County Council for secondary education—an arrangement which led to bureaucratic squabble, but not much else. Secondary education became universal, and fees were abolished —but the responsibility remained where it had been, with the county councils and (in larger cities, like Oxford itself) the county borough, which exercised precisely the same powers.

John Maud constantly used, but later in his life with hints of nostalgia and regret, the language of consensus and partnership. Inexorably, the growth of central-government interest and power soon disturbed the delicate balances of 1902 and 1944. Education was, no doubt, 'a national service locally administered' but what precisely did that mean?

The service was there in order to allow parents to fulfil their legal obligations. The 1944 Act ruled that 'It shall be the duty of the parent of every child of compulsory school age to cause him to receive efficient and full-time education suitable to his age, ability and aptitude, either by regular attendance at school, or otherwise.' The corresponding duty of the Local Education Authority was to pursue parents who failed in the obligation and 'to ensure that there shall be available sufficient schools for providing primary and secondary education'. One effect of the 1944 Act, by the abolition of the anomalous Part Three authorities, was to reduce the number of Local Education Authorities in England and Wales from some 300 to 163.

Each Local Education Authority was required by statute to appoint a Chief Education Officer (or Director of Education) and an education committee. In practice, the education committee enjoyed a wide delegation of powers, and was dependent upon the county council—except, of course, in financial matters—only in a formal sense. In the urban areas, that is to say the LCC (London County Council) and the county boroughs, political parties were active and organization often detailed and elaborate: changes in control often produced significant shifts in policy. In most of the shire counties, however, the mood was more relaxed, and political organization tended to be correspondingly weaker. In both types of Local Education Authority the relationship between the chairman of the education committee and the Chief Education Officer often provided the key to policy and the explanation of change. A determined Chief Education Officer, and especially one with clearly articulated ideals, could set a strong personal mark upon the policy and practice of a county. John Newsom in Hertfordshire,

Henry Morris in Cambridgeshire, Alec Clegg in the West Riding, Stuart Mason in Leicestershire: all provided this style of effective leadership, and changed the nature of the secondary schools under their influence. It will be more difficult, and perhaps should be so, for their successors to achieve this kind of dominance.

The assumptions and practices of Local Education Authorities did not change in any fundamental way across the three decades between the 1944 Act and the 1974 reorganization. London underwent a major piece of administrative surgery in 1965, when the Greater London Council was created, but even then the Inner London Education Authority preserved responsibility for the area which had previously been administered by the London County Council: it therefore became the only single-purpose, *ad hoc*, education authority in the country. In other areas, the pattern remained unchanged as the education service was expanded. Chief Education Officers, with their deputies and assistants, became a highly professional cadre. A network of advisory services, both to inspect and to support teaching in schools, was established: by the mid-1970s there were 1,874 advisers, working in a wide range of specialisms. By then local authorities, which had of course responsibilities wider than education alone, employed 2,900,000 people, representing 11.3 per cent of the country's work-force and a doubling since 1952: 541,890 of them were teachers.

Education represented, in terms of expenditure, the largest commitment of the all-purpose local authorities and—given the importance and visibility of this activity—it is not surprising that it achieved a sense of distinctiveness, even of separateness, within local government. Many outside the charmed circle came to resent this powerful coalition of education committees, their chairmen, Chief Education Officers, elaborate supporting services, and an expanding army of teachers. Although the county councils and the boroughs had their own co-operative organizations, which acted as powerful levers upon central government, the Association of Education Committees mobilized the whole of the educational/ administrative establishment as a unitary force. For the last thirty years of its seventy-year life (1904–74) it was dominated by Sir

William (later Lord) Alexander, reputedly the most powerful figure in the brokerage of educational influence.

I have been, on three occasions and in three different capacities, a member of the Oxfordshire County Council Education Committee: first in the 1960s as a teacher representative, then for a brief period during the turbulence of reorganization as a representative of the university, and now as a 'person of experience' appointed directly by the county council. Education committees have always had members—representing the Churches, for example—who are not county councillors, and this also tended to mark them off as different from other committees of the council. Certainly, in the 1960s the education committee was a peaceful if constructive place. Councils still had aldermen, who were persons of distinction exempt from the contentious business of being elected, and the Earl of Macclesfield still presided over the county from his castle in Watlington. He was matched at the other end of the county by Lord Saye and Sele of Broughton Castle, who was an active member of the Education Committee and chairman of the governors of Banbury Grammar School. The chairman of the Education Committee was a gentleman farmer, who called himself an Independent, and was precisely that. His voting habits at general elections were unpredictable, and his vice-chairman was a member of the Labour party who was a union official at Cowley. Both now have Oxfordshire comprehensive schools named after them.

The Director of Education for the County, never in those days to be confused with the City, had worked with John Newsom, thought deeply about educational development and, like most visionaries, had about him a touch of the autocrat. His alliance with his chairman assisted the smooth evolution of most of the county's secondary schools towards comprehensiveness, allowed the development of a philosophy of primary education closely attuned to that of the Plowden Report, and minimized contention in the Committee. Those days already seem long distant; it is not surprising if some critics found such confident habits of progressive government a little too liberal, or too cosy, or insufficiently radical, or inadequately cost-effective for their taste.

The report of 1967, by a committee also under the chairmanship of John Maud, on the Management of Local Government, had drawn attention to other weaknesses: only 12 per cent of councillors were women, their average age was fifty-five, the professional classes (and the retired) predominated, and it was hardly surprising that the turn-out figures for local elections were—even in the more contentious cities—disconcertingly low. The report of the Royal Commission (1969) proposed sweeping changes, designed to increase both the accountability and the influence of elected local governments.

The 1969 Redcliffe-Maud Report was based upon a few clear axioms: the political problems arose in their application. It was argued that the existing complexities—with a wide variety of local authorities deploying overlapping powers—should be replaced by one simple pattern. The new authorities should be unitary: responsibility for environmental services (such as planning) and for personal services (such as education) should be integrated at one level of government. Elaborate, but ultimately speculative, discussion about the proper size of such authorities led to the conclusion that their population should be at least one-quarter of a million. London had, of course, already been dealt with separately earlier in the 1960s. As a general rule the government of the cities and of the countryside in which they were set should now be integrated: distinction between county borough and counties had produced such anomalies as the formal separation of the education and other services of the city of Oxford from those of the county in which it was embedded. Exceptions would be needed in only three major conurbations—Liverpool, Manchester, and Birmingham—where the particular problems of population and geography would dictate the necessity of two tiers of government, environmental responsibilities being associated with the higher, and personal services (education, again) with the lower. There should be, alongside these three metropolitan areas with their constituent districts, fifty-eight unitary authorities (the shire counties) providing all local-government services in England and Wales.

The Labour government, which received the Report but remained in power only until 1970, tinkered with these proposals by changing the number and location of the metropolitan authorities and by assigning responsibility for education within them to the higher tier. Conservatives were, and are, suspicious of the power of the metropolitan areas—where traditionally the Labour party has enjoyed the advantage over them—and when Heath became Prime Minister in 1970 with Margaret Thatcher at Education and Science made even more fundamental changes to the principles of the Report. There was now to be two-tier government throughout England and Wales, with county councils (the shire counties) taking the strategic responsibilities, and a multitude of district councils operating below them. Education, in all its stages, was assigned to the shire counties, the higher tier of government. As for the metropolitan counties, there were now to be six of them—but, in their case, the government of education was to go to the lower level, the metropolitan district. The opportunity for a clear and definitive reform of local government had been sacrificed to expediency and political interest.

Since 1 April 1974, after a preliminary and difficult period of transitional adjustment, there have therefore been in England and Wales 105 Local Education Authorities—47 shire counties, 36 metropolitan districts, 20 outer-London boroughs, the Inner London Education Authority, and (always peculiar) the Isles of Scilly, each with its own education committee and Chief Education Officer. The informal, and in some cases unintended, effects of local-government reorganization have been in some ways even more profound than this redrawing of the administrative map. Local government became, after 1974, more political, and more contentious. Large local authorities, and larger electoral districts within them, have generated more political organization, in the shire counties as well as within the metropolitan counties. 'Independents' have become scarce, local party leaders more visible and powerful, the formal adoption of policy and tactics within the opposing groups very much more common. The relaxed alliance of Chief Education Officer and chairman is now a thing of the past.

So, of course, is the proud sense of the distinctiveness of education among local-government services. The deliberate elimination in 1974, by the hard men of the new order, of the Association of Education Committees has already been cited as an important index of this change of attitude. The distinctiveness of the education service has been eroded in other ways, too. The Royal Commission, and the work which preceded it, laid stress upon the importance of integrating the various services provided by local government. The Bains Report (1972) accelerated change in this direction by celebrating the virtues of corporate management, within which the Chief Education Officer should be one member of a team of professional administrators, no different in kind from his other professional colleagues, and subject to the same disciplines of accountability and co-operation. Corporate management has been matched at the political level by a related effort to integrate the policies of a council through a policy and resources committee, on which the chairmen of the major committees sit but from which they are required to accept direction. A new figure began to appear in the town and county halls, in which the senior officer had previously been the clerk or secretary, a mild and scrupulous legal figure with modest ambitions in management. The Chief Executive now occupies a key place in government, and therefore exercises profound influence upon educational policy, as a managerial agent negotiating with politicians and directing the total effort of the local authority. The politicization of local government, the emergence of leaders and leaders of the opposition, the role of the leader as chairman of the policy and resources committee, the doctrine of corporate management, and the growing sophistication of its techniques, the centrality of the Chief Executive—all these, taken in concert with the reorganization of 1974—have shifted the mainstream of influence. What is more, they reflect and are a reinforcing cause of a more general doubt about the achievement of schools, with which the next chapter will be concerned.

The years since 1974 have also been marked by growing strains in the relationship between central and local government, manifested especially in the difficulties associated with the financing of local services, and especially of education. Education, being labour-intensive, is an expensive business, and the expansion of schooling across the thirty years after the War had multiplied the burdens. That expansion had, moreover, distorted the framework of partnership within which the system took shape after 1944. That growth had been funded very largely through local-government expenditure: 86 per cent of all national educational provision is financed in this way, and of the residue 11 per cent is assigned directly for the support of universities through the University Grants Committee, so that only a meagre 3 per cent remains under the direct control of the DES. None of that residue, save a small amount indirectly in the form of research grants, finds its way into the support of statutory schooling. That schooling is, in financial as in legal terms, the preserve of the local authority, whose budgets have increasingly been dominated by the insistent demands of education. Education, as a proportion of all local-authority expenditure, had risen from 21.8 per cent in 1947/8 to 38.3 per cent by the late sixties.

Where does this money come from, and how does its channelling affect the scale of provision for schools? Local authorities raise money by rates, that is to say by a tax on property. Nevertheless, in 1973/4 the revenue from rates accounted for only 28 per cent of all local-authority income: fees, charges, and other miscellaneous income provided for 27 per cent, but the rest (45 per cent of the total, therefore) came from central government in the shape of the Rate Support Grant. The Rate Support Grant, cumbersome and complex as it is, remains the Government's principal instrument in determining national expenditure on education, as on other services provided by local authorities. The Government's share of that total expenditure had risen to the figure of 45 per cent from 36 per cent in 1953.

The origins of this complex system were simple enough. In the nineteenth century Government grants were made for specific purposes and on a modest scale—to support the provision of elementary schools by voluntary bodies, for example, or the teaching of science in secondary schools. In 1918, H. A. L. Fisher consolidated and enlarged these subventions in a percentage grant system: the Board of Education agreed to support approved educational expenditure by local authorities, on a percentage basis. This was to be an enlightened method of encouraging such local authorities to take a generous view of their enlarging responsibilities, and over the years the level of grant was adjusted in order to match the educational enthusiasms of the Government of the day, or (more frequently) the economic state of the nation.

It was an instrument directly in the hands of the Board and later the Ministry of Education, and regarded as a central element in its own budget. It chimed sweetly with a perception of education as 'a national service locally administered', and as enjoying a special and privileged place within local government. It was as much a part of the stable and established scene as the Association of Education Committees.

This obliging system was fundamentally modified in 1958—to the dismay of many who valued educational causes, and to the concern of Edward Boyle, then Parliamentary Secretary for Education in Macmillan's government. In its place there was now to be a block grant, administered directly by the Ministry of Housing and Local Government (later absorbed into a new Department of the Environment) under the insistent tutelage of the Treasury. The theory of the 'block grant' was that central-government support for education and other services should be neither specific nor based upon a promised percentage, and that democratically elected local authorities should themselves determine priorities and levels of expenditure. Sceptics observed that this could prove a useful formula for Whitehall and Westminister to spend less on education, and then blame somebody else for their parsimony. It certainly became simpler for central government to pile new responsibilities upon local government, without providing the matching resources.

In 1967, this system was further refined into the Rate Support Grant, which has since been based on an elaborate formula designed to make allowances for variations in need and wealth among all authorities. Throughout the 1970s (and changes in the 1980s will find a place in Chapter 12), the negotiations leading to the fixing of the Rate Support Grant became increasingly elaborate. Representatives of the Department of Education and Science are, of course, involved in them but power shifted decisively towards the Treasury and the Department of the Environment. Government attempted to set the total level of expenditure on the Rate Support Grant. 'Relevant expenditure' by each local authority was then calculated, the equalizing and balancing formula applied, and the appropriate Rate Support Grant calculated. This naturally varied from one authority to another both in volume and in proportion, but in 1973/4 it amounted nationally to 60 per cent of all relevant expenditure by local authorities alongside the 40 per cent furnished from the rates. Very few people understood, or understand, the system. It cannot be related in any precise way to any 'educational' elements within the Grant. 'Money' fought for in Cabinet, and notionally assigned to such purposes, simply disappeared into the pipes. Cash 'for' nursery education was spent, or so it was in one case alleged, on the provision of traffic-lights. It is not surprising if the Department of Education and Science, both politicians and administrators, were frustrated. The formula is neither service-specific, nor does it represent a simple percentage of what any given local authority does actually spend.

The debate continues to trouble the 1980s. The Layfield Committee reported in 1976, in the wake of local-government reorganization, on alternative ways of financing such services as education. The Labour government responded with a Green Paper in May 1977, turning aside the proposals for a local income tax and proposing the so-called 'unitary grant', which would give central government a more direct say in determining, in precise terms, the spending needs of each authority. The Conservatives, when they came to power, muddied the waters by carrying forward their own very similar proposals under the label of a 'block grant'—which is, of course, precisely what it is not. By then, Government was preoccupied with holding down national expenditure, and penalizing those authorities which persisted in 'overspending'. Central-government powers in finance which were originally used to produce a 'uniform minimum' are now being applied to generate a 'maximum of uniformity'. The terms of the argument have been reversed.

The financial question is important, for it reflects a growing uncertainty about precisely where rights of control and management lie. The system which sustains the schools cannot comfortably survive when financial power and the power to take national and strategic decisions lie in one place, whereas democratic responsibility for applying that policy reposes elsewhere. The strains inherent in such a system have also exposed the ambiguities latent in the 1944 Act. Section 1 required the Minister 'to secure the effective execution by local authorities, under his control and direction, of the national policy for providing a varied and comprehensive education service in every area'. Given that the Act of 1899 had spoken only of the duty 'to superintend and co-ordinate', what precisely were 'control and direction' to mean?

The growth of the system after 1944 made it increasingly difficult to sustain the metaphors of 'partnership'. The Ministry was compelled by circumstances to become more interventionist, and more directive. The turning-point was the relatively long, although interrupted, tenure as Minister of Sir David Eccles (now Lord Eccles). Further education, teacher supply, the expansion of higher education, and even the shape of the curriculum—all these, with the doubtful exception of the last, were perceived as matters of national rather than of local concern. The problem of teachers' salaries, like that of the Rate Support Grant, illustrates well the difficulties inseparable from the running of a system in which one 'partner' provides the schools and employs the teacher, and another furnishes most of the cash for training and paying the teachers. After 1944, the Minister had no place on the Burnham Committees and no direct say in determining the shape or level of the salary settlements with which those Committees had been, since the days of Fisher, concerned. He could accept or reject the recommendations, but not modify them. The unacceptability to the Ministry of the 1963 recommendations led, first, to a special act imposing a settlement, and then, in 1965, to legislation which incorporates representation of the Minister on the various Committees.

The Minister enjoyed other wide powers under the 1944 Act—including detailed regulations about standards of school building, the right to issue administrative Memoranda and Circulars (of which 10/65 remains the most dramatic example) on a wide range of matters, to hear appeals against the conduct of Local Education Authorities, and to approve or reject proposals for a change in the character of a school. This last power is still frequently exercised by the Secretary of State to prevent reorganization of which he disapproves—proposals, say (to take an example which has already been cited), to establish sixth-form colleges which would, in his view, seriously damage existing secondary schools of proven quality. He also has the right to intervene whenever he believes a local authority has acted unreasonably. However, in 1976 the courts checked the exercise of this last power in Tameside, ruling that the Secretary of State must himself act reasonably and noting that the dispute under review was between two legitimate and elected authorities. 'The Act does not leave the national policy to be determined by successive Secretaries of State. Where authorities have statutory discretion the Minister cannot substitute his opinions for theirs.' Small wonder, then, if authorities like Buckinghamshire, Oxfordshire's neighbour, have successfully resisted attempts by successive Labour governments to oblige them to adopt a system of comprehensive schools.

The power of the Secretary of State is, therefore, closer to an exercise of influence than to an imposition of control. But influence can be diffuse, and its effects leisurely. The Department of Education and Science, with a staff of 2,500 civil servants in 1979, is unusual among the great departments of State in having very little *direct* control over the system for which it is responsible to Parliament. Its remoteness from so many of the springs of action explains, and perhaps excuses, many of the strictures produced in 1975 by an OECD review. In particular, the Department was accused of weakness in the overall planning of the system. The civil servants were complimented upon their quality and professionalism, and yet represented as being both opportunist and overpowerful. They remain in control of policies (when there are any) which are not always visible to the public. Their political masters are often not in effective control: the average tenure of a Minister between 1945 and 1980 was only twenty months, whereas a Permanent Secretary is usually in his post for some six years, and often after a long career within the Department.

Uncertainties about the realities of power and responsibility amplified the growing doubts about the quality and appropriateness of secondary schooling in the 1970s. They were further complicated by a growing mood of interventionism, even of centralism, within a vulnerable Department of Education and Science, by unresolved questions about the relationship between central and local government as that had been redefined in 1944, and by a wholesale reorganization of local government in 1974. The elections for the new councils took place in the spring and early summer of 1973. All six of the metropolitan counties fell to Labour. They contained, as Local Education Authorities, thirty-six metropolitan districts: no fewer than twenty-six were under Labour control, with five Conservative and five with no clear overall party majority.

The forty-seven shire counties also went to the polls, and eighteen of them passed into the Conservative camp, eleven into the Labour, and eighteen sat in the no man's land. Oxfordshire changed its shape, by taking in some juicy parts of Berkshire, and Didcot. The city of Oxford ceased to be a Local Education Authority, and grumbled about that for several years to come. The new education committees and its officers had therefore, as far as secondary schools were concerned, to draw into some kind of unity the old county (where comprehensive reorganization had been completed, with relatively little fuss), parts of Berkshire (where it had hardly been contemplated), and the city of Oxford (where a particular form of reorganization had been adopted after a fierce and partisan battle).

The debates about comprehensive reorganization in the city of Oxford took place in the chamber where Dick Crossman and John Maud had sharpened their political wits in the 1930s, only a few hundred yards from County Hall, where things were very different. Unlike the county of those days, the city had long conducted its debate in sharply political terms, complicated by the presence (until the reform of 1974 removed such anomalies) of university representatives. Labour attitudes towards secondary schooling mirrored those national doubts and hesitations of the

1960s, which have already been reported. Members tended to favour traditional arrangements and were sensitive to the advantages of grammar schools. Extensive use was also made of the two direct-grant schools in the city. Within the broad consensus of attitude there was, however, a growing hostility to the eleven-plus, and by 1964 the Labour group on the Council was committed to bringing selection to an end. But how?

The local elections of May 1964 gave power in Oxford, but not an overall majority, to the Labour group: there were no fewer than twelve, more or less independent and certainly unpredictable, university members on the council. A working party proposed for discussion two alternatives: relatively small 11–18 neighbourhood comprehensive schools, which would probably have to be linked in some way to provide adequate sixth-form opportunities; or a junior college for all pupils at sixteen-plus, and not only for an élite following A-level courses, to be built on the same site as the College of Further Education, with which it would co-operate closely. The problem for the city was that it had deliberately built relatively small neighbourhood schools, and these could not conveniently be turned into all-through comprehensives.

The Labour group, undeterred by the unwelcoming paragraphs of Circular 10/65, preferred a junior college, for all the reasons already given in the national context for a new institution of this kind. It would merge the academic and vocational traditions, and mix from the age of sixteen the very different populations from the various parts of the city. Predictably, the Conservatives saw the college as a threat to sixth-form standards, as a piece of social engineering, as a decapitation of good schools. Although the general election of March 1966 increased the Labour majority at Westminster, the local elections in May recorded, as usual, a political shift in the opposite direction: in Oxford, the Conservatives recovered their small overall majority. On the Education Committee they had eight seats, with eight Labour representatives (still including the chairman of the Education Committee), three university members, and no less than eleven co-opted members following their consciences or their prejudices.

In October the junior-college proposal was, as a result, defeated, but Janet Young as the vigorous leader of the Conservatives proposed that there be a third scheme, with middle schools for the nine- to thirteen-year-olds. This made more appeal to some Conservatives, left open the possibility of taking up places for pupils at the age of thirteen in the direct-grant schools, annoyed the Labour group, who were suspicious of delaying tactics and uneasily defending a simple 11–18 solution, and attracted the approval of the Archdeacon of Oxford, a Hebrew scholar who liked the closeness of this new proposal to the arrangements made in the independent sector. The Chief Education Officer, always and inevitably in places like Oxford the professional servant of a volatile committee, produced the necessary report on this alternative.

Its narrow rejection in January 1967 by the Education Committee did not deter Janet Young—who, as a friend and ally of Margaret Thatcher, became a life peeress in 1971 and an Education Minister in 1979. She took the unusual step of giving notice that she would raise the question again in the full council, where the absence of co-opted members (although not of aldermen, like herself) might produce a different result. It did, after an acrimonious debate in March, and in January 1968 the Secretary of State, exercising his powers under the 1944 Act, approved the three-tier pattern of organization for the city schools. Margaret Thatcher, as Secretary of State from 1970, modified the proposals by requiring that two of the upper schools (in fact, and unsurprisingly, the two former boys' and girls' grammar schools) should continue to provide single-sex schooling for the parents of those children who wanted it. Parental choice was becoming a major issue.

Oxford's new pattern of comprehensive schooling was inaugurated in September 1973, just as the city council which had battled over it was transferring its responsibilities to the newly constituted county council. September 1973 was also the month in which my three children needed to take their places in Oxford schools, as we all left Banbury behind us. In 1973 Simon was nearly fourteen, and he left Broughton Hall in Banbury School to go to that upper school in Oxford which had until that day been the boys' grammar school. Hilary was eleven, and left her primary school in Banbury to go to the nearest middle school in Oxford, which until that day had been a primary school. Emma, who was seven years old, left the same Banbury primary school to go to the nearest first school in Oxford, and had to walk along a long road to get there. Within a few years my wife, Mary, began to teach in the College of Further Education, which was not to have a junior college as a twin.

Until then, the children had all grown up in Banbury. Hilary and Emma used to walk home from school each day hand in hand, along another road to the Principal's House at the very time when two thousand larger pupils surged in the opposite direction, leaving Banbury School behind them at the end of the day. From my office window, I could see their heads (just) appearing above the low wall which marked the school boundary. I now moved office, too, to the Department of Educational Studies in Norham Gardens. It was in the house in which I had lived for a while twenty years before.

CHAPTER 11

Doubt

On 18 October 1976, I climbed Headington Hill from Oxford in order to listen to a speech by the Prime Minister of the day. Mr Callaghan, who had presided over the Government only since April, was to make a major statement on education. That, in itself, was sufficiently unusual. When had any Prime Minister last chosen to speak at any length on this subject? Even more unusual was the long series of leaks, hints, and rumours which preceded Callaghan's Oxford speech.

The Labour party had been back in power since early 1974, and had already taken a number of controversial if predictable steps directly affecting secondary schools. The last year of Heath's Conservative government, with Mrs Thatcher still at the Department of Education, had been painful. In 1973, a strike by gas-workers in January had been followed by the hospital workers in March, and, later in the year, bans on overtime working by railwaymen and miners. Heath's attempt to confront the organized power of the unions was to end in ignominious defeat. The outbreak of the Yom Kippur war in October led to a world crisis in the supply and pricing of oil, which undermined the economies of all developed countries. By the end of the year, the Chancellor of the Exchequer was obliged to make massive cuts in public expenditure: all hopes for the expansion which Mrs Thatcher had promised as recently as December 1972 grew pale and dim. The Bank Rate rose to its highest level since 1914. The year 1974 began, with magnificent inappropriateness, with a newly ordained bank holiday on 1 January. Shortage of fuel had already produced a state of emergency and a three-day working week for industry. The miners then threw down the gauntlet by agreeing on an all-out strike, and Heath belatedly decided to go to the country.

The general election of 28 February 1974 produced an inconclusive result. For the first time since 1929, no party had an overall majority, and the balance of power lay with the Liberals, the Ulster Unionists, and the Welsh and Scottish Nationalist parties. The established order, and the integrity of the United Kingdom itself, seemed to be at risk. The results were a disaster for the Tories, who lost 1.2 million votes; but the Labour party also lost votes, to a total of half a million. Labour had 301 seats (in a House of 635) against 297 Conservative. Harold Wilson returned as Prime Minister, and his tactical powers were stretched to the full in what was to prove the shortest Parliament since 1681. In April, as has already been noted, the new local authorities assumed responsibility for the education service, and uncertainties about future policy were compounded. Dick Crossman was still working on his diaries when he died on 5 April 1974. His son Patrick died tragically just a year later; his daughter Virginia later became a history undergraduate at Brasenose College, Oxford. On 5 September 1974, Sir Keith Joseph (whose brooding figure dominates the educational scene as the last chapters of this book are written) made a speech attributing the perilous state of the economy to the errors of pursuing full employment, and called for strict monetary control. Another general election in the following month confirmed the Labour party in power, with a gain of eighteen seats in the House of Commons. The Conservatives lost twenty more seats (and resolved to change their policies and their leaders), and Wilson was left with a tiny overall majority—smaller than he had enjoyed in 1964, when Crossman and Crosland came to power with him, but sufficient to preserve him in office. Within three months, Margaret Thatcher had succeeded Edward Heath as Leader of the Opposition. She had learnt her lessons well, speaking out later in 1975 and appropriately in the United States, against the 'persistent expansion of the role of the State and the relentless pursuit of equality'.

Reg Prentice, as Secretary of State for Education and Science from March 1974 until June 1975, pursued 'equality' in the field of secondary schooling by picking up the unfinished business of the 1964–70 administration and by enlarging State control of educational policy. There were, or seemed to be, no new ideas. At the beginning of 1975, the termination of direct grants was announced, and no serious attempt was made (certainly nothing in harmony with the proposals of the Public Schools Commission) to incorporate the schools affected into the comprehensive sector. They were, in any case, notably unenthusiastic about such absorption, and the prospect of falling numbers in secondary schools generally left the new Local Education Authorities relatively indifferent to their fate. Nevertheless, fifty-one of the schools (forty-eight of them Roman Catholic) passed into the maintained sector as voluntary schools. In most cases, such schools had little choice—they were an integral part of local denominational provision, indistinguishable in most ways from voluntary-aided grammar schools after the 1944 Act, and could not have survived by charging fees. Four schools were closed, but one hundred and nineteen—including most of the prestigious academic schools—became fully independent and charged fees.

When the House of Lords, later in 1975, debated this ominous change, many voices and echoes from the past made themselves heard. Lord Belstead, formerly one of Mrs Thatcher's junior ministers, led the Conservative opposition—citing some published arguments of my own intended to moderate an absolute and doctrinaire opposition to selection of any kind and at any age. Lord Butler returned magisterially to his Act of 1944, roundly asserting that 'I regard the direct-grant schools as an absolutely integral part of equality of opportunity', and recalling how Shinwell had patted him on the back. Shinwell, too, was a friend of grammar schools. Lord Eccles recalled the strenuous attempts made by Conservative administrations to pour resources into the secondary schools (as indeed they had) in the hope that steadily rising standards would close any gap of quality and esteem between maintained and independent schools. Lord James of Rusholme pointed to the real dangers of a loss of opportunity in inner-city areas, where clever working-class boys would be confined to their neighbourhood schools: doubtless, he had Manchester in mind. Unrepentant, he claimed that 'It is a commentary on our society—and perhaps one reason for its decline—

that selection by intellectual ability should be, of all kinds of selection, the most distasteful to so many people of good will.'

There seemed plenty of evidence for decline in 1975, and Lord Alexander, in this same debate and now at the end of a long period of unprecedented influence over educational policy, approved the principle of withdrawing direct grants but attacked the timing: there was simply not enough money now to permit this extravagance. And indeed, in April, public spending had already been cut by £900m. To some critics, the ending of direct grants (ideological and expensive) had much in common with Barbara Castle's banishment of private beds from public hospitals. In September, £175m. was made available to help the unemployed, and especially the school-leavers. In October, a 2½ per cent fall in real disposable income marked the largest drop in living standards for the past twenty years, and unemployment rose above one million for the first time since the War.

At the end of 1975, the Government introduced a bill designed to press forward the advances already made towards comprehensive reorganization since the promulgation of Circular 10/65. The Act, eventually passed in 1976, required local authorities which had not already done so to submit plans for such reorganization, and empowered the Secretary of State to impose a settlement where none could be agreed. The recalcitrance of a small number of Local Education Authorities had persuaded the previous Labour government to attempt a similar measure in 1969, but it had been overtaken by the general election of 1970. Margaret Thatcher then rapidly issued Circular 10/70, cancelling 10/65, but Local Education Authorities continued to submit plans for reorganization: under Heath's administration, the number of comprehensive schools in England and Wales rose from 1,250 to 2,677. The situation was necessarily complicated by the local-government reorganization of 1974, but of the 105 new Local Education Authorities only 7 refused to commit themselves to the principle of comprehensive reorganization, until and unless they were required by law to do so. Of that same 105, however, only one authority had no comprehensives in 1976, 27 were fully comprehensive, 19 had reorganized all except the voluntary schools, and the remaining 58 were comprehensive in part. Over the previous decade, the number of comprehensive schools had risen from 262 to 3,387, and the proportion of secondary-school pupils in them from 8.5 per cent to 69.7 per cent. A law was now thought necessary to encourage the laggards; its effect was to accelerate the shift in power over schools towards central government.

The ending of direct grants and the making of the 1976 Education Act also hardened the distinctions between Tory and Labour policy—hardly obtrusive when Butler and Eccles had been in power—and further sharpened anxieties that quality in secondary schools was being sacrificed on an altar of remorseless equality. Norman St John Stevas, at that time the Conservative spokesman on education, advised local authorities to be dilatory in responding to pressures from the Department of Education and Science, and so allow the next Conservative government to rescue them from Labour insistence—as, indeed, it did. Doubts about a universal comprehensive system became noisier—especially as the resources of the 1960s were no longer available, and falling school rolls led to a matching decline of investment in school building. Would the Upper School in Banbury have been built in the circumstances of the later 1970s? Even Labour party supporters were volatile: in a national poll in 1977, 58 per cent of them were in favour of keeping those grammar schools which still remained, and in 1975 seventy-eight Local Education Authorities still had at least one such school.

Parental and political opposition to the elimination of grammar schools had always, of course, been well organized. As early as 1967, the local authority for Enfield had been successfully challenged in a celebrated series of court cases, in which Mr Geoffrey Howe, later to serve Mrs Thatcher as a minister, represented the parents. The movement to respect the rights of parents to be properly consulted began to gather strength. At Tameside, a metropolitan district within Greater Manchester, when the Conservatives were returned to power in February 1976 they immediately overturned the comprehensive plans of their predecessors. Plans for ending eleven-plus selection in that very year were promptly scrapped: the new councillors attributed part of their electoral success to the falling reputation of comprehensive schools in the city of Manchester.

The Secretary of State, claiming the authority of the 1944 Act, ordered the Tameside councillors to reverse their decision, on the grounds that they were acting 'unreasonably', but the courts overruled him. The constitutional significance of this episode has already been discussed: in the context of 1976 and of the enlarging debate about comprehensives, it illustrates the mood of growing contention, and the will in some places to preserve a long-established order. Comprehensive 'experiments' were associated with undisciplined and irresponsible teaching, aimed at subverting the prevailing orthodoxies of society. Various episodes in 1976 furnished magnificent ammunition to those who had been arguing, and especially since the publication of the first 'Black Paper' in 1969, that the values of British education had been systematically subverted. 'Back to basics' became the battle-cry of the later 1970s, as 'expansion' had been the slogan inspiring the missionaries of the 1960s.

The Black Papers soon came to be identified with the opinions and style of Dr Rhodes Boyson: an MP who had been a headmaster, with robust populist opinions, a commitment to the ethics of work and competition, and a contempt for left-wing sociologists. But he became a Black Paper editor only in 1975, when the fourth in the series appeared; a fifth (and last) was to follow in 1976. The name most closely associated with the polemical publications from the outset was that of Professor Brian Cox, Professor of English at Manchester—one of the most troubled and politicized of the inner-city areas. He had been a pupil of F. R. Leavis at Cambridge, and in 1958 founded the *Critical Quarterly*. His traditionalist views, on the role of the teacher or on academic rigour classically defined, were reinforced when he spent some time in 1964 at the University of California at Berkeley. The radical, anti-war, civil-rights movement of the 1960s distressed him, as did the doctrine that students had an important part to play in determining the curriculum and objectives of a university. After returning to Britain, his worst fears were confirmed by the debilitating experiences of his own children at a progressive, and apparently purposeless, primary school; the doctrines shortly to be canonized by Plowden, and exaggerations of them, were in the ascendant, and ill-prepared teachers were pouring into the schools. He determined to issue the (first) Black Paper as a special supplement to the *Critical Quarterly* and widened its target from student militancy (his first preoccupation) to include schools. Four years after 10/65, and three years after the publication of the Plowden Report, there were plenty of dissident voices and pens to recruit.

The Black Papers owed part of their success to the inevitable disenchantment of the late sixties, to the student troubles, to anxieties generated by recent expansion and school reorganization, and (doubtless) to the literary skills of writers as gifted as Kingsley Amis and Iris Murdoch. They appealed not only to rigid traditionalists, but also to many moderates who—like the authors just cited—had voted steadily on the Left, but were now worried by some of the unforeseen consequences of reform. But it was the Labour government's own Secretary of State at the Department of Education and Science, Edward Short, who at the 1969 conference of the National Union of Teachers guaranteed publicity and a modest immortality for the first Paper. He dignified its publication as 'one of the blackest days for education in the last one hundred years'. Nevertheless, within seven years, a Labour Prime Minister was, by implication at least, to endorse some of the criticisms which Mr Short, a former headmaster, had so peremptorily brushed aside.

Why did this happen? Underlying the political, and perhaps opportunist, decision of 1976 was a heavy groundswell of public discontent, sustained by some creditable research and a good deal of professional anxiety. The refusal of so many members of the educational establishment to admit that anything was, or ever could be, wrong made matters a great deal worse. Work by Start and Wells, published in 1972 when Mrs Thatcher was Secretary of State, suggested that the improvement of reading standards demonstrable until about 1964 appeared not to have been sustained since. She appointed Sir Alan Bullock, now Lord Bullock and at that time the Master of St Catherine's College, Oxford, to chair an inquiry into standards of literacy. Their report, *A Language for Life*, was published in 1975. It has had a profound effect upon teachers in schools, and generated a new awareness of the importance of language, but some of its conclusions in the matter of standards and their maintenance appear contradictory. One member of the committee refused to accept the cautiously optimistic conclusion of the majority. The Bullock Report did, however, recommend that standards of performance should be monitored in order to provide regular and reputable information, upon which proper judgement could in future be based. As a consequence, the Assessment of Performance Unit was created by the Department of Education and Science, and began to produce its first results in the later 1970s. Controversy surrounded its origins: many feared that it would be a mechanistic device to measure and control standards, and would restrain imaginative developments in teaching and in the curriculum. Analogies with some contemporary developments in the United States, where a 'Back to Basics' movement was also gaining ground, were uncomfortably close. In the event, the Assessment of Performance Unit decided to concentrate on light sampling and on addressing questions of national, rather than local or individual standards. It will concentrate on broad 'areas of experience'—language, mathematics, science, physical/ethical/aesthetic development—rather than on subjects as conventionally defined. The difficulties which have so far arisen have been technical, rather than philosophical or political, and relate to problems of item-banking (of comparability, that is) and of statistical techniques. Nevertheless, the work of the Assessment of Performance Unit is part of a changing pattern of government intervention and of public concern with what is taught.

Carefully sifted and objective evidence was, and is, hard to come by. In 1975 Rhodes Boyson published *Crisis in Education*, declamatory in style, packed with anecdote and assertion and peppered with terms like breakdown, illiteracy, violence, disorder, collapse, decline, retreat, fashion, millenarian, over-expansion —all contrasted with a plan for revival. Statements like 'adolescent violence has increased twenty fold in ten years' persuaded only those who were already convinced. More convincing was the publication in 1976 of the latest results of the National Child Development Study, an analysis of the progress and attitudes of 16,000 boys and girls born in 1958. They had been among the first to be required to spend an extra year at secondary school. Of them 11 per cent had found schooling 'a waste of time', 15 per cent claimed that they never took work seriously, 29 per cent did not like school, and for 54 per cent homework was a bore. Unfortunately, a constructive and agreed approach to real problems was inhibited by the media, and by the posturing of politicians of both main parties. Only now, in 1984, is some of the damage being repaired.

Effective discussion was also obstructed by the defensiveness of much of the teaching profession, and the aggressiveness of a small part of it. Gentility was sacrificed, and had been in the 1960s, in the increasingly abrasive salary negotiations, the growth of unionism in all parts of public life, and the tensions among the various unions representing teachers. The Houghton Report on teachers' salaries, in 1975, was a determined attempt by Government to place salaries upon an equitable basis. The public response to the award was to expect a better performance from teachers, and a greater measure of accountability. 'Accountability' had been fashionable in the United States for a number of years, and became so in Britain after 1975. It was one form of an effort to break through professional secrecy and security, to insist upon value for money, to require some measure of power-sharing in the conduct of the publicly owned schools.

Such demands were resisted by the teachers' unions, and suspicions were fed. Even more damage to public perceptions of schooling was caused by the statements and actions of various radicalizing groups among the teachers, and notably in 'Rank and File', a group of mostly young teachers within the National Union of Teachers, which was conspicuous in the early 1970s, but fragmented into smaller factions after 1976. Its membership was never more than 1,000, but that small and vocal number could be relied upon to attract attention, all of it unfavourable. Hostile to contemporary society and critical of the attempts of a servile system of schooling to mould pupils after its will, they gave the impression that standards were not only falling, but that they should be deliberately forced down even further.

Even more of a gift to disaster-hungry media was the deeply disturbing case of the William Tyndale school, which generated news and anxiety in 1975 and 1976. William Tyndale was a primary school in Islington and therefore lying within the empire of the Inner London Education Authority. Its head and his colleagues believed in what they themselves called a 'democratic, egalitarian and non-sexist philosophy'. They systematically opposed competition, orthodox discipline, any version of a formal curriculum, any suggestion that the school should be used to encourage conventional success in its pupils. Parents protested and withdrew their children until the ILEA was obliged to intervene formally. Seven of the teachers refused to co-operate in any way with the Inspectors, and went on strike. An inquiry of a semi-judicial character and conducted by a barrister, was established, and its report—after seven months, including sixty-three days of taking evidence—was scathing in its criticisms. Those criticisms were directed not only at the teachers (who were finally dismissed) but also at the failure of the ILEA to act promptly and decisively. Underlying that failure was a conventional belief, now shown to be obsolete, that schools should be allowed to manage their own affairs, that a Local Education Authority should provide not direct management but resources and support with (less frequently) polite criticism, that central government could take for granted an unwritten consensus about the nature of the curriculum and the purposes of schooling.

Questions of control and of the curriculum now intersected. In July 1976 the Permanent Secretary at the Department of Education, not a home-grown mandarin but an engineer imported from the Cabinet Office, claimed that 'The key to the secret garden of the curriculum has to be found and turned.' The criticisms of the OECD, and of the House of Commons Expenditure Committee in 1976, made it increasingly difficult for the Department of Education and Science—even if it wished to—to hold a restricted view of its responsibilities within a 'partnership'. Intervention was in the air, and in the early autumn (with John Maud, Jerome Bruner, and others) I was involved in a conference in Oxford with a group of HMIs who were promulgating the language of the core curriculum. They claimed that their renewed interest in these matters (which was to bear much fruit) bore no relationship to the growing rumours of imminent political intervention. I am sure that they believed precisely that.

Nevertheless, and in the next month, Jim Callaghan came to Oxford on 18 October to make his speech. The Tyndale affair had not been the largest problem of the year. In January, the Government made its second approach for support to the International Monetary Fund: a third was to follow in September. The pound continued to slide, and after gales and floods in January, a long period of drought dominated a leaden summer. People stood in queues at stand-pipes for water, the Oxford Canal was closed, and *Scholar Gypsy* had difficulty in navigating. The Conservatives made considerable gains in the local elections in May, and in October outlined their new policies in *The Right Approach*: they were no longer interested in the crumbling centre ground where Butler and Boyle had stood firm. Meanwhile, in March, Harold Wilson announced his retirement (at the age of sixty, and to a symphony of unfounded speculations), and on 5 April Callaghan was elected leader, and succeeded him as Prime Minister. Tony Crosland, Secretary of State for the Environment since the general election of 1974, took Callaghan's place as Foreign Secretary. Less than a year later, he suffered a stroke in the Oxfordshire village where, advised by the Crossmans, he had recently bought a house, and died in Oxford on 19 February 1977: he was fifty-six.

James Callaghan was born in 1912, and educated at elementary and secondary schools in Portsmouth: he was the only post-war Prime Minister not to be a university graduate, and prided himself (at least in public) on holding to a plain man's view of what schools should do. Starting his career as a tax officer in the civil service, he became a Cardiff MP in 1945, when I was taking the Higher School Certificate in that city, and has remained one ever since. He was a junior minister in Attlee's government and, after the thirteen years of Conservative rule so often lamented by Wilson, became Chancellor of the Exchequer in 1964, changing places with Roy Jenkins (who had been at the Home Office) after the devaluation crisis of 1967. Callaghan had been Foreign Secretary from the first general election of 1974 until becoming Prime Minister in April 1976.

Soon after becoming Prime Minister he asked the Department of Education and Science for a briefing, and the so-called 'Yellow Book' produced in response found its way into the columns of the *Guardian* and the *Times Educational Supplement* in September. It was not alarmist, but neither did it make comfortable reading. Progressive methods in primary schools could be a trap for the inexperienced teacher, which hardly came as a surprise. The secondary curriculum was unbalanced, and allowed too many exclusive choices to be made too early. It was not sufficiently relevant to the needs of the modern world and, in particular, pupils were not prepared adequately for their role in the economy. A 'core curriculum' had much to commend it, and in its develop-ment a leading role should be assigned to the Department of Education and Science and Her Majesty's Inspectorate. Teacher unions had dominated the Schools Council, the performance of which was brutally described as 'mediocre'.

Ruskin College, associated with but not a part of Oxford University, is a centre specializing in trade-union and industrial studies, and that is where the Prime Minister chose to make his statement. The students, wishing to register miscellaneous protests, tried to sing 'The Red Flag', but faltered, and the Prime Minister rightly claimed to know the words better than they. He spoke cautiously, and mostly in commonplaces, for twenty minutes. His intention was to launch a Great Debate, managed through a series of nine regional conferences, and engaging in discussion parents, employers, trade unions, as well as Local Education Authorities and teachers. The main stress of the speech lay on the relationship of education with industry and employment, but the Debate would also revolve around such principal themes as the curriculum and teaching methods, standards and assessment, and the training of teachers. Shirley Williams had, in September, been appointed

Secretary of State and was responsible for drawing together the conclusions of the Debate in a consultative document, called *Education in Schools* and presented to Parliament in July 1977.

Soured commentators observed that, in the Ruskin speech and all the diffuse talk that followed it, nothing new (or even very interesting) had been said. The Prime Minister had acted in order to catch votes, to outflank the criticisms of the Conservative party, to direct attention away from economic catastrophe, and, at the same time, to pin some unspecified responsibility for that catastrophe upon the defenceless schools. The discussions did, at least, serve as a rough form of stock-taking on educational achievements and anxieties. *Education in Schools* accorded a refreshing priority to the importance of improving and supporting teachers, rather than simply exhorting them to be somehow better. The doctrine that an overcrowded curriculum and an embarrassing number of choices were pushing out the essentials now received official approval. Variation from school to school had, it was asserted, reached unacceptable levels—generating inequality between one school and another, and making movement from one part of the country to another unnecessarily difficult for the pupil. Above all, it seems, schools were out of sympathy and out of tune with modern industrial society, and failing to impart the necessary skills to all school-leavers. A core curriculum should be pursued, and a framework established. To that end, all Local Education Authorities would be asked for information and comment, on the basis of which the Department of Education and Science would issue further guidance. This it did, in 1980, under the title of *A Framework for the Curriculum*. Her Majesty's Inspectorate at the same time published *A View of the Curriculum*—a title that was, presumably, meant to be less prescriptive and mechanical.

There is, indeed, a marked difference of emphasis in the two documents. The HMI contribution belongs to the tradition represented by their own discussion booklet *Curriculum 11–16*. That text seeks only to identify the necessary 'areas of experience' to which every pupil should have access—the aesthetic and creative, the ethical, the linguistic, the mathematical, the physical, the scientific, the social and political, and the spiritual. But the difference of emphasis is less important for secondary schools in the 1980s than the underlying assumptions about the necessity of a larger measure of central influence, a greater overall uniformity, a sustained effort to improve quality and a better matching of the work of schools to the needs of society and, in particular, the economy. These assumptions, and the policies seeking to make them effective, were not significantly modified by the political changes of 1979. Their persistence across a change of Government underlines the continuities of the past decade, and points to the importance of the Ruskin speech as marking a significant—perhaps even permanent—change in attitudes. The age of limitation and contraction had begun.

That speech, and the agenda for the debate, omitted two themes of importance. Unsurprisingly, questions about the control of the school and the role in that of parents and the community were left on one side: these matters were being considered at the same time by the Taylor Committee specially constituted for the purpose and due to report in 1977. More surprisingly, little reference was initially made to the growing concerns about schooling in a multicultural society, or to the acute problems of inner-city decay. But in August 1977 there were serious clashes at a National Front demonstration at Lewisham and, before the end of the month, violence and riots at the Notting Hill Carnival.

The omission from the original agenda of the Great Debate of education for the ethnic minorities was surprising in more ways than one: without the support of the immigrants from the New Commonwealth, the Labour party would not have won the general election of 1974 in the first place. By the end of the 1970s the new minorities formed some 5 per cent of the whole population, and 7 per cent of the child population. Their presence offered a novel, and still in the 1980s an unresolved, challenge to the orthodox conventions of the 1944 settlement. Nor can it be plausibly argued that their absence from many parts of the country means that most secondary schools simply need not bother about them. Prejudice and ignorance, or simply insensitivity, need to be overcome in all-white areas if tension in schools and society is to be adequately managed. Nevertheless, it is in the areas of concentration that the problems are most urgent. In inner-city areas (like Bradford, Birmingham, Leicester, Wolverhampton, and parts of London), immigrants and their descendants constitute 20 per cent of the total annual entry to schools. The availability of cheap, and inadequate, housing links cultural problems (of teaching, and of the curriculum) to those of disadvantage and of urban decay. Of West Indians, who are particularly at risk, 18 per cent suffer from 'multiple deprivation': the comparable figure for the indigenous population is 6 per cent.

The ILEA policy of 'banding' was designed to manipulate admissions to secondary schools in order to avoid a dangerous concentration of difficulties in any one school. It involves selection for purposes exactly opposed to those underlying the eleven-plus selection arrangements of the 1950s. Nevertheless, the 1976 Education Act allowed the practice to continue only in a grudging spirit and for a transitional period. The general strategy of the banding policy is to direct into each school, in so far as this is practicable, 25 per cent of eleven-year-olds from Band I, 50 per cent from Band II, and 25 per cent from Band III. On tests of verbal reasoning only 12 per cent of ethnic-minority children qualified for Band I, only 13 per cent on English tests, and only 14 per cent on mathematics. The Asian children did a great deal better than this, for reasons which remain speculative but are closely linked to factors of language and cultural style, and it is the West Indian pupils who stand most in need of help. After early attempts to apply rules limiting the number of immigrants in any one school, there has been little sign of any coherent national policy. Professor Alan Little has observed that the responses of successive Governments have been to limit immigration, and to introduce anti-discrimination legislation. He argues that special national policies are now needed if a downward spiral is to be avoided, and that immigrant school-leavers are even more at risk during a period of rising, and perhaps ineradicable, unemployment for teenagers.

Although this range of problems was indeed omitted from the agenda of the Great Debate, it found a place in the consultative document of 1977: *Education in Schools* promised to set up a committee, and this took shape as the Rampton Committee (now the Swann Committee), which hopes to complete its work in 1984. In 1977 the House of Commons (through the Education, Arts, and Home Office Sub-Committee of the Expenditure Committee) picked up the popular themes and turned its attention to the attainments of the school-leaver. By a curious coincidence, the Sub-Committee met to decide on a subject for the next phase of its work on the very day that Mr Callaghan gave his twenty-minute speech. It called many witnesses, and in May I travelled to London to argue before it that secondary schools would become more effective if they were given a better and more precise sense of what society—through employers, parents, and Government—was now requiring of them, and that heads of schools (given the desirable scope of their authority and autonomy) should not be irremovable from office, and should have fixed-term appointments. Fortunately, I had already been saying that while still the head of a secondary school. The Report of the Sub-Committee served a useful purpose by removing some of the rhetoric and nonsense from the contemporary debate. It helped to consolidate the constructive notion that standards may not have fallen in secondary schools, but that the requirements laid upon their pupils had risen and that the task was, therefore, to accelerate a matching rise in achievement.

Government leaders were, in 1977, in trouble with their own Labour party and responded at the October Conference with a crisp appeal to 'back us or sack us'. It did not do much good. The prolonged Grunwick affair, involving workers in a small North London factory who did not wish to accept a 'closed shop', further tarnished the image of the trade-union movement. In November the firemen went on strike, and sat picketing by blazing fires outside the fire stations as passing motorists (or some of them) sounded their horns in support. The Liberals had made a pact with the Government—not an alliance, but an agreement that Labour legislative proposals would not be introduced in the Commons without Liberal consent. In May, the Liberal leader (David Steel) announced that the pact would end with that session of Parliament. The Government had, if it was lucky, an overall majority of one. *The Times* was in deep trouble with the printing unions, largely as a result of its attempts to introduce new technology. Management decided, in an attempt to restore sanity, to stop publication altogether, and the last edition appeared on 30 November 1978. The supplements, including the *Times Educational Supplement*, were suspended as well. For twelve months there would be no educational news, and not everybody thought that a bad thing.

CHAPTER 12

Contraction

For the first half of 1979 I was on sabbatical leave from my appointment in Educational Studies in Oxford, and accepted an invitation from the Ford Foundation to spend part of that time in the United States. There was to be a general election in Britain on 3 May, and I cast a postal vote. Margaret Thatcher became Prime Minister, and many Americans noted this change with approval. The creeping softness of British society was now to be decisively attacked.

My commission in the States, the results of which appeared in a short book in 1982, was to study the graduate schools of education at a small number of research universities. These graduate schools, relatively unconcerned with teacher training and heavily committed to the education of researchers and administrators, had separated themselves from the problems of teachers in elementary and secondary schools: they had pursued ethereality at the expense of practicality and influence. The reasons for that retreat lay near the surface of the problem. Schools, and especially secondary schools in the inner cities, had been battered in the accelerating social changes of the years after 1960. Teachers, subject to administrative, political, and parental control, had never achieved even a modest degree of professional autonomy. Their work was undervalued and, in a competitive world hungry for talent and ready to pay for it, underpaid. Their initial training was sketchy and inadequate, dispersed over a large number of institutions and entangled in undergraduate courses. The 'back to basics' movement, associated with demands for competence and accountability, generated a continuing crisis of confidence in American schooling. There were many analogies with British attitudes in the late 1970s.

The graduate schools of education, or rather that small number of them leading the field in universities like Stanford or Harvard, were themselves locked in a competitive struggle—with one another, to be top of the national league, and within their own universities for reputation and resources. These could be secured not by a commitment to the messy yet important cause of public schooling, but by earning a name for scholarship. This, in turn, would be won—the American academic market being what it is —by publications esteemed by sociologists, psychologists, and economists (for example) working within securely established disciplines. The problems of relating the values and habits of a prestigious university to the needs of systems of common schools in a complex society were presented in stark form.

It was, I believe, my own experience in British secondary schools and my continuing preoccupations at Oxford that prompted the invitation to examine these particular problems. Certainly my work in Oxford since 1973 had been dominated by a concern with the relationship of that university and its Department of Educational Studies to the world of secondary schools. That concern survives, and the work which derives from it is far from achievement. The Department in Oxford had existed for nearly a century, and for much of that time in the dubious shadows inhabited by most English Schools or Departments of Education: the James Committee had recently confirmed that prevailing impression. Academics generally, for obvious and often for good reasons, are not respectful of the work of such places. Engaged themselves in the business of education (but not of Education), they are scornful of those who make a profession or a mystery of it and suspicious of attempts to manufacture a new subject. Many of them show a general if sometimes naïve prejucide that the training of teachers, a respectable and necessary task, should be given a sharper and more professional edge: an opinion shared by many of the public, and by most practising teachers themselves.

Most of the effort of the Department, in 1973, was directed at the initial training of teachers: the provision, that is, of the Post-graduate Certificate of Education already described in Chapter 9. This had been designed mainly for those who were going on to teach in grammar or Public Schools, and a first requirement was to bring it more into line with a changing pattern of secondary schooling. This in turn required a close partnership with the comprehensive schools of Oxfordshire, and with the Local Education Authority. In time, it led to the development in those schools of the role of the professional tutor, and (by the early 1980s) to a number of joint appointments involving schools and the Department. The emphasis within the Department shifted from social science towards teaching and the curriculum. The model was, and is, that of the teaching hospital, rather than of the American graduate school.

Equally important has been the parallel shift of emphasis from initial training to post-experience work with teachers—the central theme of the James Report. The anticipated decline in the demand for teachers offered an opportunity to reduce by over one hundred the number of students taking a PGCE (and so to improve the quality), and to introduce over sixty teachers each year on full-time courses leading to the degree of M.Sc. or to a special diploma. Most of these are seconded teachers, working on problems of central interest to the schools. Their presence, coupled with a change in the style of the PGCE, brings the Department into a close—some would argue, too close—association with schools as they are, and with their ambitions for change.

Oxford, then, has been my window on changing secondary schools for most of the 1970s and into the 1980s, as Banbury was in the 1960s. The concern of the university with research has taken a particular shape, owing much to the particular local circumstances in 1973. By a fortunate coincidence, the early 1970s had brought together in Oxford a group of people deeply concerned with the needs of public education and distributed at strategic points around the university. John Maud was on record (in evidence to the Franks Commission of 1964) as arguing that 'the present situation, in which the study of education is segregated from the main stream of academic activity in the university, is unsatisfactory and ought to be changed . . . There is an opportunity here for Oxford to take an initiative and provide something which this country has not yet got, and very much needs: a centre for research and study in education, in which scholars from a variety of fields combine in a joint examination of the problems and in setting academic standards comparable to those in the primary disciplines.'

Associated with John Maud in that plea was Alan Bullock, first chairman of the Schools Council, chairman of the committee recently appointed by Mrs Thatcher to inquire into the teaching of English in schools, and at the time of my arrival in Oxford, Vice-Chancellor. Geoffrey Caston, Registrar of the University, had been Joint Secretary of the Schools Council. Jerome Bruner was the Watts Professor of Psychology, and A. H. Halsey Director of the Department of Social and Administrative Studies. They came together to form the Oxford Educational Research Group (OERG), my task being to engage this enterprise closely through the Department with the work of schools. The Oxford Educational Research Group has undertaken research in the provision of education for the under-fives (in the wake of Mrs Thatcher's *Framework for Expansion*), mixed-ability teaching, the teaching of foreign languages, mathematics, the impact of science and technology upon the curriculum, the identification and support of more-able pupils, and provision for pupils with special educational needs. These are concerns which will reappear in the discussion in the rest of this chapter of the themes of secondary schooling which weave their way across the years 1979 to 1984. I have identified these themes as *control, choice, contraction, diversity, utility,* and *quality,* trying to help the reader by italicizing the keywords at critical points of transition in the discussion. But, I should like to emphasize, the themes are all interconnected and not neatly separable into distinct sections.

The year 1979 began with Arctic weather, and on the second day of the year the lorry drivers went on strike. Later in the month, an eight-week period of disruption in schools and hospitals brought painfully home the financial difficulties of the social services. At the end of March, the Labour government lost by one vote a vote of confidence in the House of Commons, and Mr Callaghan announced the dissolution of Parliament. The general election took place on 3 May, when I was in New York. The

Conservatives secured a comfortable majority of forty-three, Mrs Thatcher became the country's first woman Prime Minister, and Mark Carlisle replaced Shirley Williams at Education and Science. Janet Young, the former Oxford city councillor who had championed middle schools in the city and been made a life peeress in 1971, supported him as Minister of State, with a special responsibility for schools. The 1976 Act, which imposed upon local authorities the legal obligation to submit plans for comprehensive reorganization, was promptly repealed. This was no less than the Conservatives had promised—grammar schools might be kept if the local electors wanted them and, in any case, it was not the business of a Government elected 'to roll back the frontiers of the State' to impose the preferences of Westminister and Whitehall upon every county and metropolitan district. The councillors of Tameside had been correct.

Nevertheless, questions of *control*—the issues discussed in Chapter 10 under the looser heading of 'Influence'—did continue to obsess central government, and the continuities of policy across the general election of 1979 proved remarkably strong. Whereas Government might indeed be prepared to leave to its local-government 'partners' details of secondary-school organization, it was compelled to carry forward the concerns of its Labour predecessor in the management of local-government expenditure. The key doctrine of the Rate Support Grant, of leaving to the elected councils the right to determine priorities within spending and (to some extent) its total level, had worn threadbare by 1979. In that year, Education accounted for 13 per cent of all public expenditure, coming second only to social-security payments of all kinds (25 per cent) and forging ahead of Health and Social Services at 12 per cent, Defence at 10 per cent, Housing at 7 per cent, and all the rest at 33 per cent. Under the new, and unhelpfully misnamed, Block Grant—introduced by the Local Government Planning and Land (No. 2) Act of 1980—the Government itself assesses how much each local authority 'should' spend on its various services, how much that authority might properly expect to raise through the rates, and pays a grant to make up the difference. It therefore becomes in principle more difficult, in terms of political argument, for a local authority to rearrange national priorities: the basis for the calculation of the grant is now more open and explicit. In fact, the new arrangements are at least as complex as those they were meant to simplify, and many of the detailed calculations remain obscure. Nevertheless, central government—in the interests of managing the economy—has taken to itself the right of more detailed prescription. Moreover, any local authority which ignores the guide-lines and chooses to levy higher rates to pay for services (such as education) will be harshly penalized, and its grant will be progressively cut.

The Government has moved in other ways to extend its influence in the key sector of spending on education. In 1982, it made directly available to Local Education Authorities some £5m. in the form of in-service training-grants. This was the kind of money which, after being won in ministerial discussions, had previously been lost in the hidden and rumbling pipes in the plumbing of the Rate Support Grant. The Secretary of State therefore now exercises the right, important in terms of the leverage on the system, to determine which parts of the educational enterprise shall receive some special attention and finance. In 1982 he chose training for headship, the teaching of mathematics, special needs, and pre-vocational education. In 1983 the Department of Education and Science, stressing that nothing in the existing habits of 'partnership' would be affected, formally announced the introduction of Education Support Grants. The principle is, again and however modest the initial scale of the operation, an important one. A small part of the education budget is now to be withheld from the Block Grant, to remain at the disposal of the Department of Education and Science itself in order to help Local Education Authorities to respond quickly to new developments at national level, to promote improvements in schools, to encourage them to release and redeploy some of their existing resources.

Nor will the Government leave unquestioned the structural changes in local government completed as recently as 1974. It is no secret that it does not like the Greater London Council and Inner London Education Authority, increasingly dominated by a radical leadership and glaring from its fortress across the Thames at the Houses of Parliament. The Inner London Education Authority, even given the special problems of the capital, has long enjoyed a reputation for generous spending. Until 1980, it received all its income from precepts upon the Inner London boroughs— themselves heavily supported through the Rate Support Grant. Under the 1980 Act, the grant will be payed directly to the ILEA, with predictable consequences.

But attitudes are as important as money in these matters. The ILEA decided, under the very shadow of the invasion of the Falklands, to withold (albeit temporarily and pending an inquiry) its usual grants to the Scouts—suspecting the movement of en- couraging militarist, sexist, and racist tendencies. Such actions did not pass unremarked. A similar, if less powerful, blend of economic and ideological interests permeates the Conservatives' dislike of the metropolitan counties. In 1983 the Government proposed that they, too, should be disbanded. It was, of course, the Conservatives who had rejected the proposals of an earlier Labour government that these counties, like the safer shires, should also be education authorities.

The perceived necessity of more *control* from the centre (which will reappear in discussions about the curriculum and examin- ations) sits uncomfortably with a deeply held commitment to a widening of *choice* (in education, as elsewhere), which in turn jars with the necessities of managing a system in *contraction*. Under- lying the emphasis upon choice, and running across any simple political divisions, is a steadily growing public disenchantment with decisions made unilaterally or covertly by bureaucrats and professionals, such as teachers. Objections to a monopoly of this kind have been mounted as much from the Left as from the Right. The power of teachers in the deliberations of the Schools Council, the monarchical authority of heads in matters of curriculum and discipline, the empty formalities of many school governing bodies —these were among the targets for reformers. The Taylor Com- mittee reported in 1977 in favour of strengthening the authority of governing bodies (at the expense of teachers, professionals, and politicians) and of changing their composition: equal membership for parents, teachers, Local Education Authority representatives, and the community at large (not always clearly defined, but to include employers). The changes sponsored by the Labour government of the day were much more modest, and for good reason.

That reason lies in the tension between *control* and *choice* at a time of *contraction*, and is well illustrated in the 1980 Education Act. That Act requires the publication of information about schools—their policies, their curriculum, their examination results. Within certain necessary constraints, parents are now allowed to choose a school, which need not even be within the boundaries of their own Local Education Authority. If they are not satisfied with the decision, then there is a right of appeal to formally constituted panels. The problems are obvious, and especially if too many pupils choose one particular school. That difficulty is manageable, not without awkwardness, when all or most schools are under heavy pressure. Parents will accept that if a school is already full then some pupils—possibly those from a greater distance—will have to go elsewhere.

But, whatever may be true of particular schools, the 'system' as a whole is no longer full, and even more space will become available within it. The Act therefore requires Local Education Authorities to state the maximum capacity of each school, and then fix a Planned Admission Limit, which may be up to 20 per cent below this maximum. As numbers in secondary schools fall, and as some schools continue to be more popular than others, it will be increasingly difficult to persuade parents that places are not available, when desks and rooms are empty. And yet, if some schools are filled to capacity, others will be perilously small, expensive, and inefficient. 'Consumerism' will widen the gap between good schools and bad schools, and make it more difficult for Local Education Authorities to plan rationally for the contraction of the system.

Such a contraction is inevitable, and the only question is whether it will be handled well or ill. For the first time—and whatever happens to the economy and whatever political decisions on investment in education are taken—some decline is inevitable. In 1900 there were 5.7m. pupils in elementary and secondary schools, and by 1950 (largely because of declining birth-rates, and in spite of the raising to fifteen of the school-leaving age) the corresponding figure was still only 5.8m. By 1977, it was 9.0m., but by 1990 it will be only 7.0m. The number of pupils in secondary schools will fall from 3.6m. in 1979 to 2.5m. in 1990. Shrinkage of this order places the school system under severe financial strain. Given the uneven and haphazard incidence of this contraction it is not possible to reduce the number of teachers or the number of buildings in step with the overall decline in numbers, but the argument that the costs of education must go down when the number of pupils declines cannot be resisted. The curriculum will be under pressure, and attempts to maintain or increase diversity at risk. Fewer new teachers will be needed, and those already in post will have to be rescued from the dangers of staleness. New arrangements will have to be devised for linking, or even federating, schools. Yet all these necessary tasks will be complicated, as they might well have been under any administration, by paying greater attention to the preferences and wishes of parents. The Government had included in the Bill, which as amended became the 1980 Act, other provisions which ran into difficulty with some of its own supporters. The overriding need for economy and the wish to reduce the weight of central-government requirements had prompted it to try to remove the obligation upon Local Education Authorities to provide free transport for children having to travel more than three miles to school. This was a blow to rural constituencies and to denominational schools, especially Roman Catholic ones. The forces of tradition grumbled and gathered in the House of Lords. The Duke of Norfolk observed that the 'villagers of England' had written to him. Lords Boyle, Alexander, and Redcliffe-Maud all voted against the Government. Lord Butler, now Master of Trinity College, Cambridge, protested that the transport agreement had been vital to the settlement of 1944 and recalled that the Conservative party had always been strongest when it supported the rural areas. The Government gave way.

The wishes and opinions of parents will also, and backed for the first time with the authority of law, become a major determinant in the provision to be made for children with special educational needs. The Warnock Report of 1978 and the Education Act of 1981, which was largely based upon the Report's recommendations, illustrate the strength of the continuities across the political divide of 1979. The Committee, under the chairmanship of Mrs Mary Warnock, was constituted by Mrs Thatcher when she was Secretary of State in 1973, with a brief covering the education of handicapped children and young people. The 1944 Act had referred to 'disability of mind or body', and the practice which was developed after that Act reflected a 'medical' view of educational handicap. Eleven categories of such handicap were defined, reduced to ten in 1953, the concept of causation was a relatively uncomplicated one, and much of the diagnosis and prescription was therefore in the hands of medical experts. The prevailing assumption was that education for such pupils could best be provided in special schools, designed and staffed to deal with them in relative isolation from the rest of the system of primary and secondary schools. The growing engagement of sociology and psychology in the framing of educational policy—illustrated, as has already been explained, in questions of selection and secondary-school organization—generated a more sophisticated and complex understanding of the nature of educational handicap. This change was reflected in the requirement, after 1975, that the assessment of such pupils should incorporate an educational and psychological element, as well as a medical. The notion that 'special education' was uniquely 'special'—different and separate —slowly dissolved.

In its place, the 1981 Act places the working concept of 'special educational needs'. The Act therefore embraces any kind of learning difficulty, provided that it is significantly greater than that of the majority of children of the same age. Included within this broad category, at some stage of their school careers and for a longer or shorter period, will be some 20 per cent of all children. For a smaller proportion, of the order of 2 per cent, precise and formal action will be required. The Local Education Authority will have the responsibility of preparing a Statement, analysing the needs of the pupil and indicating the methods—which may include assignment to a special school—by which those needs will be met. Parents will, by law, be involved in discussions about that Statement, and now have rights of appeal and redress if a Local Education Authority fails to make a Statement, or to involve parents in its preparation, or to deliver the services specified as necessary. Such procedures, taken with those of the 1980 Act, represent an important new emphasis. They register a decline in the authority of the autonomous professional, and a strengthening of the principles of consumerism. Their influence cannot be confined to the area of special educational needs, themselves now broadly defined.

This legislation is important, too, within another context. Underlying it is a belief that, wherever this is practicable, pupils with special needs should be integrated within the general system of schooling. It follows that ordinary schools will need to develop new skills, and in many cases new attitudes, if this general principle is to become a reality. Secondary schools are being required, in this and in other ways, to develop a greater measure of *diversity*, and to do so at a time of *contraction* while paying greater regard to principles of *choice*. The Conservative government elected in 1979 chose to pursue a different, and at some levels conflicting, policy with regard to the education of the more able—or some of them. Its policy of an Assisted Places scheme reflects a Government belief that the independent schools are likely to achieve higher academic standards than most maintained secondary schools, that such schools deserve a modest measure of public support, and that the abolition of direct grants by its Labour predecessor had weakened the national system of education. The Assisted Places scheme, included within the 1980 Education Act, remains controversial and its outcome uncertain. It is very different from, and simpler than, the old direct-grant scheme. It enables the parents of an able pupil to apply to an independent school approved for this purpose. The successful pupil pays tuition fees, but on a means-tested basis: the scheme is designed to assist pupils, whose parents could not otherwise afford it, to win a competitive place. No Government assistance is available for boarding costs, and the Local Education Authority is involved neither in the selection nor in the financing of pupils. Some Local

Education Authorities see the scheme as a further example of the growth of the influence of central government upon educational provision. Some of the spokesmen for the independent schools have for other reasons been uneasy about the limitation of the scheme to pupils with high academic ability, arguing that it should be extended to cover those categories of boarding need described in the Report of John Newsom's Public Schools Commission. Nevertheless, 230 independent schools were in 1983 part of a scheme which supported some 14,000 pupils at an annual cost of £10m. Some comprehensive schools have recently become more aware of the special needs of more-able pupils, knowing that if their potentialities are not realized then influential public opinion will become critical. Across the years 1979 to 1984 the Department of Education and Science has, through its research funds, supported an inquiry by the Oxford Educational Research Group into the identification of and provision for more-able pupils in comprehensive schools. The inquiry suggests that, to an extent not previously appreciated, high ability may be subject-specific (for example, in physics or in English) and that present methods of identification can be significantly improved.

If some contemporary pressures thrust secondary schools towards greater diversity—in special needs, in provision for the more able, in (as will appear) placing more stress for some pupils upon vocational courses—other countervailing pressures point towards a greater measure of uniformity. Variety and diversity were given a bad name by the Great Debate and all that surrounded it—in my view, unjustifiably so. One interim product of that Debate was the Department of Education and Science paper, published in January 1980 when Mark Carlisle was still Secretary of State. That outlined a core curriculum for all, to include English, mathematics, science, a foreign language, religious education, and physical education. English and mathematics should be taken by all pupils to the age of sixteen, and each should take about 10 per cent of the available time. Science, to take between a further 10 and 20 per cent of that time, should be provided for all—with a stress upon its applications. Most pupils should attempt a foreign language, to be available to all for a minimum of two years in the secondary school. Religious education should be linked with 'wider considerations of personal and social needs'. Preparation for adult and working life should be given a high priority, as should the special needs of the ethnic minorities, the handicapped, the gifted, and girls. The curriculum could not be static. At the end of the Great Debate the Department of Education and Science was still offering no more than an agenda, and the final document in the series (*The School Curriculum*, March 1981) advanced matters very little. All this, in terms of the life of secondary schools, was harmless enough—if somewhat dampening to the spirits. In September 1981, the Prime Minister reshuffled her Cabinet: Sir Keith Joseph moved into Education and Science, Norman Tebbit took over Employment. The mood and pace of educational policy were changed.

Mrs Thatcher had been showing a growing impatience with those who had come to be called the 'wets' within her own Government: the doubters who had protested at the pain of cuts in public expenditure, and resented the growing toughness of the policies. In the June Budget of 1979, public-expenditure cuts of £4,000m. had already been imposed and further cuts for the following year were announced in November. The minimum lending rate rose to a record 15 per cent. In May 1980 the TUC mobilized itself for a 'Day of Action', which made less impression on the public imagination than the eruption of the volcano at Mount St Helens a few days later. The strikes in Poland, and the recognition of Lech Walesa's Solidarity, reminded the West of some of the disagreeable realities of the socialist State. In November Ronald Reagan defeated Jimmy Carter in the Presidential election in the United States, and a few days later (on a second ballot) Michael Foot defeated Denis Healey in the contest to succeed Callaghan. By Christmas 1980, United Kingdom unemployment figures were up to 2,133,000.

In 1981, the map of British politics began to shift. In January, the Council for Social Democracy was founded by four disenchanted Labour MPs (including Dr David Owen and Mrs Shirley Williams, Callaghan's choice for Education), and early in March twelve MPs resigned the Labour whip. The Brixton race riots (although so to label them is to simplify their causes) flared on 11 April, and there were serious disturbances later in the summer in Liverpool and Manchester. There were predictable Labour gains in the local elections of May 1981, and three days later François Mitterand became the Socialist President of France. The policies he then initiated were derived from a fundamental contradiction of all the principles being applied across the Channel.

In April, unemployment in Britain passed the 2.5m. mark for the first time since the 1930s and trapped over 10 per cent of the work-force. A £500m. package of measures to reduce unemployment was announced on 27 July, and two days later the nation took a holiday to celebrate the marriage of the Prince of Wales. In September 1981, Margaret Thatcher reshuffled her Cabinet, in the interests of holding a strong line against internal criticism. On 28 September 1981, Edward Boyle, who had been a member of the House of Lords and a distinguished Vice-Chancellor of the University of Leeds since 1970, died at the age of fifty-eight. Both the expansionist Ministers of the 1960s, Boyle and Crosland, died before they were sixty. In November the Queen's speech gave warning of a Bill to curb local-government spending. On 26 November Shirley Williams won the first victory for the new Social Democratic Party at Crosby, on Merseyside. Just before Christmas martial law was imposed in Poland, and that particular experiment in moderated State socialism seemed to be at an end.

With a hard-headed Tebbit at Employment and Keith Joseph at Education, and against a background of growing unemployment throughout Europe, it was inevitable that interest shifted towards the unemployed school-leaver. The relationship of secondary education to the world of work had been a persistent theme for at least the previous five years, but the growing scale of the economic problem threw into even sharper relief the preoccupation with utility, with the capacity of education and training both to produce employable youngsters and to increase national wealth. The simplistic notion that education in itself, almost without regard to its content, would have these effects—a notion that underlay the expansionist reports of the 1960s—was by now finally discredited. Equally plain was a growing conviction, not confined to Whitehall, that the educational establishment could no longer be relied upon to direct a wise investment of the considerable resources committed to it. It was feared that more money for education and training, unless its purposes could be effectively specified, might produce no more than large and diluted sixth forms—just as Crosland, nearly twenty years before, had feared that, without a clear two-track policy in higher education, more investment would have financed too many traditional university courses.

This association of the theme of *utility* with those of *control* and *contraction* was, again, not simply a novelty of the years after 1979. The Manpower Services Commission—the creation of the Department of Employment and not of Education and Science—had been funded by the Labour government of 1974–9. Its influence and budget grew in step with unemployment. In September 1983, various smaller schemes were drawn into the grand strategy of the Youth Training Scheme. This, in spite of the hurry and worry surrounding its birth in 1983, is not a temporary device, but an enterprise to extend, at the earliest practicable date, to all those young people under the age of eighteen who are not in full-time education training of one kind or another. Priority in the first year of operation will be given to those just leaving school at about the age of sixteen, and the 452,000 places available during that year cost £1,000m.

Most of these places (some 300,000 in all, in the so-called Mode A) were provided by employers, and the balance more directly by the Manpower Services Commission itself, either through various community schemes and workshops or through the Colleges of Further Education. All trainees accepted under Mode A should receive three months' off-the-job education and training—in life and social skills, and not only in vocational expertise. The probability is that, at least with the employer who first takes them on, there will be paid work at the end of the year for only two out of every five. All will receive a payment of £25.00 per week, provided by the Government through the Scheme, although that sum may be supplemented in some cases.

The Youth Training Scheme has suffered from a multitude of critics, objecting that it is a device to keep down the wages of the young, to mask the brutal realities of unemployment, to delay for a year after leaving school the probability of being without work. But, with the refinements which will follow it, it has permanently changed the map of training provision and economic activity for the 16–19 age group, and introduced a new factor of unpredictable force into the discussions outlined in Chapter 8. It is a response of the greatest significance to the changes registered in the previous decade, and a late attempt—forced by urgent necessity —to repair Britain's lamentable record in providing adequate and flexible training for its young work-force. In January 1974, 36 per cent of sixteen-year-olds were in full-time education—26 per cent in secondary schools, and 10 per cent in further education. No less than 61 per cent had moved straight from school into employment, and only one in three of these received any part-time education or training; 3 per cent were unemployed. By 1982, 10 per cent of sixteen-year-olds were in Youth Opportunity Programmes (one of the predecessors of the Youth Training Scheme of 1983), and 14 per cent unemployed. The number in employment had shrunk from 61 to 28 per cent, and the number in full-time education enlarged from 36 to 48 per cent.

The Youth Training Scheme, and the deep changes underlying and justifying it, is modifying the philosophy and practice of 16–19 education, and therefore of secondary schools. Most of the responsibility for the education and training of this group no longer lies with the educational agencies created in 1944 and redefined in 1974. It may be that, long before the end of this century, change on this scale will have the effect—desired or not—of terminating secondary education at the age of sixteen, and of stimulating further the growth of a separate tertiary system, operating within different financial structures and under different control.

Even in the mean time, the effects upon secondary schools in their present form cannot be predicted with any certainty. There is an obvious danger that schools in their present form will become less, instead of more, open to 'the world of work'. If jobs are not there for leavers at the age of sixteen, schools will have little motivation to prepare pupils for them, and pupils will become sceptical or dismissive of attempts by schools to do so. It is already alleged that lack of employment opportunities, in a society where the expectation has been that more than half of the age group can find jobs at the age of sixteen, erodes the motivation of pupils to work hard or prepare for examinations. The pressure of the Youth Training Scheme upon employers will make them less willing, or simply less able, to provide work-experience opportunities for pupils within secondary schools.

Such pressures render problematic the future of the new Certificate of Prevocational Education, available from September 1983 for pupils in sixth forms. The CPVE is part of a planned effort to shift the emphasis in schools from the general towards the vocational, the technical, the useful. It is planned as a qualification at the end of a balanced one-year course preparing for a number of occupations, and acting as the 'educational counterpart' (whatever that may prove to mean) to the Youth Training Scheme. Notice of death has been served upon the Certificate of Extended Education—to perish in 1985 as one of the last survivors of an attempt (inappropriate and doomed to failure) to provide a general yet academic counterpart to A level for those who wished to enjoy some of the advantages of a sixth-form education without being willing, or in most cases able, to make good sense of a full A level course. The 'new sixth form' may soon look very ancient indeed.

This same effort to shift the emphasis in schools from the general towards the vocational, the technical, and the useful explains the joint Manpower Services Commission/Department of Education and Science development—with the money coming from the Manpower Services Commission—known as the New Technical and Vocational Education Initiative. The NTVEI is sponsoring, from September 1983, fourteen pilot schemes for special courses within schools for pupils from the age of fourteen. It is therefore a remarkable affront to the orthodox doctrine that courses in comprehensive schools should remain general rather than vocational in character, and (even) that a common curriculum should prevail. Local Educational Authorities were, and perhaps still are, jealous of the direct funding of this initiative, although—after a ritual howl of complaint at the lack of consultation—they did not find it possible to refuse the money. The issues of *utility*, *control*, and *diversity* are all embedded in the NTVEI.

The youthful Certificate of Prevocational Education does not represent the only change in the debate about school examinations, although—after ten years of searching—it is the solitary innovation. Keith Joseph abolished the Schools Council, disliking its ponderous constitution, its quango-like qualities, and its dubiously radical record. In its place, the Secretary of State has constituted an Examinations Council and a Curriculum Council, showing no sympathy for those who argued ten short years before that the curriculum and the examinations associated with it could not be rationally separated. In fact, examinations raise so many complex issues of power and control that their strategic management is inevitably political: the creation of a new committee, appointed by the Secretary of State, advised directly by his Inspectorate, and accountable to him, may be the formula for producing change when the effort to find consensus has demonstrably failed. The Secretary of State himself has shown a marked taste for intervening in matters on which his predecessors had remained prudently if unhelpfully silent.

The future of the sixteen-plus examination system is to be resolved (perhaps) in the second quarter of 1984, and—unless the arguments for unification are very powerful indeed—it is hard to foresee a Conservative government 'abolishing O level'. But the work on establishing the new criteria has continued, again not without commentary from the Secretary of State. He does not wish a tender respect for the cultures of the ethnic minorities to blunt a concern for the teaching of 'standard' English, nor does he wish the teaching of physics to be diluted by a consideration of the social implications of the applications of science. Pending any agreement, or decision, about the sixteen-plus examination at national level, several local enterprises have flourished. Prominent among them has been the work stimulated by Tim Brighouse, Chief Education Officer for Oxfordshire since 1978 and a key member of the Oxford Educational Research Group. He has drawn three other Local Education Authorities into a partnership with the Oxford Delegacy of Local Examinations (now well into the second century of its work) in order to develop an Oxford Certificate of Educational Achievement. The Oxford Certificate of Educational Achievement will record success in recognized examinations (GCE, CSE, CPVE, and so on) and level of performance in graded assessments (initially in English, mathematics, science, and a modern language), and also give an extended record of the pupil's achievement and attitudes while at secondary school of the kind outlined no less than forty years ago in the Norwood Report. Central to this work will be teachers seconded from the four Local Education Authorities to the Department of Educational Studies and working with the tutors there. The Oxford Certificate of Educational Achievement, unlike so many of the developments sketched in this chapter, represents an attempt—within the necessary constraints of national policy—to sponsor development based upon local initiative.

The balance between local control and central influence has also been upset by the changes of style, especially over the nine years from 1974 when Sheila Browne was at its head, in the work of Her Majesty's Inspectorate. A scrutiny of the Inspectorate, ordered by Margaret Thatcher as part of the work of a special group commissioned to sniff out waste and inefficiency in and around Whitehall, completed its work in the summer of 1981— although it was March 1983 before the report was published, together with the Government's response. In the earlier 1970s there had been a good deal of sour criticism of the Inspectorate, and some thought that it had lost its way. The Schools Council had distracted attention from HMI as an authoritative source of curriculum development and of professional advice to the Secretary of State. HMI had, in its origins, been associated with inspection and examination as a means of securing public accountability for the expenditure of Government grants to elementary schools. That work was enlarged, and debased, by the operation of the system of payment by results. In the twentieth century greater emphasis was placed upon the general and formal inspection of particular schools, upon which unpublished reports were made to Local Education Authorities and governors, and on the inspection of individual teachers, mostly during their probationary year. A liberal tendency to emphasize advising rather than inspecting, the growth of Local Education Authorities and their own professional services, the expansion of the system: all these developments eroded the historic function of HMI, without substituting any clear and new role.

That definition was achieved during the 1970s by a campaign of sustained and intelligent aggression. HMI asserted its independence, its visibility, its right to publish contributions to and comments upon educational policy. A greater expertise was achieved by the better use of specialist services, and by a closer integration of the national network—many HMI now spend a good proportion of their time at the Department of Education and Science in London, or working on particular aspects of the curriculum, such as mathematics, or modern languages. There are, in 1984, about 490 Inspectors in England and Wales, most of them with good experience of teaching and high qualifications. They furnish information on the working of the system to the Department of Education and Science, undertake and publish surveys of schools or of the curriculum, contribute extensively to in-service work with teachers, and consult with Chief Education Officers and heads of schools. As they are concerned with 32,000 schools and 580 Colleges of Further Education (as well as 5,400 evening institutes) they can no longer report on the work of individual teachers, and their capacity to report on particular institutions is necessarily limited. They do nevertheless conduct some 260 full and formal inspections of institutions each year, including a handful of the Local Education Authorities themselves. Their reports on schools and colleges have been published since January 1983, and constitute important and objective information and comment available to the public. The ending of the older convention of secrecy directly relates, of course, to a wish to extend the areas of *choice* within the school system. Bad schools will now be more easily recognized. The contribution of HMI is not identical with that of the Department of Education and Science, with which it needs to be intimately linked but from the politics at which it needs to maintain a cool distance. The tensions here are real, and it may be that in recent years the capacity of the Department of Education and Science to contribute effectively to the formulation of educational policy has been limited by its ambivalent relationship to its own professional advisory body. HMI is therefore an essential ingredient in any discussion about changing patterns of *control*, and the moving balance between central and local influences.

The disappearance of the Central Advisory Councils (the sponsors of the Hadow, Spens, Crowther, Newsom, and Plowden Reports) and, even more abruptly, of the Schools Council has left HMI with an eminence which may not be lonely but is certainly powerful. The HMI report on *Aspects of Secondary Education in England* (1979) illustrates the importance of its work both in exercising *control* within a diverse system, and of preserving that *quality* which is another of the emphatic interests of the years since 1979. The 1979 report on secondary schools satisfied neither those who wished to believe that the decline of grammar schools had been fatal to standards, nor the optimists who were neurotically defensive about any criticisms of the schools. HMI found that 'in most schools teachers and pupils alike work hard and have some solid achievements to show. A minority of schools have work of real distinction'. The report challenges the assumption, increasingly pervasive since October 1976, that *diversity* within the schools had produced a chaotic variety in the curriculum. On the contrary, it found that—given the large measure of self-determination still enjoyed by secondary schools—the similarities were more striking than the differences. It observed, somewhat sadly, that comprehension and the raising of the school-leaving age had not led to any radical reshaping of the curriculum, and called for 'a more explicit rationale of the curriculum as a whole'. It was less helpful in attempting to define what that rationale might be, and took somewhat for granted that an all-embracing rationale would, in fact, be desirable. HMI doubted whether the ablest pupils were always sufficiently challenged, but found that the greatest cause for concern often lay in the work and achievement of those of below-average ability—those in the third quartile. It openly criticized the subservience of schools and teaching to the sixteen-plus examination system—confronting but not weakening the harsh realities within that system which guarantee that this can hardly be avoided.

HMI has also been active in the attempts, now vigorously sponsored by the Secretary of State, to improve the quality of teaching and to give it a sharper professional edge. The opportunity for this improvement of *quality* is, of course, offered by *contraction*. In 1982, it was made clear that the number of candidates admitted to teacher-training courses in 1985 would again be cut. The total, for primary and secondary combined, is to be (unless further reductions are made) 17,350, and within the global figure the balance shifts towards primary; 8,750 will be admitted to courses of training to teach in secondary schools—only 1,850 for the B.Ed., but 6,900 for the PGCE. The universities are to provide just over half of this secondary cohort, and the recommendations of the James Committee have turned out to be predictions. Of every five teachers going in to secondary schools, four will have taken the route through a first degree followed by a one-year course of training. All entrants to teacher training now follow undergraduate or graduate courses, the old Certificate of Education has disappeared, two A levels are required of all entrants (as well as O levels in English and Mathematics), and the last dispensations from proper training (for science and mathematics graduates) have disappeared. Fewer will mean better, even if Kingsley Amis had not necessarily been right in arguing in the Black Papers that more might mean worse.

But changes in the content of initial training, of the kind pursued since 1972 by many places (including Oxford), are as important as an improvement in the entry, and a framework for such changes was provided in the Government White Paper on *Teaching Quality*, published in 1983. Quality is to be the keynote of the 1980s, as quantity had to be for Tony Crosland's decade. Unifying the decisions and proposals of the Secretary of State is a concern to raise the standards of teaching by placing it more firmly within a professional, some might argue a utilitarian, discipline. More care is to be taken in the selection of candidates, in which experienced class-room teachers as well as lecturers and tutors should (quite rightly) be involved. Tutors in departments like the one in which I work should have recent experience in schools, and this must if necessary be secured by a policy of exchanges and secondments. Obviously, appointments shared by secondary schools and universities will be a key element in making this principle effective. New criteria are to be established, in the place of the anarchy since the early 1970s, to ensure that teacher-training courses are of the necessary quality and relevance. The elaboration and application of these criteria, by the Secretary of State or anybody to whom he commits this responsibility, will move the *control* of teacher training, and specifically of its contents, towards the centre. Not, in this case, from the Local Education Authorities or from schools, but from nowhere to somewhere. Local Education Authorities are required, by an amendment of the regulations, to pay more careful attention to the precise qualifications of an applicant before making an appointment. The effective management of the teaching force during a period of contraction makes it sensible that such appointments should be to the service of a Local Education Authority rather than a particular school: an apparently modest comment which nevertheless strikes at the heart of older concepts of the autonomy and distinctive character of each school. Control shifts from the head to the Local Education Authority, and perhaps it should.

Whatever is now done to improve the quality of new entrants to teaching, it remains disconcertingly true that most of the teachers who will be in the class-rooms in the year 2000 are there already in 1984. *Teaching Quality* addresses the problem by extending the arrangements for premature retirements (suggesting that 5,000 to 10,000 per annum might be an appropriate target over the next few years) and promising a further enlargement of the in-service training programme. This programme, no doubt further stimulated by the power now enjoyed at the centre to offer some direct funding for it, moves to the heart of the policies designed to produce better teachers for the schools.

These concerns have been as much part of my own life since

1971 as an engagement in the extension of secondary-school opportunities had been in the 1960s. But they have not been my only task. When I came to Oxford in 1973 I became a Fellow of Brasenose College, and in 1980 readily agreed to become for a few years its Tutor for Admissions. This task has given me a supplementary angle of vision upon the world of secondary schools, and in particular on the difficulties of matching the high values of that world to the traditions of a university proud, and with good cause, of its élitist reputation. I shall write the last chapter of this book in my room in Brasenose, looking out from a small window past the staircase in which I lived as an undergraduate and towards the gate through which I first walked as a schoolboy, forty years ago.

CHAPTER 13

Forty years on

Forty years on, growing older and older,
Shorter in wind, as in memory long,
Feeble of foot, and rheumatic of shoulder,
What will it help you that once you were strong?
God give us bases to guard or beleaguer,
Games to play out, whether earnest or fun;
Fights for the fearless, and goals for the eager,
Twenty, and thirty, and forty years on!

Harrow School Song, v. 4

A Tutor for Admissions in an Oxford college has little power, but plenty to interest him and keep him busy. All the colleges have, since 1962, worked closely together on admissions but it is still the tutors in a particular subject within each college who finally decide whom to admit—usually on the basis of a special entrance examination, taken in November. The work of the Tutor for Admissions is to assist this process to run smoothly and—even more important—to help sixth-formers and teachers in secondary schools of all kinds to learn about Oxford, its courses of study, and its colleges. If he is wise, he will spend time visiting schools, sixth-form colleges and tertiary colleges. Of course, his main concern is with those students in them who are thinking about university applications, but what is happening to this minority cannot be separated from the changes within their own communities and among their contemporaries. On a recent visit to a tertiary college in the North, for example, I learnt a great deal about the introduction of the Youth Training Scheme in that particular area. These tasks have therefore enabled me to integrate a career in secondary schools, the interests of a Department of Educational Studies, and membership of a University.

They have been undertaken at the end of a period of expanding opportunities in higher education for those leaving secondary schools. In the year 1970/1 there were in Great Britain 210,000 home (United Kingdom) full-time students in universities and 212,000 in advanced further education (many in the polytechnics). That total of 422,000 had ten years later risen to 492,000, with six-sevenths of the increase in the university sector. The undoubtedly more dramatic expansion of the 1960s did not end at midnight on 31 December 1970. In 1970/1 the APR (the age participation rate, that is the percentage of eighteen-year-olds going into higher education) was 13.8, and by 1980/1 it was 13.2. This is, however, a misleading comparison as the earlier figure—referring to the year before the James Report when recruitment to Colleges of Education was at its peak—included many school-leavers without two A levels, embarking on three-year teacher-training courses. If these are excluded from the calculation, the 13.8 drops to 11.8.

The size of the eighteen-year-old population passed its peak in 1982/3, and this should on the surface mean that more space is becoming available in higher education—especially as there is some evidence of a levelling off, or even a slight decline, in demand. However, the Government is anxious to reduce expenditure—in higher education as elsewhere—and (in the short term at least) pressure on places and resources will remain severe. But across the second half of the forty-year period with which this book is concerned, the underlying trend is one of expansion of opportunity for secondary-school-leavers—from an APR of 7.2 per cent in 1962/3, when I started to work in Banbury, to a peak of 14.6 per cent ten years later.

That compares ill—or, depending upon your point of view, well—with 42 per cent in the United States and with other, but less striking, figures within Europe. The English system of higher education is small and expensive—students receive support, generous by any international standard, in meeting fees and maintenance costs, the staff–student ratio is exceptionally high, laboratories and other facilities more than adequate, the drop-out rate low. In 1980/1, the cost per pupil in an English primary school was £610, £860 for a secondary pupil, £3,380 for a polytechnic student, and £4,420 for a university student. Britain provides, for a carefully selected minority of its secondary-school leavers, an intensive and specialized three-year course. The nature of that careful selection is, of course, determined by the structure of the secondary-school curriculum and by the General Certificate in Education examination at A level. Part of the problem in providing effective education for the 16–19 age group lies in the fact that 16–19 education is uncomfortably stretched between a 5–16 sector (increasingly 'common', or comprehensive, or inclusive, or open) and a sector of higher education dedicated to principles of quality and selection. Much of what happens in secondary schools is explained by this underlying mismatch. A levels would have disappeared long ago, but for the special (and for many of us attractive) nature of higher education.

The eighteen-plus frontier is, therefore, as was suggested in Chapter 8, of high strategic importance—and nowhere more than in entrance to Oxford and Cambridge. These universities have traditionally been particularly favoured, for good and obvious reasons, by the Public Schools, whose place in the secondary-school system and whose increasingly academic (or meritocratic) character were discussed in Chapter 6. It was important for the two older universities, voluntary and independent in their origins but increasingly (now, in effect, totally) dependent upon public funds, to attract able pupils from maintained secondary schools. It was the argument of the Franks Commission of 1964, composed in the shadow of the Robbins Report, that not enough such pupils were coming to Oxford. They were deterred perhaps by the complexity of the system as it then was, by a sense of the private inwardness of the place, by the myths of privilege and snobbery.

The colleges of the university have since then made a major effort to meet the self-generated criticism. The task was complicated by the comprehensive reorganization associated with Circular 10/65 and outlined in Chapter 5. There were now many more schools with sixth forms, more problems in keeping them all informed of relevant developments within the university, more difficulties for those schools in preparing candidates for the Oxford examination when secondary schools were harrassed by the inescapable problems of any large-scale reorganization. There was, and still is, no evidence that the comprehensive secondary schools which took shape in the 1960s and 1970s were unable to prepare pupils adequately for one of the most demanding and competitive examinations which any eighteen-year-old pupils anywhere in the world are asked to take. On the contrary, the proportion of entrants to Oxford with a high A-level score (that is, three Bs or better) rose in 1981 to 73.5 per cent, as compared with 22.5 per cent for the universities as a whole, and 58.6 per cent for Oxford in 1970. By 1981 the proportion coming from maintained schools rose to 50 per cent, compared with an *average* of 44 per cent for the whole period from 1968 to 1980. Problems remain, and notably the higher success rate of candidates taking the November entrance examination *after* their A levels—a luxury which few maintained schools or pupils could afford. Late in 1983, the colleges agreed that, in future, all candidates would be more fairly compared by being examined before A level. At the same time, other means of entry for able students were opened up, and (if all goes well) a larger number of them from comprehensive schools will be encouraged to apply.

Oxford, a highly visible university, has therefore modified its admissions arrangements across the years to admit more pupils from comprehensive schools and, by any standards available to it, more of higher ability. This university, in terms of numbers, directly involves only a small number of school-leavers. If, however, it had not been able to admit more pupils from comprehensive schools without lowering its standards, then the modest promises of those engaged in the 1960s in the reform of a school like Banbury would have been hollow indeed. Other evidence about the achievement of the schools, although less precise, is not discouraging. Interpretation of the statistics may be disputed, especially by those committed to over-simplification, but the thorough analysis of the results of some 16,000 pupils born in one week in 1958 and included in the National Child Development Study shows no evidence of any significant difference in the results of pupils attending comprehensive schools as compared with those going to grammar and secondary modern schools. Attempts to compare the 'performance' of Local Education Authorities keeping some grammar schools with those which are fully comprehensive have not generated clear results. Recent work, by Dr John Gray of the University of Sheffield, points towards the conclusion that *up to 80 per cent* of the differences between schools can be explained in terms of the social and intellectual composition of their *intake*, and that there is no relationship between the degree of selectivity which a Local Education Authority preserves and results in examinations. Differences between particular secondary schools remain wide, and will present more of a problem as the system contracts and parental choice is maximized. The wise observer will abstain from alarmist talk about declining standards and, until much clearer evidence is available, from relating such comment to naïve comparisons of the non-selective sector with the selective sector, both treated as though they were single wholes. Research and enquiry should concentrate on those differences between schools which can *not* be explained in terms of differences in background and intake, and on enabling the poorer schools to become better—by the means outlined in *Teaching Quality*, for example. Politicians and parents will watch very carefully the operation of the principle of choice as numbers contract, and be apprehensive if the operation of that good principle renders secondary schools unfit to meet the needs of the more able, or of that underachieving 40 per cent with which the Secretary of State is so properly concerned and who should not be consigned to secondary schools where expectations and morale are low.

The office of Secretary of State for Education and Science remained, as he so wished, in the hands of Sir Keith Joseph after the general election of June 1983. The Conservatives were then returned with an enhanced majority, and claimed that their firmness and their policies had been justified. Unemployment had risen past the three million mark in January 1982, which saw the worst snow since 1963 and the beginning of a long period of difficulties with the railway workers. Rab Butler, the architect of the 1944 Act and of new Conservative policies after their defeat in 1946, who twice failed to become Prime Minister, died on 8 March 1982. Roy Jenkins won Glasgow Hillhead for the Social

Democrats on the twenty-fifth of the month. On 2 April Argentine forces invaded the Falkland Islands, a British dependency in the South Atlantic, and a task force sailed from England two days later—'God give us bases to guard or beleaguer'. Lord Carrington resigned as Foreign Secretary and the Cabinet's image of the tough new non-aristocratic Conservatism was strengthened. The Argentine cruiser, the *General Belgrano*, was sunk on 2 May and the British *Sheffield* two days later. The Tories were encouraged by their successes in the local elections, and political analysts began to talk of 'the Falklands factor'. The Pope visited Britain at the end of the month, and in June the Argentine forces in the Falklands surrendered. In July, the Home Secretary announced that an intruder had made his way unchallenged into the Queen's bedroom, and in August unemployment figures rose to 3,292,702; one in seven of the work-force. In August too, on our family holiday, *Scholar Gypsy* took us on a long voyage through the canals of central and northern England, and across the Pennines into Yorkshire. Eric James and his wife Cordelia joined us for a long summer lunch, and we talked about schools and universities as we had known them, and we would wish them to be. He still had all the zest of the warrior. The solidarity of trade unions and their traditional willingness to strike were undermined by a 61 per cent vote against striking in the mineworkers' ballot in November. On 20 November 1982 Lord Redcliffe Maud died in Oxford, and Lord Bullock wrote about his achievements in the *Oxford Review of Education*, which they had both helped to found. The same number of the *Review* reported a meeting, in Brasenose College, Oxford, of American and European educators, at which much of the informal talk was about efforts in the States to revive sagging confidence in public education. On 1 April 1983 demonstrations, estimated in number from 40,000 to 100,000, formed a human chain from the US Air Force base at Greenham Common in Berkshire to the Atomic Weapons Research Establishment at Aldermaston, to protest against the plan to base cruise missiles in Britain. The Easter weekend witnessed many such demonstrations throughout Europe. The Prime Minister announced on 9 May that a general election would be held on 9 June. The Conservatives won their biggest majority since the War, although they had a lower share of the popular vote than in 1979. Since 1979, partly as a result of the increased burden of unemployment payments and in spite of strenuous efforts by the Government, public expenditure had risen by 3 per cent in real terms. Margaret Thatcher rearranged her Cabinet, but Government changes at Education and Science affected only the junior ministers. Rhodes Boyson, who had worked in that capacity since 1979, left the educational world. Shirley Williams lost her seat in the Commons, and in October Neil Kinnock was elected to succeed Michael Foot as leader of the Labour party. In the same month, the rate of inflation rose to 5.1 per cent: in June (at 3.7 per cent) it had been the lowest for fifteen years. In February unemployment reached a new peak, but in September 1983 it fell for the first time since 1979.

Many of the initiatives taken in education by the Conservative Government before and after their election victory in 1983 have already been noted. The urgent need to keep expenditure within tighter bounds has dominated policy. Such expenditure had soared across many of the forty years of this book, and especially when the school population was surging forward. If a baseline is drawn in the year 1960–1 and the figure 100 taken to represent national expenditure on education, the corresponding figure for 1970–1 was 170, for 1976–7, when the peak was reached, 213, and for 1980–1, 207. Educational expenditure in the United Kingdom in 1978 (the last year for which fully comparable figures are available) represented 5.4 per cent of Gross National Product compared with 5.3 per cent for France, 4.6 per cent for West Germany, and 4.6 per cent for Italy—the other countries within the European Community with populations of over fifty million. Planned expenditure for 1982–3 was £12,548m., of which £9,428m. was assigned to the grant-related expenditure by local authorities, under the new procedures. For various technical reasons, however, this did not represent the full sum spent on education by local authorities. Declining numbers of pupils in schools meant that, in spite of the cuts, more money per pupil was being spent than ever before, and that the pupil–teacher ratio (PTR) was more favourable than it had ever been.

Some of the contemporary pessimism in and about education may, therefore, seem to be misplaced. But the problems for secondary schools, as for all parts of the education service, are severe. This is largely because of the political and administrative dilemmas related to the management of contraction. Schools cannot simply be taken out of use as *overall* demand declines, and unit costs must therefore rise. The effort to extend parental choice (for example, in the 1980 Act) and the reluctance of communities to sacrifice their own schools inhibit the effective management by Local Education Authorities of shrinking resources. The stubborn autonomy of schools, the formerly legitimate determination of heads to recruit and keep their own staff, the reluctance to lose sixth forms or to engage in difficult but necessary co-operative arrangements—all these, too, produce rigidities. Even more fundamental, in my view, is that complex of attitudes with which so many of these pages have been concerned. Attitudes about secondary schools are not separable from attitudes towards politics, equality, the rights of the citizen, authority, competition, or the economy. Schools have an easier and better time when they know that most of their leavers can find jobs: at present the blight of unemployment lies heavily on many countries. In one which has a notoriously weak tradition of education and training for the young adult, the misery is exacerbated. Equally important as a determinant of attitudes, and logically distinct, is the declining school population. In the summer of 1983, Mrs Thatcher reminded the public that if total Government expenditure for 1984–5 was to be kept at £126,400m. then there would be no room for tax cuts—and there had already been, even since the general election of June, a further £500m. cut in spending. Underlying this immediate problem of balancing the books was the longer-term crisis in public provision: the number of those over the age of eighty-five would, before the end of the century, double to a figure of one million, whereas the working-age population, upon whom both the younger and the older most depend, would increase only from 30.5 to 32 million. Geriatrics and not education will be the most demanding of the social services: Beveridge, Bevan, and contraception have done their work only too well.

But the picture is far from being one of unrelieved gloom, and anyone who denied that substantial and permanent progress had been made in the generation since 1944 would invite and deserve ridicule. The blacker spots in the system naturally attract most comment, and the unevenness of provision which the 'partnership' system allows must sometimes amplify such comment. The over-all parent–teacher ratio, to take one example, is now 18.5, and 16.6 for secondary schools only. But the national figure conceals variations: between 14.2 for the ILEA and 19.2 for Sutton within the Greater London area, between 16.2 and 19.8 in the metropoli-tan districts, between 17.9 and 21.0 in the shire counties. HMI keeps a careful watch upon Local Education Authority policies, and in the summer of 1983 published a report comparing provision in all the English LEAs. They found that twenty-two had im-proved on their performance since 1981, and nine deterioriated. Although four Local Education Authorities were giving cause for serious concern, the system was not on the whole getting any worse. The Chartered Institute of Public Finance and Accountancy reviewing later figures was less sanguine: expenditure in the 104 Local Education Authorities for the year 1983–4 was set to go up by 5.6 per cent, but inflation by 6 per cent.

Financial problems will give a sharper edge to the complex issues identified in Chapter 12. They will produce strong pressure towards measures of rationalization, especially within each Local Education Authority, which will be popular neither in secondary schools nor in education committees. But if those pressures can be accommodated, and if public discussion about secondary schools can avoid the sharp evils of divisiveness (grammar versus compre-hensive, for example) and concentrate instead upon the pursuit of quality within a smaller system, then these schools will be better than their predecessors of the sixties and seventies. The system remains large and buoyant—with 4,622 schools in January 1982, and a decline in the number of pupils under the school-leaving age (73,000 down, compared with 1980) partly offset by a rise (31,000) in the number of pupils over that age. The rise of three percentage points over the previous year in the staying-on rate represents the largest annual increase since the raising of the school-leaving age. There were 228,400 teachers in secondary schools, 2,500 less than in the previous year. For the first time ever, more girls than boys attempted A levels.

The year 1984 is the last in which any of my own children will be in secondary schools. Emma takes A levels this summer—in physics, mathematics, further mathematics, and English. She is one of that 26 per cent of all A-level candidates (10 per cent in 1962) who spread their choice outside the confines of arts subjects only or science only, and one of the 20 per cent of girls among the A-level candidates taking physics. She hopes to study physics at university. Hilary left school when she was seventeen, one of the interim generation who took a Certificate of Extended Education (with other things) after a course of O levels and CSE. She is now taking an A level in her spare time, while Simon is working towards his Ph.D. in mathematics at Cambridge, the subject his grandfather was prevented from pursuing. All three attended comprehensive schools in Oxfordshire.

The schools which this book has taken as examples, that is those which happened to be associated with my own life and career or with my family, are not as they were. Cardiff High School disappeared, and not without controversy in a stormy reorganization of schools in the city, into a newly formed comprehensive school in the suburbs. Emanuel, the voluntary-aided grammar school at which I began teaching, gave a chilly reception to Tony Crosland's Circular 10/65, and did not cherish the idea of merging with anyone else. The change in the political control of London—the first since 1934, when Herbert Morrison ruled in the name of Labour—delayed execution, but the return of the Labour party to power in London in 1970 and at Westminster in 1974, accelerated events. In May 1975 the Inner London Education Authority served a Section 13 Notice under the 1944 Act, indicating its intention to cease to maintain the school, and was not deterred by a petition with 36,000 signatures. In 1976, the school became an independent fee-paying day-school, and as such welcomed the academic enrichment of its intake under the Assisted Places Scheme introduced four years later.

Wallington, the maintained grammar school where I was head

of history, has since enjoyed its share of drama. Part of Surrey when I knew it, in 1965 it was moved into the new London Borough of Sutton, which then acquired four selective grammar schools, admitting 20 per cent of the ability range. A new and firmly Conservative council did as little as possible about 10/65, and eventually proposed with a show of innocence that all the present secondary schools might become high schools but that 'the four schools at present designated grammar schools shall continue to specialise in pre-university courses'. Opinions, and votes, seemed slowly to shift, for by the end of 1971 (when the Conservatives were back at Westminster, Mrs Thatcher as Secretary of State was busily approving comprehensive schemes, and I was working on the James Committee) the council agreed to abolish 'selection by ability' and was working on plans for a system based on middle schools. In Wallington, as previously in Enfield, the groups in favour of preserving the grammar schools mobilized their forces, protesting when the Section 13 Notices were published, and the Secretary of State rejected the proposals. That was in January 1974, shortly before the defeat of the Conservatives in the general election. In 1974, the newly elected borough council voted to retain a selective system, and the director of education resigned. Acting under the new 1976 Act, the Department of Education and Science, with a Labour Secretary of State, insisted that comprehensive plans must be submitted: and so they were, with unrealistic proposals for changes in 1986, a comfortable ten years ahead. Shirley Williams, as Secretary of State, rejected these plans in September 1977 (a year after the Ruskin speech) and insisted on better and faster proposals. Sutton delayed, and the Secretary of State instituted proceedings, under Section 99 of the 1944 Act, on the grounds that the Local Education Authority was failing in its duty. Sutton moved to take legal action, but the general election of 1979 intervened, the 1976 Act was repealed, and the grammar school survived.

Within Oxfordshire, Banbury School remains upon its course (although now somewhat smaller than it once was), and several of the teachers there have come to spend a year working in the Department of Educational Studies in Oxford. Lord Williams'

School in Thame was steered through the difficult years of re-organization and is now a comprehensive school. The eleven-year-olds of Kidlington no longer have to leave the village to go to secondary school: it has one of its own. It also has four primary schools: one of them a voluntary-controlled Church of England school, operating within the terms of the 1944 Act. This is the school where my father was once a boy, working for his scholar-ship examination in the evenings. The old buildings no longer exist and the school several years ago moved to share a site with the new secondary school. But when everything was being packed, the headmaster—trained in a punctilious tradition—did not forget to take with him the log-books.

On 27 January 1978 he wrote in the current volume:

The Headmaster this morning attended the funeral service for Mr. George Arthur Judge, who died on January 22nd, aged 91. Mr. Judge was formerly a pupil of Kidlington School. It is recorded in the first log book by the then Headmaster on the 5th February 1900 that 'George Arthur Judge a VI Standard boy in this school has gained an Oxford County Council Junior Scholarship of £30 per annum for four years tenable at Thame Grammar School.'

NOTES ON QUOTATIONS

Some of the quotations used in this book are identified in the text itself. In Chapter 1, Stanley Baldwin's comment made in 1923 is to be found in Olive Banks (1955), p. 119. The remarks of the President of the Board of Education in 1932 are recorded in Brian Simon (1974), p. 186. The account by Goronwy Rees of life in Cardiff High School in the 1920s is given in his autobiography *A Chapter of Accidents* (Chatto and Windus, 1972), pp. 35–9. T. O. Lloyd's celebration of the queue is on p. 246 of his volume *From Empire to Welfare State* (Oxford University Press, 1970).

The observations of the senior civil servants on the discussions leading up to the 1944 Act are identified in P. H. J. H. Gosden (1976), pp. 248, 257, and 258. The comments made by Butler and those attributed to the Chief Whip are drawn from the chapter on 'William Temple and Educational Reform' in R. A. Butler's *Art of Memory* (Hodder and Stoughton, 1982). The opinions of the Chancellor of the Exchequer are given in P. H. J. H. Gosden (1976), p. 285. Churchill's characteristic grumble about 'Rome on the taxes' is in the same volume, p. 312.

Ellen Wilkinson's definition of 'parity of esteem', recorded in Chapter 2, is quoted in Rodney Barker (1972), p. 88, and A. J. P. Taylor's advice to 'run away to sea rather than go to a secondary modern' was proffered in the October 1957 issue of *The Twentieth Century*. Butler's distinction between equal educational opportunity and identical educational opportunity was developed in the 1952 *Year Book of Education*. The objective of making 'Mary Smith more Mary Smith' is recorded in William Taylor (1963), p. 111, and the poetic lines about Oxford are taken from *Alma Mater* by Sir Arther Quiller-Couch. The London County Council's definition of 'a system of comprehensive high schools' is developed in Stuart Maclure's *One Hundred Years of London Education 1870–1970* (Allen Lane, the Penguin Press, 1970), p. 130.

In Chapter 4, Jeremy Thorpe's remark on 'the night of the long knives' is noted on p. 205 of the history by Alan Sked and Chris Cook (1979). The alarming comparison, in the following chapter, between an aerodrome and a comprehensive school is to be found in I. G. K. Fenwick (1976), p. 52, and Michael Stewart's preference to 'wait a bit' on p. 131 of the same volume.

In Chapter 6, Crosland's agreement with Maurice Kogan is recorded in Maurice Kogan (1971), p. 124. A convenient version of Crosland's

Woolwich speech is in Willem van der Eyken (1973), pp. 468–73. Crosland's preference for consulting his friends before giving them anything to drink is also attested by Maurice Kogan (1971), p. 186, while his dismissal of Crossman's policy on the raising of the school-leaving age as 'crazy' is in Susan Crosland (1982), p. 195. The prayer of the small boy at an independent school is in Royston Lambert (1968), p. 277.

Thomas Arnold's characterization of the sixth form, quoted in Chapter 8, was first printed in A. P. Stanley, *Life and Correspondence of Thomas Arnold* (John Murray, 1881), vol. I., p. 104.

The quotations from the House of Lords debate on the abolition of direct-grant schools are in *Hansard*, 365. 165, 12 Nov. 1975. The description of the philosophy of the William Tyndale School as 'democratic, egalitarian and non-sexist' is quoted in Adam Hopkins (1978), p. 97.

FURTHER READING

Armytage, W. H. G., *Four Hundred Years of English Education*, Cambridge University Press, 1964.

Banks, Olive, *Parity and Prestige in English Secondary Education*, Routledge and Kegan Paul, 1955.

Barker, Rodney, *Education and Politics, 1900–1951*, Oxford University Press, 1972.

Becher, T., and Maclure, J. S., *The Politics of Curriculum Change*, Hutchinson, 1978.

Benn, Caroline, and Simon, Brian, *Half Way There*, 2nd edn., Penguin, 1972.

Boyson, Rhodes, *Crisis in Education*, Woburn Press, 1975.

Bruner, Jerome S., *The Process of Education*, Harvard University Press, 1960.

Crosland, C. A. R., *The Future of Socialism*, Jonathan Cape, 1956.

Crosland, Susan, *Tony Crosland*, Jonathan Cape, 1982.

Crossman, R. H. S., *Diaries of a Cabinet Minister, Volume I: 1964–1966*, Hamish Hamilton and Jonathan Cape, 1977.

Dent, H. C., *Education in England and Wales*, 2nd edn., Hodder and Stoughton, 1981.

Douglas, J. W. B., *The Home and the School*, MacGibbon and Kee, 1964.

Eyken, Willem van der, *Education, the Child and Society. A Documentary History 1900–1973*, Penguin, 1973.

Fenwick, I. G. K., *The Comprehensive School 1944–1970*, Methuen, 1976.

Fenwick, Keith, and McBride, Peter, *The Government of Education*, Martin Robertson, 1981.

Gathorne-Hardy, Jonathan, *The Public School Phenomenon, 597–1977*, Hodder and Stoughton, 1977.

Gosden, P. H. J. H., *Education in the Second World War*, Methuen, 1976.

Hargreaves, David H., *The Challenge for the Comprehensive School*, Routledge and Kegan Paul, 1982.

Hencke, David, *Colleges in Crisis*, Penguin, 1978.

Hoggart, Richard, *The Uses of Literacy*, Chatto and Windus, 1957 (Penguin, 1958).

Hopkins, Adam, *The School Debate*, Penguin, 1978.

Jackson, Brian, and Marsden, Dennis, *Education and the Working Class*, Routledge and Kegan Paul, 1962 (Pelican, 1966).

James, Philip, H., *The Reorganisation of Secondary Education: a Study of Local Policy Making*, National Foundation for Educational Research, 1983.

Judge, Harry, *School is Not Yet Dead*, Longman, 1974.

Kalton, Graham, *The Public Schools: a Factual Survey*, Longman, 1966.

Kogan, Maurice, *The Politics of Education*, Penguin, 1971.

Lacey, Colin, *Hightown Grammar*, Manchester University Press, 1970.

Lambert, Royston, *The Hothouse Society*, Weidenfeld and Nicolson, 1968.

Lawson, John, and Silver, Harold, *A Social History of Education in England*, Methuen, 1973.

Maclure, J. Stuart, *Educational Documents England and Wales 1816–*, Methuen, 1979.

Mann, John, *Education*, Pitman, 1979.

Marwick, Arthur, *British Society since 1945*, Penguin, 1982.

Montgomery, Robert, *A New Examination of Examinations*, Routledge and Kegan Paul, 1978.

Parkinson, Michael, *The Labour Party and the Organisation of Secondary Education, 1918–65*, Routledge and Kegan Paul, 1970.

Pedley, Robin, *The Comprehensive School*, 3rd edn., Penguin, 1978.

Rae, John, *The Public School Revolution*, Faber, 1981.

Reid, William, and Philby, Jane, *The Sixth: an Essay in Education and Democracy*, Falmer Press, 1982.

Rogers, Rick, *Crowther to Warnock*, Heinemann, 1980.

Simon, Brian, *The Politics of Educational Reform 1920–1940*, Lawrence and Wishart, 1974.

Simon, Brian, and Taylor, William (eds.), *Education in the Eighties*, Batsford, 1981.

Sked, Alan, and Cook, Chris, *Post-War Britain: a Political History*, Penguin, 1979.

Stevens, Auriol, *Clever Children in Comprehensive Schools*, Penguin, 1980.

Taylor, William, *The Secondary Modern School*, Faber, 1963.

Vernon, Betty, *Red Ellen: Ellen Wilkinson*, Croom Helm, 1982.

Watkins, Peter, *The Sixth Form College in Practice*, Edward Arnold, 1982.

Wright, Nigel, *Progress in Education*, Croom Helm, 1977.

Yates, Alfred, and Pidgeon, D. A., *Admission to Grammar Schools*, National Foundation for Educational Research, 1957.

Young, Michael, *The Rise of the Meritocracy*, Thames and Hudson, 1958 (Penguin, 1961).

The information on secondary reorganization in Oxford and Sutton is drawn from two useful articles, both published in the *Oxford Review of Education:*

Prichard, Mari, 'Which Scheme? Oxford City Council's Debate on Comprehensive Reorganisation, 1964–1967', III.3, 1977.

Pattison, Mark, 'Intergovernmental Relations and the Limitations of Central Control', VI.1, 1980.

INDEX